## | READING |

Basic

Intermediate

Advanced

Expert

## | LISTENING |

Basic

Intermediate

Advanced

Expert

## Informative passages

HACKERS APEX READING includes informative and interesting passages on a variety of topics, such as science, art, and history.

## Useful online study materials

HACKERS APEX READING provides access to quality online study materials at HackersBook.com. These include streaming audio recordings of all passages accessible through QR codes in the book.

# HACKERS
# APEX
# READING
# for the
# TOEFL iBT®

## Basic

HACKERS

# Preface

[ H A I C K I E R I S ]

APEX

READING

for the

TOEFL iBT

Basic

II

# Preface

Thank you for purchasing HACKERS APEX READING for the TOEFL iBT Basic. The TOEFL iBT is a highly challenging exam, so it is important to select an effective study guide. All of us at Hackers Language Research Institute are confident that this publication will be an invaluable resource as you prepare for the TOEFL iBT.

HACKERS APEX READING for the TOEFL iBT is a series of comprehensive study guides for students planning to take the TOEFL iBT or for those wanting to improve their general English reading skills. This series includes four books that progress in difficulty. Students can begin at the level that matches their current abilities and then move on to the higher ones. All of the books in this series provide step-by-step question-solving strategies for every TOEFL question type. These are based on thorough research and years of instructional experience. Each book also includes informative and interesting passages that enable students to improve their English reading skills and expand their background knowledge at the same time. Furthermore, students will receive access to quality online study materials that are designed to help them get the most out of the books in this series. Key features of HACKERS APEX READING for the TOEFL iBT books include:

- Detailed explanations and question-solving strategies for all TOEFL Reading question types
- A large number of high-quality TOEFL Reading passages and questions
- Two full-length TOEFL Reading tests
- Vocabulary exercises to review essential vocabulary that appeared in the passages
- An answer book with Korean translations and lists of key vocabulary
- Access to streaming audio recordings of all passages through QR codes
- Access to supplementary study materials online (www.HackersBook.com)

Thank you again for choosing HACKERS APEX READING for the TOEFL iBT Basic, and we wish you all the best whether you are preparing to take the TOEFL iBT in the near future or simply hoping to develop your English reading skills overall.

# Table of Contents

# How to Use This Book

## 1   Understand the Question Type

Each chapter includes an Overview page that provides essential information about the featured question type and key strategies for answering it. Make sure you fully understand the strategies before moving on to the Example section, which provides a short passage with one or two questions to apply the key strategies to.

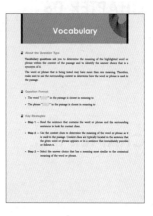

## 2   Improve Your Skills with Reading Practice Exercises

Each chapter includes four Reading Practice exercises. These will help you become more familiar with the featured question type, as well as other question types. Each exercise is accompanied by a vocabulary quiz so that you can review the key vocabulary from the passage.

## 3   Take the iBT Reading Test

Each chapter includes an iBT Reading Test, which consists of a longer passage and 10 questions that are similar to those that appear on the TOEFL iBT. Taking this test will enable you to improve your reading comprehension skills and prepare for the TOEFL iBT.

## 4 Review Essential Vocabulary

At the end of each chapter is a Vocabulary Review, which includes questions on essential vocabulary from the chapter. You will be able to easily memorize the vocabulary words by seeing them in sentences with various contexts.

## 5 Evaluate Your Progress with Actual Tests

The book includes two Actual Tests, which are full-length reading tests that include passages and questions that closely match what appears on the TOEFL iBT. They provide an excellent opportunity to apply the skills you have learned and evaluate your progress.

## 6 Check the Answer Book

The Answer Book specifies the correct answer choice for all questions and provides Korean translations of all passages and questions. It also includes a list of key vocabulary words from each passage with definitions.

# About the TOEFL iBT

## What Is the TOEFL iBT?

The TOEFL (Test of English as a Foreign Language) iBT (Internet-Based test) includes Reading, Listening, Speaking, and Writing sections to comprehensively assess English ability. Although most tasks require the application of only one of these skills, some require the use of two or more. The TOEFL iBT is designed to measure a student's capacity to use and understand English at a university level and is, therefore, much more difficult than many other English proficiency tests.

## TOEFL iBT Structure

| Section | No. of passages and questions | Time (min.) | Score | Notable Features |
|---|---|---|---|---|
| Reading | • 2 Passages<br>• 10 Questions/Passage | 36 | 30 | • Each passage is approximately 700 words long. |
| Listening | • 2 Conversations<br>• 5 Questions/Conversation<br>• 3 Lectures<br>• 6 Questions/Lecture | 41 | 30 | • Speakers have various accents, including American, British, Australian, etc. |
| Speaking | • 1 Independent Task<br>• 3 Integrated Tasks | 17 | 30 | • Independent Task asks you to state your opinion about a specific topic.<br>• Integrated Tasks ask you to provide a response based on reading and listening content. |
| Writing | • 1 Integrated Task<br>• 1 Academic Discussion Task | 35 | 30 | • Integrated Task asks you to provide a response based on reading and listening content.<br>• Academic Discussion Task asks you to state your opinion about a specific topic in an online classroom. |

Total Time: Approximately 2 hours  /  Total Score: 120

## ■ TOEFL iBT Reading Section

The TOEFL iBT Reading Section evaluates a student's ability to read and comprehend English texts that are comparable to those encountered in a typical first- or second-year university class. Although the passages cover a wide variety of academic topics, there is no requirement to be familiar with the subject matter. The information in the passage is all that is needed to answer the questions.

## ■ TOEFL iBT Reading Question Types

| Question Type | Description | Score | No. of Questions (per passage) |
|---|---|---|---|
| Vocabulary | Choose the answer choice that is closest in meaning to the given word or phrase. | 1 | 1-2 |
| Reference | Choose the answer choice that the given word or phrase refers to. | 1 | 0-1 |
| Sentence Simplification | Choose the answer choice that accurately and completely summarizes the key information in the given sentence. | 1 | 0-1 |
| Fact & Negative Fact | Choose the answer choice that restates (Fact) or contradicts (Negative Fact) the relevant information in the passage. | 1 | 2-5 |
| Inference | Choose the answer choice that can be inferred based on the relevant information in the passage. | 1 | 0-2 |
| Rhetorical Purpose | Choose the answer choice that best describes the function of a specific piece of information in relation to the immediate context or the passage as a whole. | 1 | 0-3 |
| Sentence Insertion | Choose the answer choice that corresponds to the correct location in the passage to insert the given sentence. Each possible location in the passage is marked by a square [ ■ ]. | 1 | 1 |
| Summary | Choose three answer choices that best summarize the main points of the passage. | 2 | 0-1 |
| Category Chart | Choose the answer choices that match the given categories. | 3-4 | 0-1 |

# CHAPTER 01

# Vocabulary

# Vocabulary

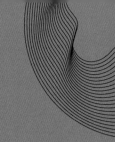

## ■ About the Question Type

**Vocabulary questions** ask you to determine the meaning of the highlighted word or phrase within the context of the passage and to identify the answer choice that is a synonym of it.

The word or phrase that is being tested may have more than one meaning. Therefore, make sure to use the surrounding context to determine how the word or phrase is used in the passage.

## ■ Question Format

- The word "      " in the passage is closest in meaning to

- The phrase "      " in the passage is closest in meaning to

## ■ Key Strategies

- **Step 1** — Read the sentence that contains the word or phrase and the surrounding sentences to look for context clues.

- **Step 2** — Use the context clues to determine the meaning of the word or phrase as it is used in the passage. Context clues are typically located in the sentence that the given word or phrase appears or in a sentence that immediately precedes or follows it.

- **Step 3** — Select the answer choice that has a meaning most similar to the contextual meaning of the word or phrase.

# Example

## Animal Camouflage

Animals usually blend into their natural background by producing colors similar to their natural surroundings. This technique is known as camouflage. It can be used both to protect animals against predators and to disguise animals hunting for prey. Camouflage makes it 5 difficult to distinguish animals in the wild because their colors match those of their environment.

Some animals change colors through multiple tiny physical structures. Just as a prism scatters visible light to reflect the colors of the rainbow, these structures convert available light into a particular mix of colors. Polar bears, for example, 10 actually have black skin and clear hairs. But when light shines on a polar bear, each of its hairs bends the light, bouncing it around so that the animal appears white.

Other animals actually change the color of their skin by producing pigments called biochromes. These pigments absorb some light waves and reflect others. 15 Octopuses use biochromes to change not only the color of their skin but also the pattern. When an octopus feels threatened, it can seemingly disappear into the surrounding terrain.

1   The word "distinguish" in the passage is closest in meaning to

(A) remember

(B) protect

(C) encounter

(D) recognize

2   The word "convert" in the passage is closest in meaning to

(A) ignore

(B) transform

(C) erase

(D) utilize

## Pop Art

After World War II, the United States began to enjoy a period of peace and prosperity, during which Americans found they had more money and leisure time. The mass-produced consumer goods that flooded stores were marketed in colorful advertisements. This led to the emergence of a new type of culture. Rock and roll music became popular and television shows began to replace radio shows 5 for entertainment. In the art world, the pop art movement responded to these changes.

Until then, the dominant style of art was abstract expressionism, which was mostly appreciated by elites. But pop art was based on everyday objects instead of philosophical ideas. Pop artists depicted them in realistic images modeled 10 after advertisements, and they reproduced their artwork in large quantities using the tools of commercial mass-production. The aim was to destroy ideas about originality and to blur the lines between "high" art and "low" art.

Roy Lichtenstein, renowned for his comic book-inspired works, and Jasper Johns were some of the pioneers of the movement. But Andy Warhol was perhaps 15 the most well-known. In addition to creating paintings of Campbell's Soup cans, he used images of prominent figures such as Marilyn Monroe, Elvis Presley, and Michael Jackson for his portraits. Furthermore, he developed his own technique to produce art, combining traditional paintings with printed images. The blend of old and new methods created unique works. 20

The pop art movement was important because art became accessible to everyone and not just rich people. Because pop art incorporated elements from mass media and everyday items, it was well-liked by the general public. In fact, many regarded it as "art for everyone."

1 The word "prosperity" in the passage is closest in meaning to

(A) change
(B) conflict
(C) wealth
(D) justice

2 The word "them" in the passage refers to

(A) elites
(B) everyday objects
(C) philosophical ideas
(D) Pop artists

3 The word "accessible" in the passage is closest in meaning to

(A) debatable
(B) approachable
(C) reasonable
(D) valuable

4 According to the passage, why was Pop Art popular with regular people?

(A) It was based on things that people often saw or used.
(B) It was regarded as "high" art by elites.
(C) It became trendy among famous celebrities.
(D) It mixed traditional and newer art techniques.

• Vocabulary Quiz •

The word ☐ is closest in meaning to

| 1 emergence | 2 depicted | 3 originality | 4 regarded |
|---|---|---|---|
| ⓐ arrival | ⓐ transported | ⓐ creativity | ⓐ admired |
| ⓑ acclaim | ⓑ portrayed | ⓑ equality | ⓑ considered |
| ⓒ decree | ⓒ attached | ⓒ sophistication | ⓒ announced |

## The Environmental Threat of Avocados

Over the past decade, global avocado production has more than doubled. This trend will likely continue as more consumers are familiar with the health benefits of avocados, which are an excellent source of vitamins and healthy fat. Unfortunately, the increased popularity of avocados has had a negative effect on the environment.

One issue is that the cultivation of avocados contributes to deforestation. The cultivation of this fruit is highly profitable, so more and more land is being cleared to grow it. For example, approximately 30,000 acres of forest are lost annually in Mexico to create new avocado farms, which is a concern because the destruction of forests is linked to global warming. It also puts an increasing number of native plant and animal species at risk due to habitat loss.

Avocados cause further problems because the trees that produce this fruit are water intensive. On average, 70 liters of water is needed to produce a single avocado. By comparison, only 22 liters is used to grow an orange. Avocado cultivation has depleted water resources in many parts of the world, and, in some cases, it has even led to significant water shortages for the local people.

The amount of energy used to transport avocados is also a concern. Although avocados are primarily grown in Central and South America, the largest markets for this fruit are in Europe and the United States. Avocados must be kept below 13 degrees Celsius during shipment as they will ripen early if they are exposed to higher temperatures. Therefore, a large amount of energy is required to transport avocados from producers to consumers.

1  The phrase "contributes to" in the passage is closest in meaning to

(A) maintains
(B) causes
(C) harms
(D) prevents

2  According to paragraph 2, which of the following is true of Mexico?

(A) It intends to pass laws to prevent deforestation.
(B) It has become the largest producer of avocados.
(C) It brings new land under cultivation each year.
(D) It sets aside areas to protect endangered species.

3  The word "depleted" in the passage is closest in meaning to

(A) injured
(B) replaced
(C) modified
(D) reduced

4  According to paragraph 4, a lot of energy is required to transport avocados because they

(A) must be moved after ripening
(B) have to be transported in large quantities
(C) should be processed before delivery
(D) need to be kept cool during shipment

● Vocabulary Quiz ●

The word [        ] is closest in meaning to

1  cultivation
ⓐ preparation
ⓑ farming
ⓒ improvement

2  profitable
ⓐ lucrative
ⓑ relevant
ⓒ capable

3  concern
ⓐ debate
ⓑ worry
ⓒ prejudice

4  shortages
ⓐ neglect
ⓑ intensifies
ⓒ deficiencies

# Reading Practice 3

## Right-Handedness among Humans

Handedness is a preference for using either the right or left hand. By some estimates, over 90 percent of people are right-handed. This makes humans unique. Population groups of other primates, such as chimpanzees, include roughly the same number of right- and left-handed individuals.

The tendency toward right-handedness among humans is not a new 5 phenomenon. Archaeologists who study our early ancestors have found evidence that many individuals shared this characteristic in the past. For example, they examined a large number of stone tools created from 1.9 to 1.4 million years ago. Right-handed individuals produced slightly more than half of these tools. Studies of preserved teeth from 600,000 years ago show that this trend became stronger 10 over time. The wear on the teeth indicates that the vast majority of individuals used their right hand to put food in their mouth.

While there is much evidence of right-handedness being a common human trait for a long period of time, scientists are still uncertain of the reason. One theory is that it is related to social cooperation. Early humans shared tools and worked 15 together on tasks. This is easier if most members of a group have the same handedness. Therefore, it is possible that humans became mainly right-handed as they resided in groups and cooperated with each other over many generations.

Another potential explanation is based on how the brain is split into two hemispheres. The left side controls the right part of the body and vice versa. In 20 humans, the left hemisphere also handles language. It is likely that as humans began to use the language regularly, the left side of the brain became dominant. This could result in a preference for using the right side of the body.

### Glossary
· hemisphere: one half of the brain
· vice versa: the reverse of what is said is true

1 The word "tendency" in the passage is closest in meaning to

(A) attitude

(B) support

(C) progress

(D) inclination

2 The word "they" in the passage refers to

(A) humans

(B) archaeologists

(C) ancestors

(D) individuals

3 The word "resided" in the passage is closest in meaning to

(A) formed

(B) lived

(C) worked

(D) resisted

4 According to paragraph 4, which of the following is true of the human brain?

(A) The right part controls the right side of the body.

(B) Each hemisphere developed separately.

(C) Both halves have developed new functions over time.

(D) One side is responsible for language use.

• Vocabulary Quiz •

The word ☐ is closest in meaning to

1 roughly
ⓐ naturally
ⓑ approximately
ⓒ frequently

2 characteristic
ⓐ trait
ⓑ idea
ⓒ temper

3 potential
ⓐ inherent
ⓑ precise
ⓒ possible

4 dominant
ⓐ powerful
ⓑ effective
ⓒ useless

Answer Book p. 4

## How a Camel Survives in the Desert

Deserts are areas of land with very little water. Most are characterized by extreme heat throughout the year. Therefore, desert animals must be able to cope with the lack of moisture and high temperatures. An example of an animal that has 5 successfully adapted to the desert ecosystem is the camel.

A camel is able to survive in the desert because it uses water very efficiently. In fact, most camels can go for 7 to 10 days without drinking. One reason for this is that the inside of a camel's nose is extremely cool and dry. As a result, the 10 water vapor in a camel's breath is changed into a liquid before it escapes into the air. This then returns to the camel's body. A camel is also able to conserve water because it does not sweat until its body temperature reaches 41 degrees Celsius. Most animals begin sweating when they are much cooler than this.

The ability to tolerate heat is another factor that makes a camel well suited to 15 a desert environment. Most importantly, a camel's fat is stored primarily in the hump on its back. The lack of fat on the rest of the body means that heat can be released very quickly. In addition, a camel's body temperature drops significantly at night. Starting each day with a low body temperature allows a camel to endure the heat for a long period of time. Finally, a camel has thick pads on its feet. 20 These offer protection from the hot desert sand as a camel walks.

### Glossary
·ecosystem: a community of organisms and their environment

1 The word "adapted" in the passage is closest in meaning to
(A) protected
(B) tolerated
(C) depended
(D) adjusted

2 The word "This" in the passage refers to
(A) camel
(B) breath
(C) liquid
(D) air

3 The word "conserve" in the passage is closest in meaning to
(A) save
(B) lose
(C) increase
(D) provide

4 What is NOT mentioned as a reason a camel can tolerate high temperatures?
(A) It stores most of its fat in the hump.
(B) Its nose is wet during the day.
(C) Its body cools drastically at night.
(D) Its feet are protected from hot sand.

• Vocabulary Quiz •

The word [＿＿＿＿] is closest in meaning to

| 1  extreme | 2  suited | 3  released | 4  drops |
|------------|-----------|-------------|----------|
| ⓐ severe   | ⓐ devoted | ⓐ gathered  | ⓐ differs |
| ⓑ moderate | ⓑ advanced | ⓑ discharged | ⓑ decreases |
| ⓒ supreme  | ⓒ adapted | ⓒ hidden    | ⓒ warms |

Answer Book p. 5

## The Great Pyramid of Giza

➡ The Great Pyramid of Giza is the only one of the Seven Wonders of the Ancient World that still exists. Construction was completed around 2560 BC. For about 3,800 years, the pyramid was the tallest manmade structure until the Lincoln Cathedral was ⁵ erected in AD 1311.

➡ Archaeologists are uncertain about how the ancient Egyptians built such a massive structure. In particular, the method used to transport the 2.3 million stone blocks that comprise the pyramid is not known. The smallest of these weighs 1.3 tons while the largest is almost 80 tons. One theory is that the blocks were placed ¹⁰ on sleds and then dragged to the site of the pyramid. As the pyramid became taller, ramps were placed around it. **A** This allowed blocks to be added to the upper levels. **B** The labor would have been done entirely by people as the ancient Egyptians did not use oxen or horses as work animals. **C** It is believed that it took 30,000 workers 20 years to construct the Great Pyramid. **D** Significant resources ¹⁵ were also needed to feed and accommodate so many workers.

➡ The obvious question is why so much effort was put into building this structure. The Great Pyramid served as a tomb for the Egyptian ruler Khufu. The ancient Egyptians believed that their kings—known as pharaohs—were gods rather than mortals. Therefore, they had to have impressive tombs. These burial places included ²⁰ not only the body but also the things needed to enjoy the afterlife. For example, pharaohs were usually buried with beautiful robes, expensive wines, and treasures such as rings and necklaces. Also, the interior walls were painted with pictures of the dead person's life. In effect, the pyramids were monuments to the pharaohs.

| Glossary | ☒ |
| --- | --- |
| **mortal:** a human being | |
| **afterlife:** life after death | |

**1** In paragraph 1, why does the author mention "the Lincoln Cathedral"?

   Ⓐ To emphasize the magnitude of the pyramid

   Ⓑ To explain the difference between the two structures

   Ⓒ To give an example of another architectural wonder

   Ⓓ To argue that it is still the world's tallest manmade structure

Paragraph 1 is marked with an arrow [➡].

**2** Which of the sentences below best expresses the essential information in the highlighted sentence in the passage? *Incorrect* choices change the meaning in important ways or leave out essential information.

   Ⓐ Archaeologists wonder about the purpose of the Egyptian Pyramids.

   Ⓑ The Egyptians built the giant structure for no particular reason.

   Ⓒ The methods the Egyptians used to build the pyramid are not known.

   Ⓓ Archaeologists try to solve the mystery of the Great Pyramid.

**3** The word "comprise" in the passage is closest in meaning to

   Ⓐ surround

   Ⓑ complete

   Ⓒ contain

   Ⓓ compose

**4** According to paragraph 2, which of the following is true about the stone blocks?

   Ⓐ They were cut into square shapes.

   Ⓑ They come from the same spot.

   Ⓒ They show damage from transport.

   Ⓓ They vary greatly in terms of weight.

Paragraph 2 is marked with an arrow [➡].

**5** According to paragraph 2, the construction of the Great Pyramid

    Ⓐ did not last for longer than a decade

    Ⓑ caused the deaths of many workers

    Ⓒ did not involve the use of animals

    Ⓓ required resources from other countries

Paragraph 2 is marked with an arrow [➡].


**6** The word "served" in the passage is closest in meaning to

    Ⓐ prepared

    Ⓑ delivered

    Ⓒ functioned

    Ⓓ assisted


**7** The word "they" in the passage refers to

    Ⓐ workers

    Ⓑ Egyptians

    Ⓒ kings

    Ⓓ mortals


**8** According to paragraph 3, pharaohs were typically buried with all of the following EXCEPT

    Ⓐ picture books

    Ⓑ valuable jewelry

    Ⓒ alcoholic beverages

    Ⓓ clothing items

Paragraph 3 is marked with an arrow [➡].

Volume  Review  Help  Back  Next

**9** Look at the four squares [■] that indicate where the following sentence could be added to the passage.

**This represented a major investment in terms of manpower.**

Where would the sentence best fit?

Click on a square [■] to add the sentence to the passage.

**10 Directions:** An introductory sentence for a brief summary of the passage is provided below. Complete the summary by selecting the THREE answer choices that express the most important ideas in the passage. Some sentences do not belong in the summary because they express ideas that are not presented in the passage or are minor ideas in the passage. **This question is worth 2 points.**

Drag your answer choices to the spaces where they belong.
To remove an answer choice, click on it. To review the passage, click on **View Text**.

---

**The Great Pyramid of Giza is a unique structure.**

- 
- 
- 

---

Answer Choices

Ⓐ Scientists are uncertain about the building methods used.

Ⓑ Later buildings were modeled after the Great Pyramid.

Ⓒ Egyptians constructed the Great Pyramid as a burial site.

Ⓓ The Great Pyramid was built several thousand years ago.

Ⓔ The number of workers varied from year to year.

Ⓕ The pharaoh's treasures were included in the tomb.

Answer Book p. 5

# Vocabulary Review

## A. Fill in the blanks with the appropriate words from the box.

| disguise | preference | impressive |
|---|---|---|
| absorb | transport | seemingly |

1  Martin likes all kinds of music, but he has a strong _____ for jazz.

2  The company can _____ the microchips by ship or by plane.

3  The spy wore a wig and some sunglasses to _____ himself.

4  These new paper towels can _____ more water than regular ones.

5  The ten-year-old started a charity by himself, which is _____.

6  The math problem was _____ easy, but it was actually difficult to solve.

## B. Choose the closest meaning for each highlighted word.

7  This sauce is primarily made of tomatoes, with just a little bit of cream.
  (A) traditionally      (B) immediately      (C) mainly      (D) probably

8  Planning ahead helps you manage your time more efficiently.
  (A) carefully      (B) effectively      (C) partially      (D) creatively

9  We must reach the station by 8:30 or else we will miss the train.
  (A) agree with      (B) arrive at      (C) give up      (D) call for

10  Although his parents smiled, it was obvious that they were sad to see their son move away.
  (A) curious      (B) compelling      (C) ambiguous      (D) apparent

11  The massive blue whale is the world's largest animal and weighs more than 100 tons.
  (A) worthless      (B) appropriate      (C) trivial      (D) enormous

12  The animal shelter relied entirely on volunteers and had no paid employees.
  (A) respectively      (B) completely      (C) possibly      (D) ordinarily

13  This boat can accommodate ten people, but it can probably take in one more person.
  (A) release      (B) enhance      (C) control      (D) hold

14  It is slightly cold outside, so you should take a light jacket with you.
  (A) properly      (B) marginally      (C) thoroughly      (D) occasionally

# CHAPTER 02

# Reference

# Reference

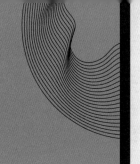

## About the Question Type

**Reference questions** ask you to identify what the highlighted word or phrase refers to in the passage.

The highlighted word or phrase is usually a pronoun (*it*, *they*, *this*, etc.). The correct answer choice will be the noun that the highlighted word or phrase refers to. The incorrect answer choices will be nouns that appear in the preceding sentences but are not referred to by the highlighted word or phrase.

## Question Format

- The word "⬜⬜⬜" in the passage refers to

- The phrase "⬜⬜⬜" in the passage refers to

## Key Strategies

- **Step 1** — Read the sentence that contains the highlighted word or phrase and the sentences that immediately precede it.

- **Step 2** — Find the noun that the highlighted word or phrase refers to. Determining whether the highlighted word or phrase is singular or plural can make it easier to identify its referent.

- **Step 3** — Substitute your answer choice for the highlighted word or phrase, and confirm that it makes sense.

# Example

## Placebo Effect

A placebo is a medical treatment such as a pill that has no actual medical properties. Placebos are often used when a new medication is being tested. Some patients are given placebos and others are given active medications, and the effectiveness of each is compared. When a person's physical or mental condition improves after taking a placebo, this is called the Placebo Effect. In some cases, placebos can produce favorable outcomes like real medicine. Experiments have demonstrated this possibility. Some studies have revealed that half of those who took placebos reported an improvement in their condition.

So, what causes the placebo effect? A recent study shows that expectations regarding treatment are the reason for this phenomenon. When a person believes that it will be effective, a positive outcome is more likely. In other words, the mind has a powerful influence over the body and can even help it heal.

Of course, placebos cannot actually shrink tumors or lower cholesterol. They will not cure patients in the traditional sense. Instead, placebos work on symptoms that are controlled by the brain. They are most likely to alleviate pain, stress, and fatigue.

**Glossary**

·tumor: an abnormal growth of cells in tissue

1  The phrase "this possibility" in the passage refers to

(A) testing a new medication
(B) improving someone's condition
(C) producing beneficial results
(D) taking real medicine

2  The word "it" in the passage refers to

(A) outcome
(B) mind
(C) influence
(D) body

Answer Book p. 6

## Growth of the US Frozen Food Industry

The frozen food industry in the United States began in 1929 when the inventor Clarence Birdseye developed the technology to instantly freeze any food. However, it did not expand very rapidly in the early years. The public's disinterest in frozen foods was partially attributable to the limited selection of products available—mainly fish and a few vegetables—as well as the lack of freezers in homes to store these items for long periods of time. The main reason, though, was that people preferred canned goods, which were cheap and convenient.

World War II played an important role in making frozen foods more acceptable to American consumers. Tin, the metal used for canned food containers, was in short supply, so the US government put strict controls in place to conserve this resource. Furthermore, most of the canned goods that were produced were used by the military to feed its personnel. As a result, American food companies began to make a much wider selection of frozen items, and major grocery store chains in all areas of the country aggressively advertised these to the public.

Frozen foods found even greater acceptance in the post-war years. In the 1940s, the introduction of the freezer for residential use, usually as a component of a refrigerator, allowed people to keep frozen foods in their residences indefinitely. The industry experienced another boost in the 1950s with the invention of TV dinners. These were complete frozen meals with an entrée, vegetable, and dessert that were already cooked and simply had to be reheated in the oven. Making both shopping and cooking extremely easy, they quickly caught on with the American public. Soon, food manufacturers were offering a variety of precooked frozen foods, ranging from pizzas to chicken cutlets.

1 The word "it" in the passage refers to

(A) industry
(B) inventor
(C) technology
(D) food

2 According to paragraph 1, which of the following was NOT a reason for the initial unpopularity of frozen foods?

(A) Companies did not offer a wide range of options.
(B) Freezers were costly to operate over the long term.
(C) Residences did not include a suitable storage space.
(D) Consumers had a preference for another product type.

3 The word "these" in the passage refers to

(A) companies
(B) items
(C) chains
(D) areas

4 The word "indefinitely" in the passage is closest in meaning to

(A) unusually
(B) frequently
(C) endlessly
(D) generally

• Vocabulary Quiz •

The word [          ] is closest in meaning to

1 instantly
ⓐ sharply
ⓑ immediately
ⓒ tremendously

2 expand
ⓐ collect
ⓑ increase
ⓒ vanish

3 convenient
ⓐ effortless
ⓑ delicious
ⓒ outstanding

4 extremely
ⓐ highly
ⓑ briefly
ⓒ directly

Answer Book p. 7

## Otis's Elevator

The modern elevator was developed during the 1800s. The first types used steam or water pressure to move platforms up and down. These elevators were used only to transport cargo since they were too dangerous to carry people. 5

Then, in 1852, American inventor Elisha Otis designed the first passenger elevator. Otis was employed at a furniture manufacturer, and the workers needed a way to lift heavy materials up to the higher floors. The cargo elevators were very unreliable for moving them 10 because the ropes would often break. Equipment could be damaged and workers could be injured, too. So, Otis designed a safety device using metal rods and springs. If the cable broke, the device would prevent the elevator from falling and crashing into the ground.

Otis introduced his new invention at the 1853 World's Fair with a dramatic 15 demonstration. In front of a crowd, Otis rode on a platform high into the air. He ordered the rope on the pulley to be cut. The onlookers gasped, but, thanks to his invention, the elevator on the shaft only fell a few inches before it stopped.

After that, elevators became secure enough to move people. But, more than that, Otis's invention revolutionized architecture. Very tall buildings had not been 20 practical because people could not regularly walk up and down many flights of stairs. However, once elevators were safe, buildings could be built higher and higher. Today, our modern cities are filled with skyscrapers with elevators that all use the same type of safety device that was invented more than a century ago.

1 The word "them" in the passage refers to

(A) people

(B) workers

(C) materials

(D) floors

2 According to paragraph 2, which of the following is true about Otis's elevator?

(A) It moved faster than the previous elevators.

(B) Otis designed it to find a way to move supplies.

(C) It was the most popular invention at the 1853 World's Fair.

(D) It had a cable that rarely broke.

3 The phrase "his new invention" in the passage refers to

(A) equipment

(B) safety device

(C) cable

(D) elevator

4 The word "practical" in the passage is closest in meaning to

(A) elegant

(B) critical

(C) useful

(D) essential

• Vocabulary Quiz •

The word _____ is closest in meaning to

| 1 employed | 2 injured | 3 onlookers | 4 secure |
|---|---|---|---|
| ⓐ detected | ⓐ hurt | ⓐ spectators | ⓐ common |
| ⓑ confronted | ⓑ affected | ⓑ pessimists | ⓑ safe |
| ⓒ hired | ⓒ spoiled | ⓒ critics | ⓒ nice |

Answer Book p. 7

## Mexican Cavefish

The Mexican cavefish is a species that lives in underwater limestone caves in Mexico. The habitat of these small, colorless fish has no light, little oxygen, and almost nothing to eat. To survive in this environment, they have developed a number 5 of unique physical characteristics.

Since they live in complete darkness, the cavefish rely on smell and taste to find food in the cave. To help them search for it, they have larger and more numerous taste buds than their cousins that live in the river. In addition, they have developed the ability to detect changes in pressure, so they are sensitive to 10 the slightest movements in the water. Cavefish gills are also bigger than those of other types of fish. This allows them to extract oxygen from water much more efficiently.

Perhaps the most interesting adaptation of the cavefish is that they lost their eyes completely. Over a period of millions of years, their eyes gradually grew 15 smaller and smaller until they disappeared altogether. Their eye sockets are now covered with scales and appear as dark spots. In the past, it was thought that the cavefish's eyes gradually disappeared because of disuse, but new studies show that they probably went away for a different reason. Cavefish have smaller brains than river-dwelling fish because they do not need to process images. This is an 20 advantage because their small brains use up to 30 percent less energy. Thus, it is likely that the cavefish lost their eyes in order to conserve energy, which helped them survive in a harsh habitat.

1 The word "it" in the passage refers to
(A) darkness
(B) taste
(C) food
(D) cave

2 According to paragraph 2, which of the following is true of the cavefish?
(A) Its gills need more oxygen to function.
(B) It has a limited number of large taste buds.
(C) It is capable of detecting small motions in the water.
(D) It has small gills due to oxygen restrictions.

3 The word "they" in the passage refers to
(A) scales
(B) dark spots
(C) cavefish
(D) eyes

4 The word "harsh" in the passage is closest in meaning to
(A) irregular
(B) rare
(C) gloomy
(D) severe

• Vocabulary Quiz •

The word [         ] is closest in meaning to

1 unique
ⓐ natural
ⓑ general
ⓒ special

2 rely on
ⓐ depend on
ⓑ relate to
ⓒ carry on

3 adaptation
ⓐ adjustment
ⓑ regulation
ⓒ creation

4 advantage
ⓐ authority
ⓑ benefit
ⓒ weakness

# Reading Practice 4

## Why Is Pluto Not a Planet?

When Pluto was first discovered in 1930, it became the ninth and smallest planet in the solar system. But, in 2006, that changed when scientists declared that it was no longer a planet at all. The surprising news came about because of the ⁵ discovery of a new planet in the Kuiper Belt, a region that is located in the outer solar system beyond Neptune. The new planet, Eris, was actually larger in mass than Pluto, and its composition was similar to the ninth planet as well.

Now, astronomers had to make a decision. Should Eris be the tenth planet ₁₀ in the solar system or, if not, should Pluto be considered a planet? After some careful consideration, they decided to change the definition of a planet. To be a planet, a celestial body must meet three requirements: it must orbit the Sun, be mostly round in shape, and have a gravity strong enough to clear the area around it of objects. Pluto had no problems with the first two requirements, but ₁₅ there was an issue with the third. Pluto was unable to either pull all of the nearby rocks and other debris into its own orbit or push them out to space. Therefore, its classification needed to be changed.

In response, scientists created an entirely new category called a dwarf planet for Pluto and its neighbor Eris. Dwarf planets, as their name suggests, refer to the ₂₀ planets that are smaller in size and lack sufficient gravitational force. Now, Pluto is no longer the last planet in the solar system. Instead, of all the celestial objects in the Kuiper Belt, it is the closest.

### Glossary
· celestial body: an object in the universe, such as a planet or star

1  The word "declared" in the passage is closest in meaning to
   (A) observed
   (B) experimented
   (C) debated
   (D) announced


2  The word "its" in the passage refers to
   (A) solar system
   (B) Neptune
   (C) Eris
   (D) Pluto


3  According to paragraph 2, why was Pluto's classification changed to a dwarf planet?
   (A) It was located outside the solar system.
   (B) It turned out not to have any gravity.
   (C) It did not remove objects around it.
   (D) It was smaller than Eris.


4  The word "it" in the passage refers to
   (A) Pluto
   (B) planet
   (C) solar system
   (D) Kuiper Belt

• Vocabulary Quiz •

The word [          ] is closest in meaning to

| 1 region | 2 consideration | 3 requirements | 4 sufficient |
| --- | --- | --- | --- |
| ⓐ facility | ⓐ transition | ⓐ profits | ⓐ enough |
| ⓑ system | ⓑ thought | ⓑ conditions | ⓑ efficient |
| ⓒ area | ⓒ experiment | ⓒ purposes | ⓒ objective |

Answer Book p. 9

## The Black Death

➡ The Black Death, also known as the plague, was one of the most fatal epidemics ever recorded in human history. It is believed to have originated in Asia, but it arrived in Europe in 1347 when trading ships for grains and seeds docked in Sicily. Sicilians were horrified to discover that most of the sailors were dead. These "death ships" were immediately sent back out to sea, but, unfortunately, it was too 5 late.

➡ The Black Death spread through fleas living on the rats from the ships. They would bite people, and then it spread quickly from person to person. People who caught the plague would develop a fever and become weak. They experienced severe swelling in the groin and armpits that would grow to the size of an apple. 10 Furthermore, the body became covered in black sores, from which the Black Death gets its name. Left untreated, people would usually die within 72 hours.

➡ While we now have medicine to treat the plague, the doctors back then did not know what to do. A common practice involved withdrawing "bad blood" from the body. **A** Many tried drinking vinegar or eating crushed minerals, like emeralds. **B** 15 Interestingly, the best chance for survival was a strategy still used today: social distancing. **C** This means that potential victims maintained a safe distance from other people. **D** However, only the wealthy were able to flee crowded cities and go to remote estates where they stayed away from everyone else.

In the end, most caught the feared illness and many died. The combination of 20 a high fatality rate, easy transmission, and no treatment killed roughly 25 million people—almost half of Europe. It would take 200 years for population levels to recover to previous levels.

| Glossary | ☒ |
| --- | --- |
| **epidemic:** an outbreak of disease that spreads quickly and affects many individuals | |

**1** The word "horrified" in the passage is closest in meaning to

(A) depressed

(B) disappointed

(C) shocked

(D) pleased

**2** According to paragraph 1, which of the following is true about the Black Death?

(A) It was first discovered by doctors in Asia.

(B) Its starting point in Europe was Sicily.

(C) Sailors caught it more than other people.

(D) It spread to other parts of Europe through seeds.

Paragraph 1 is marked with an arrow [➡].

**3** The word "They" in the passage refers to

(A) sailors

(B) fleas

(C) rats

(D) ships

**4** In paragraph 2, the author mentions "an apple" in order to

(A) suggest a possible treatment

(B) emphasize the severity of a symptom

(C) reveal a means of transmission

(D) indicate a cause of swelling

Paragraph 2 is marked with an arrow [➡].

**5** According to paragraph 2, the Black Death was given its name because

Ⓐ its symptoms included black sores

Ⓑ it was spread by black rats

Ⓒ it caused the blood to turn black

Ⓓ its victims' graves had black tombstones

Paragraph 2 is marked with an arrow [➡].

**6** The phrase "stayed away from" in the passage is closest in meaning to

Ⓐ mocked

Ⓑ avoided

Ⓒ consoled

Ⓓ criticized

**7** According to paragraph 3, people tried each of the following methods to survive the Black Death EXCEPT

Ⓐ leaving populated areas

Ⓑ letting blood out of the body

Ⓒ consuming crushed stones

Ⓓ cleaning wounds with vinegar

Paragraph 3 is marked with an arrow [➡].

**8** Which of the sentences below best expresses the essential information in the highlighted sentence in the passage? *Incorrect* choices change the meaning in important ways or leave out essential information.

Ⓐ The inability to treat this deadly and contagious disease resulted in the deaths of half of Europe.

Ⓑ Preventing the spread of this fatal illness limited the number of casualties in Europe.

Ⓒ Millions of Europeans died of the disease because an effective treatment was never discovered.

Ⓓ A large percentage of the European population was infected by this highly transmissible disease.

**9** Look at the four squares [■] that indicate where the following sentence could be added to the passage.

**Of course, none of these treatments helped.**

Where would the sentence best fit?

Click on a square [■] to add the sentence to the passage.

**10 Directions:** An introductory sentence for a brief summary of the passage is provided below. Complete the summary by selecting the THREE answer choices that express the most important ideas in the passage. Some sentences do not belong in the summary because they express ideas that are not presented in the passage or are minor ideas in the passage. **This question is worth 2 points.**

Drag your answer choices to the spaces where they belong.
To remove an answer choice, click on it. To review the passage, click on **View Text**.

---

**The Black Death was a terrible disease that spread throughout the fourteenth century.**

- 
- 
- 

---

Answer Choices

(A) The Black Death wiped out nearly the half of European population.

(B) Withdrawing blood from the body was the most effective treatment known.

(C) Medical knowledge then was not sufficient enough to deal with the plague.

(D) Most of the lives lost during the Black Death in Europe were in Sicily.

(E) After the plague ended, new medicines to treat diseases were developed.

(F) The Black Death spread quickly among humans after insects passed it on to humans.

Answer Book p. 9

# Vocabulary Review

Answer Book p. 10

**A.** Fill in the blanks with the appropriate words from the box.

| | | |
|---|---|---|
| alleviate | transmission | expectations |
| gradually | outcome | numerous |

1 The virus spread quickly because of its high rate of _____ .

2 The store received _____ complaints because of the rude employees.

3 Aspirin can _____ some symptoms of a migraine, but it cannot make it go away.

4 This book is extremely popular, so _____ for the sequel are high.

5 The underdog team won the game, which was a surprising _____ .

6 The slow boat _____ came closer and closer until it finally reached the shore.

**B.** Choose the closest meaning for each highlighted word.

7 Villagers on the mountain complained that their cell phone service was unreliable.
   (A) incorrect     (B) inappropriate     (C) undependable     (D) irregular

8 Darren goes to the gym regularly every morning at 7 a.m., which is a good habit.
   (A) routinely     (B) particularly     (C) greatly     (D) possibly

9 The doctor said it would take at least six months to recover from my broken leg.
   (A) suspend     (B) unite     (C) rebound     (D) disappear

10 Some scientists describe viruses as living things but others disagree with this definition.
   (A) regulation     (B) characterization     (C) implication     (D) collaboration

11 The man was in a fatal car accident and passed away last night.
   (A) reckless     (B) harsh     (C) lethal     (D) loose

12 The forest was partially destroyed by the fire, but the rest of the area was not damaged.
   (A) somewhat     (B) certainly     (C) seldom     (D) always

13 The cold temperature tonight is sure to freeze the lake by tomorrow morning.
   (A) chill     (B) thaw     (C) carve     (D) merge

14 "Linda" was a common name for girls in the 1950s, but it is rarely used now.
   (A) official     (B) necessary     (C) limited     (D) popular

# CHAPTER 03

## Sentence Simplification

# Sentence Simplification

## About the Question Type

**Sentence Simplification questions** ask you to choose the sentence that best summarizes the highlighted sentence in the passage.

Incorrect choices often change the original meaning of the highlighted sentence or leave out essential information. Therefore, make sure that your answer choice paraphrases the key information of the sentence.

## Question Format

Which of the sentences below best expresses the essential information in the highlighted sentence in the passage? *Incorrect* choices change the meaning in important ways or leave out essential information.

## Key Strategies

- **Step 1** — Read the highlighted sentence in the passage and identify its essential information.

- **Step 2** — Select the answer choice that most accurately paraphrases the essential information of the sentence. Keep in mind that an answer choice that does not fully restate the essential information cannot be the correct one.

# Example

## Were Dinosaurs Warm-Blooded or Cold-Blooded?

Dinosaurs have always presented many mysteries to paleontologists. One of the most puzzling has been their body temperature. Warm-blooded animals like mammals and birds produce heat within their body to maintain a constant body temperature. Cold-blooded animals like reptiles cannot regulate their body temperature and get heat from their environment. But what about dinosaurs? 5

In order to find out, scientists decided to look at metabolism. Warm-blooded animals have fast metabolisms that allow for a faster growth rate, more brainpower, and quicker movements. Cold-blooded animals lack these traits but are more economical with energy and food; that is, they can sustain themselves for long periods of time with very little food. Interestingly, studies of fossils showed 10 that dinosaurs had a combination of these characteristics. [1]They could regulate their body heat like mammals, although they could not do it continually.

Scientists believe this unique in-between stage gave dinosaurs an ecological advantage. They would have been smarter and faster than reptiles. [2]However, dinosaurs would not have required as much food as similar-sized mammals to 15 maintain these characteristics. In short, dinosaurs were truly in a category of their own. It is no wonder that we remain fascinated by these long-gone creatures.

1 Which of the sentences below best expresses the essential information in the highlighted sentence in the passage?

(A) Mammals and dinosaurs could both maintain body heat consistently.

(B) Mammals cannot regulate their body heat as well as dinosaurs.

(C) Dinosaurs could not always control their body temperature like mammals.

(D) Dinosaurs did a better job of managing body heat than mammals.

2 Which of the sentences below best expresses the essential information in the highlighted sentence in the passage?

(A) Because they had many attributes, dinosaurs had to eat much food.

(B) To preserve certain traits, dinosaurs needed less food than mammals.

(C) Mammals and dinosaurs were similar sizes because they ate a lot.

(D) The amount a dinosaur ate determined what kind of traits it had.

## How Alaska Became the 49th State

Alaska is the 49th and largest state in the US. It is a region filled with beauty and abundant natural resources. Around 5 percent of the area is covered in glaciers, and there are millions of acres of untouched wilderness. However, Alaska was not 5 always considered such an attractive place.

Native tribes had been the only inhabitants of the area for thousands of years until Russia began to expand its territory. During the seventeenth century, Russians established fur trading posts and other settlements in the region. Life there was not easy. The climate was harsh and agriculture was almost impossible. 10 [1]Since living there in general was so unpleasant and maintaining remote settlements was never very profitable, Russia eventually decided to sell Alaska to the United States.

Unfortunately, no one was interested in buying the area except for one person. US Secretary of State William Seward insisted on acquiring it because the large 15 landmass would increase the size of the US by 20 percent. He believed that Alaska would be a valuable possession for the US. [3]Most Americans, on the other hand, thought the deal was a waste of money and called it "Seward's Folly." In the end, the purchase was approved by only a single vote in the senate in 1867.

Luckily, Seward's insistence paid off. Gold was discovered there soon after the 20 deal, and hundreds of citizens headed to the northern territory. Alaska had more riches to offer. It was home to a wide variety of wildlife, including polar bears, beluga whales, and caribou. The US also gained hundreds of billions of dollars in fur, copper, fish, timber, and petroleum. Now, Alaska is one of the richest states in America, meaning that Seward's Folly was, in fact, a great achievement. 25

### Glossary

·folly: a foolish act or idea

1 Which of the sentences below best expresses the essential information in the highlighted sentence in the passage?

   (A) The US tried to purchase Alaska, even though life there was tough.

   (B) Russia chose to sell Alaska to the US because the land had no advantages.

   (C) The US hoped to gain profits by selling a useless region to Russia.

   (D) Having a colony in Alaska was too difficult and expensive for Russia.

2 The word "acquiring" in the passage is closest in meaning to

   (A) conquering

   (B) developing

   (C) requiring

   (D) obtaining

3 Which of the sentences below best expresses the essential information in the highlighted sentence in the passage?

   (A) Seward was criticized by Americans for not negotiating a better deal.

   (B) There was strong opposition in the US to the deal for financial reasons.

   (C) Opinion was divided in the US over the amount of money that should be spent.

   (D) Americans were not provided with sufficient information about Seward's plan.

4 According to paragraph 4, Seward was proved to be correct about Alaska because

   (A) its population began to increase

   (B) the region included significant natural resources

   (C) other US states contributed to its purchase

   (D) citizens of other countries relocated there

• Vocabulary Quiz •

The word [       ] is closest in meaning to

1 [abundant]
   ⓐ ample
   ⓑ standard
   ⓒ peaceful

2 [attractive]
   ⓐ legitimate
   ⓑ gigantic
   ⓒ appealing

3 [remote]
   ⓐ distant
   ⓑ informal
   ⓒ favorable

4 [insistence]
   ⓐ aptitude
   ⓑ persistence
   ⓒ estimation

# Reading Practice 2

## The Wire Mother Experiment

The Wire Mother Experiment was a famous experiment created by American psychologist Harry Harlow in the 1960s. [1]In the early 20th century, many psychologists believed that a baby became emotionally attached to its mother simply 5 because the mother provided food and water. However, Harlow was suspicious of this claim. He devised an experiment to see if it was true.

His research involved using newborn rhesus monkeys. He took the infants away from their mothers just a few hours after birth and left them to be raised by two 10 doll mothers. The first was made of wire and provided food. The second was made of soft cloth and did not provide food. Harlow observed how the monkeys behaved in these conditions.

He discovered that the baby monkeys went to the wire mother for food when they were hungry. However, they spent the majority of their time with the cloth 15 mother. The babies appeared to gain emotional comfort and security from the softness. In addition, they acted differently when they were faced with unfamiliar situations, such as being in a new room. [2]Although the young monkeys would feel safe and explore the room when placed in it with the cloth mother, they would freeze up, scream, and cry in fear if it was removed.
20

Harlow's experiment showed that love and affection were critical elements of healthy child development. They had positive effects when provided and devastating consequences when absent. His groundbreaking work is still studied to this day and continues to inform research on human behavior.

1 Which of the sentences below best expresses the essential information in the highlighted sentence in the passage?

(A) Psychologists thought mothers only provide nutrition to a baby for emotional reasons.

(B) A baby's desire for food reflected its need to have a mother, according to psychologists.

(C) Psychologists claimed that a baby bonded with its mother because it was given nourishment.

(D) Between affection and nutrition, psychologists argued that a baby would choose the latter.

2 Which of the sentences below best expresses the essential information in the highlighted sentence in the passage?

(A) When the baby monkeys were put in a new space with the cloth mother, they were frightened.

(B) Most baby monkeys were too afraid to enter the new room without the cloth mother.

(C) If the cloth mother was taken away, the baby monkeys were uncertain about how to behave.

(D) The baby monkeys felt secure with the cloth mother but panicked without it.

3 The word "devastating" in the passage is closest in meaning to

(A) unexpected

(B) harmful

(C) malicious

(D) confusing

4 According to paragraph 4, the experiment Harlow conducted

(A) provided inconclusive results

(B) was discredited by recent studies

(C) is relevant to modern research

(D) reveals a problem with human behavior

• Vocabulary Quiz •

The word [      ] is closest in meaning to

| 1 suspicious | 2 devised | 3 absent | 4 groundbreaking |
|---|---|---|---|
| ⓐ doubtful | ⓐ investigated | ⓐ away | ⓐ absolute |
| ⓑ forceful | ⓑ planned | ⓑ ready | ⓑ satisfactory |
| ⓒ clueless | ⓒ defended | ⓒ early | ⓒ innovative |

Answer Book p. 12

# Frida Kahlo

[1]Born in 1907, Frida Kahlo achieved international renown as an artist because of her self-portraits that were heavily influenced by her Mexican heritage. While she achieved success for her work, Kahlo's life was far from an easy one.

At the young age of six, she suffered from polio, which damaged her right leg. As a teenager, she was in a terrible bus accident that nearly killed her. It left her severely injured. She underwent more than 30 surgeries and spent many months recovering in bed. Unfortunately, she would continue to feel severe pain for the rest of her life.

Yet there was a silver lining. Feeling trapped in her bed and her body, Kahlo began to paint portraits of herself to pass the time and forget about her adversity. Despite never having had formal training as an artist, Kahlo showed an innate ability. She used bold, bright colors and a style that was directly inspired by Mexican folk art. [3]Even after she recovered, Kahlo continued to paint and eventually abandoned her studies in medicine to pursue a career as an artist.

Although many professional art critics considered Kahlo to be a Surrealist painter, she rejected this label. Instead, Kahlo argued that her paintings were accurate representations of her own experiences. Indeed, much of the personal pain that she suffered throughout her life is reflected in her work, as her self-portraits honestly portray her emotional states in response to the hardships she faced. By refusing to separate art from life, Kahlo created an artistic legacy that is still influential today.

### Glossary
· polio: an infectious disease usually affecting children and resulting in disability or death
· Surrealist: an artist whose work is based on the ideas of the unconscious and dreams

1 Which of the sentences below best expresses the essential information in the highlighted sentence in the passage?

(A) Kahlo was widely admired for introducing Mexican art to an international audience.

(B) Kahlo focused on self-portraits because this art form was popular in her home country.

(C) Kahlo influenced other Mexican artists by developing new portrait techniques.

(D) Kahlo became famous by creating pictures of herself that reflected her culture.

2 The word "innate" in the passage is closest in meaning to

(A) natural

(B) conscious

(C) extraordinary

(D) steady

3 Which of the sentences below best expresses the essential information in the highlighted sentence in the passage?

(A) Kahlo's interests in medicine led her to become an artist.

(B) Kahlo gave up medicine to become an artist after recovery.

(C) Kahlo had to stop studying medicine while she was recovering.

(D) Kahlo stopped her career in medicine because it interfered with her art.

4 According to paragraph 4, which of the following statements about Frida Kahlo is true?

(A) She struggled to produce art because of her challenging life.

(B) She viewed painting as a distraction from her personal difficulties.

(C) She believed herself to be a Surrealist artist.

(D) She disagreed with an expert opinion regarding her work.

• Vocabulary Quiz •

The word ⬚ is closest in meaning to

| 1 renown | 2 nearly | 3 accurate | 4 influential |
|---|---|---|---|
| ⓐ blame | ⓐ almost | ⓐ classic | ⓐ conventional |
| ⓑ fame | ⓑ someday | ⓑ precise | ⓑ enthusiastic |
| ⓒ loyalty | ⓒ likewise | ⓒ careful | ⓒ significant |

Answer Book p. 12

## The History of Hand-Washing

Hand-washing is one of the first routines we learn as children. It is an easy and highly effective way to prevent diseases. Yet, as a practice, it is a fairly recent development that did not catch on at first.

It began to take form in Europe during the 1840s. ²This was a terrible time because many new mothers were getting sick and dying regardless of social status or initial health. Shortly after giving birth, mothers would develop a rapid heart rate, a fever, and severe abdominal pain. Eventually, they would die from the sickness. The condition was known as "childbed fever." One Hungarian doctor named Ignaz Semmelweis saw this again and again as he worked at the maternity ward of the Vienna General Hospital. He was determined to find the cause.

Semmelweis observed two maternity wards that were at the hospital. One was run by doctors and the other was run by midwives. He noticed that the one the midwives were in charge of had far fewer deaths from childbed fever. After comparing the two wards and ruling out any differences, Semmelweis finally found the answer. ³While the midwives only delivered babies, doctors performed a number of other tasks at the hospital, including doing autopsies. Semmelweis hypothesized that certain "particles" were being transferred from dead bodies to new mothers by the doctors. He ordered the medical staff in the doctor's ward to wash their hands with soap and their medical tools with a chlorine solution. The effect was immediate: the mortality rate dropped dramatically.

Unfortunately, Semmelweis's thinking was ahead of his time, as his theory was initially rejected by the medical community. It was not until after his death that hand-washing became routinely accepted and ultimately changed hygiene health worldwide.

### Glossary
· autopsy: an examination of a dead body to determine the cause of death
· chlorine: a gas that is used especially as disinfectant

1 The phrase "catch on" in the passage is closest in meaning to

(A) occur

(B) approach

(C) emerge

(D) spread


2 Which of the sentences below best expresses the essential information in the highlighted sentence in the passage?

(A) The period in history when pregnant women were dying was the bleakest.

(B) Women from all classes and of varying health conditions passed away.

(C) Social standing and healthiness played a minor part in women passing away.

(D) Pregnancy was the largest cause of women becoming sick during this period.


3 Which of the sentences below best expresses the essential information in the highlighted sentence in the passage?

(A) Doctors conducted various medical procedures, but the midwives' sole job was to deliver babies.

(B) Midwives had more time to deliver babies than doctors, who had many different responsibilities.

(C) The main job of midwives was to deliver babies, while doctors' main task was doing autopsies.

(D) Midwives performed various tasks, but doctors only delivered babies.


4 According to paragraph 3, which of the following is NOT true?

(A) Semmelweis monitored a couple of different maternity wards.

(B) Semmelweis noted a difference in the mortality rates of two patient groups.

(C) The requirement to wash hands and equipment was applied to midwives.

(D) The number of deaths in the doctor's ward decreased after new measures were adopted.


• Vocabulary Quiz •

The word [        ] is closest in meaning to

1  prevent
   ⓐ block
   ⓑ attack
   ⓒ lose

2  practice
   ⓐ habit
   ⓑ addiction
   ⓒ endeavor

3  immediate
   ⓐ modest
   ⓑ different
   ⓒ instant

4  dramatically
   ⓐ usefully
   ⓑ greatly
   ⓒ solidly

## Green Icebergs

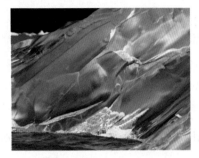

Nearly all icebergs are white or blue, but there is a small percentage that displays a dark emerald green color instead. Known as green icebergs, these oddities are only found in certain parts of Antarctica. There had been reports of green icebergs for more than a century, but no one could explain the reason for their color until recently. 5

→ Regular icebergs are made of compressed snow that turns to ice. **A** The blue color of the ice is what we typically see. **B** However, green icebergs are made of marine ice—ocean water frozen to the underside of the ice shelf—and not snow. **C** 10 The marine ice that makes green icebergs is much darker and has a distinct green hue. **D**

→ At first, scientists thought that dissolved organic matter in the ice was the reason for the coloring. It is yellowish in color, so mixing it with pure blue ice would create a green hue. However, when they sampled icebergs, they found the 15 green and blue marine ice had the same amount of organic material. In addition, researchers determined that the quantity was too small to make a difference in the coloring, which suggested that something else had to be responsible.

→ They came across a clue while measuring iron levels in the icebergs. To their surprise, green icebergs had 500 times more iron than regular ones. As iron 20 oxides in rocks are mostly yellow, scientists began to form a new theory based on the presence of the iron oxides in icebergs. As glaciers in Antarctica traveled over bedrock, they would grind the rocks into a powder called "rock flour." The rock flour would flow into the ocean and become frozen into part of the marine ice. The combination of blue ice and yellow iron oxides created green hues around the 25 edges of glaciers. When pieces of these broke off, they became the rare green icebergs.

| Glossary | ☒ |
| --- | --- |
| **bedrock:** the solid rock underlying soil | |

**1** The word "distinct" in the passage is closest in meaning to

Ⓐ organic

Ⓑ bizarre

Ⓒ noticeable

Ⓓ initial

**2** According to paragraph 2, which of the following is true about green icebergs?

Ⓐ They are more common than blue icebergs.

Ⓑ They are not as bright as regular icebergs.

Ⓒ They are made from compressed snow.

Ⓓ They are found in many different regions.

Paragraph 2 is marked with an arrow [➡].

**3** The word "It" in the passage refers to

Ⓐ snow

Ⓑ organic matter

Ⓒ ice

Ⓓ coloring

**4** Which of the sentences below best expresses the essential information in the highlighted sentence in the passage? *Incorrect* choices change the meaning in important ways or leave out essential information.

Ⓐ They found organic material in the samples of green and blue marine ice.

Ⓑ Green icebergs and blue icebergs were tested to see how much organic material each type had.

Ⓒ The quantity of organic material in green marine ice was equal to that found in blue marine ice.

Ⓓ The type of organic material in the icebergs determined whether they were blue or green.

**5** According to paragraph 3, which of the following is true?

   Ⓐ Blue marine ice did not contain organic material.

   Ⓑ Small amounts of organic material can change colors of iceberg.

   Ⓒ Blue ice and green ice can sometimes mix.

   Ⓓ Organic matter in the ice has a yellowish color.

Paragraph 3 is marked with an arrow [➡].

**6** The phrase "came across" in the passage is closest in meaning to

   Ⓐ discovered

   Ⓑ presented

   Ⓒ confirmed

   Ⓓ approached

**7** Which of the following can be inferred from paragraph 4 about iron oxide?

   Ⓐ Its color changes depending on where it is located.

   Ⓑ Its presence hinders the movement of icebergs.

   Ⓒ It is the most common mineral found in Ataractic icebergs.

   Ⓓ It is found in the bedrock of Antarctica.

Paragraph 4 is marked with an arrow [➡].

**8** According to paragraph 4, which of the following is NOT true about rock flour?

   Ⓐ It is made up of finely ground rock.

   Ⓑ It turns blue when it freezes.

   Ⓒ It is formed by a glacier's movement.

   Ⓓ It is a component of green icebergs.

Paragraph 4 is marked with an arrow [➡].

Volume | Review | Help | Back | Next

**9** Look at the four squares [■] that indicate where the following sentence could be added to the passage.

**When sunlight hits the ice, it absorbs the red light and reflects the blue light.**

Where would the sentence best fit?

> Click on a square [■] to add the sentence to the passage.

**10 Directions:** An introductory sentence for a brief summary of the passage is provided below. Complete the summary by selecting the THREE answer choices that express the most important ideas in the passage. Some sentences do not belong in the summary because they express ideas that are not presented in the passage or are minor ideas in the passage. **This question is worth 2 points.**

> Drag your answer choices to the spaces where they belong.
> To remove an answer choice, click on it. To review the passage, click on **View Text**.

---

**Despite having been around for hundreds of years, green icebergs remained a mystery to scientists.**

- 
- 
- 

---

Answer Choices

(A) Antarctica is a special place for scientists because of the unique iceberg phenomena.

(B) Icebergs that form from marine ice in Antarctica sometimes have a distinct color.

(C) Scientists spent too much time studying organic material when they should have been researching minerals.

(D) Organic matter initially became a primary candidate for the cause of green icebergs because of its yellow color.

(E) Rock flour containing iron oxides was the reason why icebergs turned green.

(F) Green icebergs are much more valuable because of their high concentration of iron.

Answer Book p. 13

# Vocabulary Review

**A.** **Fill in the blanks with the appropriate words from the box.**

| | | |
|---|---|---|
| hypothesized | hardships | sustain |
| dissolved | possessions | untouched |

1 When the earthquake damaged our house, my family lost all of its _____ .

2 The remote island is _____ by civilization, so it is a pristine environment.

3 The snow _____ quickly under the bright sun.

4 It is amazing that elephants can _____ their huge size on a diet of grass.

5 The scientist _____ that the virus would mutate, and his theory was correct.

6 Behind every successful person, there are many unknown _____ and challenges.

**B.** **Choose the closest meaning for each highlighted word.**

7 Glass frogs are oddities in the animal kingdom because they have transparent skin.
   (A) formalities      (B) anomalies      (C) properties      (D) abilities

8 We learn from our mistakes and grow stronger by overcoming adversity.
   (A) misfortune      (B) poverty      (C) fear      (D) anxiety

9 The dishwasher's instructions were puzzling, so I had to call the service center.
   (A) amazing      (B) fleeting      (C) confusing      (D) shocking

10 Tim had too many tasks, so he assigned some of his projects to another team member.
   (A) credits      (B) figures      (C) patterns      (D) duties

11 The new dam did not regulate the flow of water very well.
   (A) deceive      (B) reverse      (C) authorize      (D) control

12 The police discovered who was responsible for the crime and arrested him.
   (A) accountable      (B) elementary      (C) beneficial      (D) dependable

13 There was an unpleasant smell in the building because of the broken sewer system.
   (A) permanent      (B) disagreeable      (C) tremendous      (D) negligent

14 He and I became friends fairly recently, as we have only known each other for one month.
   (A) even      (B) quite      (C) beyond      (D) much

# CHAPTER 04

## Fact

# Fact

## About the Question Type

**Fact questions** ask you to identify specific information that is explicitly stated in the passage.

The correct answer choice restates specific information in the passage that directly answers the question. Incorrect answer choices include information that is contradicted by the passage, irrelevant to the question, or not mentioned in the passage.

## Question Format

- According to paragraph #, which of the following is true of X?

- According to paragraph #, what/how/why . . . ?

- The author's description/discussion of X mentions which of the following?

## Key Strategies

- **Step 1** — Read the question and identify the keywords. If the question indicates a specific paragraph, you can ignore the rest of the passage.

- **Step 2** — Scan the passage for the keywords, and locate the relevant information.

- **Step 3** — Select the answer choice that correctly paraphrases the relevant information in the passage.

# Example

## Monument Valley

Located in the southwestern United States, Monument Valley is a collection of large sandstone rock formations in a red-sand desert, with the most impressive of these being over 250 meters tall. This natural wonder is the result of geological ⁵ processes that occurred over an extended period of time.

Millions of years ago, the site of Monument Valley was surrounded by higher land. As a result, a large amount of rock and sand from the nearby Rocky Mountains was deposited in the area. This caused the formation of layers upon ¹⁰ layers of different types of rock. Around the same time, pressure from deep under the earth gradually elevated the lowlands, creating a raised area of flat land called a plateau.

At this point, wind and water began to break down parts of the plateau. The process of erosion affected the various rock layers differently, and the softer ones ¹⁵ wore away much more quickly than the harder ones. The formations visible in Monument Valley are composed of the most durable types of rock.

1   According to paragraph 2, which of the following is true of Monument Valley?

(A) It was surrounded by bodies of water.

(B) It was lower than the adjacent areas.

(C) It was closer to the Rocky Mountains.

(D) It was composed of a single type of rock.

2   According to paragraph 3, how did erosion lead to the formation of Monument Valley?

(A) It formed layers of different rocks.

(B) It flattened the surface of the plateau.

(C) It deposited a variety of rocks in the area.

(D) It impacted different materials at different rates.

Answer Book p. 15

## Storytelling in Silent Films

From the late 1800s until the 1920s, motion pictures were produced without sound. Known as silent films, they did not include music, sound effects, or dialogue. Therefore, they were primarily a visual form of entertainment. Despite this limitation, early filmmakers developed several methods to present stories to audiences. 5

One of the most important was the use of exaggerated facial expressions and body language by actors. This made the character's emotions obvious to audience members. For example, if a character was supposed to be surprised, the actor would throw his or her hands up in the air and open his or her eyes wide. During this type of scene, the director would often focus the camera on the actor's face. 10 A close-up shot made it easy for the audience to determine how the character was feeling.

Silent films also included title cards, which were film frames with text between the scenes. They often displayed dialogue or the inner thoughts of a character. Title cards also functioned like the narrator in a modern film. They would 15 provide background information about what was happening on screen. As silent films became more complex, the title cards became increasingly important. Filmmakers worked with professional writers to produce the content. They also employed artists to create illustrations and other decorative features.

Another method was the employment of live musicians in theaters. This 20 allowed for the use of music to create a suitable atmosphere and express mood. Film producers provided instructions for the musicians to follow while the movies played. These often included information on how to create sound effects to match the action onscreen. For instance, loud drums might be played to represent the sound of thunder during a storm. 25

1 The word "exaggerated" in the passage is closest in meaning to

(A) overemphasized
(B) understated
(C) ingenious
(D) accurate

2 According to paragraph 2, a close-up of an actor's face

(A) showed the dialogue between different characters
(B) allowed viewers to identify the emotional state
(C) encouraged audience members to follow the plot
(D) made body language hard to understand

3 How did directors of silent films provide background information to moviegoers?

(A) Artists were hired to create film sets.
(B) Musicians played popular songs about a topic.
(C) Live narrators were employed at theaters.
(D) Lines of text were included in movies.

4 The word "These" in the passage refers to

(A) theaters
(B) instructions
(C) musicians
(D) movies

• Vocabulary Quiz •

The word [          ] is closest in meaning to

1 limitation
  ⓐ result
  ⓑ investigation
  ⓒ constraint

2 displayed
  ⓐ showed
  ⓑ rejected
  ⓒ prevented

3 increasingly
  ⓐ progressively
  ⓑ overwhelmingly
  ⓒ reluctantly

4 suitable
  ⓐ lively
  ⓑ appropriate
  ⓒ believable

## Braille System

Braille is a system of writing for the blind. Each character is made up of one or more raised dots. A message written in Braille can be read with touch rather than sight. Since it was first developed, Braille has come to be used by visually  5 impaired people throughout the world.

Braille has its origins in a military code created for the French emperor Napoleon. He wanted a way for his soldiers to read messages at night without using lights. In response, the inventor Charles Barbier developed a simple system of raised dots to write numbers that can be read by touch. Louis Braille, a French  10 educator who lost his sight at a young age, improved on the system. By 1905, Braille had produced a complete form of writing for the blind, which was named after him.

Braille was based on the Latin alphabet, which is used in many regions of the world. The most basic component of Braille is the cell. This is a pattern of six  15 dots arranged in two columns of three. Different dots are raised within a cell to represent specific letters of the alphabet. For example, one raised dot in the upper left corner of a cell stands for the letter A. The system also includes other types of characters, such as punctuation marks and numbers.

As Braille spread to other countries, variations were introduced. These were  20 necessary because of the differences between languages. However, in 1951, an international conference was held to ensure consistency among the various Braille scripts. This included creating ways to match the letters in non-Latin alphabets with those in Latin ones. As a result, a blind person who achieves Braille literacy in one country can usually read the script used in other countries.  25

1 What was the purpose of the system created by Charles Barbier?

(A) It prevented military plans from being read by enemies.

(B) It enabled the army to understand an enemy's code.

(C) It allowed Napoleon to send messages to his allies.

(D) It enabled soldiers to read notes in the dark.

2 The phrase "stands for" in the passage is closest in meaning to

(A) reserves

(B) symbolizes

(C) imitates

(D) determines

3 According to paragraph 3, what is a feature of Braille?

(A) Punctuation marks can be represented.

(B) More than six dots can be utilized if necessary.

(C) Every letter can be written with the same pattern.

(D) A single dot can express an entire word.

4 According to paragraph 4, a conference on various Braille scripts was held in 1951 to

(A) determine their literacy rates

(B) introduce them to other countries

(C) eliminate errors from them

(D) make them more uniform

• Vocabulary Quiz •

The word ⬚ is closest in meaning to

| 1 sight | 2 impaired | 3 component | 4 consistency |
|---------|------------|-------------|---------------|
| ⓐ vision | ⓐ disabled | ⓐ function | ⓐ complexity |
| ⓑ temper | ⓑ appealing | ⓑ example | ⓑ uniformity |
| ⓒ faith | ⓒ diligent | ⓒ part | ⓒ accuracy |

Answer Book p. 16

## ADHD

Attention Deficit Hyperactivity Disorder (ADHD) is a common childhood mental health disorder. In the United States, this condition has been diagnosed in approximately 10 percent of all children. It can cause serious challenges for ⁵ affected individuals.

ADHD causes a range of symptoms that make it difficult to function in school. Most significantly, children with this disorder are easily distracted and, thus, cannot focus on their schoolwork for long periods. In addition, they have a hard time sitting still, and they will frequently interrupt others. As a result, children ¹⁰ with ADHD often get in trouble, which can lead to self-esteem issues.

The exact causes of ADHD have not been determined. However, researchers believe that genetics plays an important role. In fact, a recent study shows that 75 percent of children with this disorder have a relative with ADHD. There is also evidence that other factors may moderately increase the risk of developing this ¹⁵ condition. For example, exposure to certain hazardous substances, such as lead, at a young age may be a contributor. A head injury may lead to the development of ADHD as well.

Regardless of the cause, ADHD is treatable. Generally, behavioral therapy is enough to cope with mild symptoms. A therapist will work with both the child ²⁰ and the parents to develop a plan to encourage positive behaviors and discourage negative ones. For serious cases, medications to boost the production of a chemical in the brain that improves attentiveness may be prescribed. Fortunately, treatments become less necessary as a child approaches adulthood because the symptoms of ADHD are usually significantly reduced once a person reaches his ²⁵ or her 20s.

1 The word "diagnosed" in the passage is closest in meaning to
   (A) treated
   (B) prevented
   (C) identified
   (D) transmitted


2 According to paragraph 2, ADHD affects children's performance in school because it
   (A) hinders their ability to concentrate
   (B) lowers their levels of energy
   (C) causes them to avoid talking
   (D) makes them shy around others


3 According to paragraph 3, which of the following is believed to be the most common cause of ADHD in children?
   (A) Personal relationships
   (B) Inherited traits
   (C) Harmful chemicals
   (D) Physical injuries


4 According to paragraph 4, medication for ADHD is most likely to be prescribed when a patient
   (A) responds to another treatment
   (B) enters into adulthood
   (C) begins behavioral therapy
   (D) shows severe symptoms

• Vocabulary Quiz •

The word ☐ is closest in meaning to

1 distracted
   ⓐ sidetracked
   ⓑ instructed
   ⓒ disciplined

2 interrupt
   ⓐ interrogate
   ⓑ disrupt
   ⓒ embrace

3 moderately
   ⓐ somewhat
   ⓑ already
   ⓒ significantly

4 hazardous
   ⓐ undesirable
   ⓑ illegal
   ⓒ dangerous

## Babylon

Established in approximately 2300 BC, Babylon was an ancient city on the Euphrates River just south of modern-day Baghdad. It was an important center of power in the region for thousands of years. 5

Although little is known about its early history, Babylon rose to prominence in 1792 BC. This year marked the start of King Hammurabi's reign. During his almost 40 years as ruler, Hammurabi conquered most of the city-states of southern Mesopotamia. His kingdom came to be known as the First Babylonian Empire. He made Babylon his capital and reinforced its 10 walls for defensive purposes. He also established a complex system of law for his subjects called the Code of Hammurabi.

Hammurabi's descendants governed Babylon for several hundred years. During this period, the city increased in population to become one of the largest in the world. It was also a time when many impressive structures were built. These 15 included a massive temple called the Etemenanki that was supposedly over 90 meters tall. Some historians believe it was the inspiration for the tale of the Tower of Babel in the bible. Unfortunately, Babylon was conquered by a foreign state in 1595 BC. This led to an extended period of decline for the city.

In 626 BC, Babylon rebelled, marking the start of the Second Babylonian 20 Empire. The new kingdom eventually expanded beyond the borders of the original Babylonian empire to control much of the Middle East. Many of the structures that had been neglected during the time of foreign control were restored. However, in 539 BC, the city once again lost its independence. The importance of the city gradually decreased, and, by 275 BC, it had been almost completely 25 abandoned.

1 The word "reinforced" in the passage is closest in meaning to

(A) combined
(B) inspected
(C) designed
(D) strengthened

2 According to paragraph 2, which of the following is true about King Hammurabi?

(A) He established a new city.
(B) He ruled for less than a decade.
(C) He allied with a foreign empire.
(D) He created a legal system.

3 The author's discussion of the Etemenanki mentions which of the following?

(A) It was built by King Hammurabi.
(B) It inspired a story in a religious text.
(C) It was destroyed in 1595 BC.
(D) It resembled a building in a foreign city.

4 According to paragraph 4, which of the following is true of the Second Babylonian Empire?

(A) It developed new methods of agriculture.
(B) It faced several rebellions in the cities it ruled.
(C) It controlled more territory than the first one.
(D) It retained its independence until 275 BC.

• Vocabulary Quiz •

The word [ ] is closest in meaning to

| 1 conquered | 2 descendants | 3 supposedly | 4 neglected |
|---|---|---|---|
| ⓐ defeated | ⓐ subjects | ⓐ improbably | ⓐ ignored |
| ⓑ overlooked | ⓑ superiors | ⓑ immensely | ⓑ purchased |
| ⓒ oversaw | ⓒ offspring | ⓒ reportedly | ⓒ destroyed |

## Plant Defense Mechanisms

It may seem like plants have no means of defending themselves since they can appear quite passive to the human eye. However, every plant is actually hard at work utilizing different methods of protection against predators.  5

➡ Typically, the first line of defense is physical. This may take the form of a barrier, such as the numerous layers of bark on a tree that keep out all but the most determined insects. Many other plants have thorns, like roses, or prickly spines, such as those of cacti. These give the flora a fitness advantage by deterring herbivores. Some physical defenses are much more subtle. 10 For instance, one species of tropical vine has yellow markings on its leaves that resemble the eggs of Heliconius butterflies. This discourages the butterflies from laying their eggs, which is an advantage because the larvae of this insect feed on the vine.

➡ Plants also make use of chemical defenses. **A** If a plant's exterior is 15 compromised or damaged, it must resort to a different set of systems. **B** Thus, over thousands of years, plants have evolved to produce bitter-tasting chemicals or poisonous toxins that animals learn to avoid. **C** Such chemical substances, known as secondary metabolites, are not directly involved in the growth, development, or reproduction of a plant. **D**  20

➡ Although being the two most common forms of defense, physical and chemical mechanisms are not the only ones plants are capable of employing. For example, ant plants form a symbiotic relationship with ants. They produce nectar for ants to eat and have hollow internal structures that are suitable for them to build their nests in. In return, the ants will attack any herbivore that attempts to damage the 25 plant. This shows just how ingenious plants can be when it comes to protecting themselves.

| Glossary | ✕ |
|---|---|
| **herbivore:** an animal that eats mainly plants | |

**1** The word "passive" in the passage is closest in meaning to

- (A) aggressive
- (B) inactive
- (C) weak
- (D) similar

**2** According to paragraph 2, which of the following is true about trees?

- (A) Their bark is a less effective defense than thorns or spines.
- (B) Their exterior can be penetrated by only a few insects.
- (C) They can provide protection to other species of flora.
- (D) They deter herbivores by growing an inedible outer covering.

Paragraph 2 is marked with an arrow [➡].

**3** Which of the following can be inferred about Heliconius butterflies in paragraph 2?

- (A) The vegetation they mimic is found only in the tropics.
- (B) Each larva consumes a large number of vine leaves.
- (C) The yellow markings on their eggs function as camouflage.
- (D) Multiple individuals will avoid laying eggs in the same location.

Paragraph 2 is marked with an arrow [➡].

**4** The phrase "resort to" in the passage is closest in meaning to

- (A) interrupt
- (B) display
- (C) demand
- (D) utilize

**5** According to paragraph 3, how do animals respond to plants with chemical toxins?

- Ⓐ They ensure that they do not grow or develop.
- Ⓑ They develop a biological antidote for them.
- Ⓒ They figure out which ones are poisonous.
- Ⓓ They understand to stay away from them.

Paragraph 3 is marked with an arrow [➡].

**6** Which of the sentences below best expresses the essential information in the highlighted sentence in the passage? *Incorrect* choices change the meaning in important ways or leave out essential information.

- Ⓐ Plants must employ several types of defense system simultaneously in order to survive.
- Ⓑ Most plants that employ other defensive systems do not use chemical or physical ones.
- Ⓒ Physical and chemical mechanisms are most commonly used due to their effectiveness.
- Ⓓ There are other forms of defense that plants use besides physical and chemical mechanisms.

**7** The word "ingenious" is closest in meaning to

- Ⓐ clever
- Ⓑ obscure
- Ⓒ untamed
- Ⓓ generous

**8** According to paragraph 4, which of the following is NOT true of ant plants?

- Ⓐ They include areas well suited for ant habitation.
- Ⓑ They create a substance that an insect eats.
- Ⓒ They are toxic to many species of herbivores.
- Ⓓ They are defended by another type of organism.

Paragraph 4 is marked with an arrow [➡].

**9** Look at the four squares [■] that indicate where the following sentence could be added to the passage.

**In other words, they are produced solely for the purposes of defense and nothing else.**

Where would the sentence best fit?

Click on a square [■] to add the sentence to the passage.

**10 Directions:** An introductory sentence for a brief summary of the passage is provided below. Complete the summary by selecting the THREE answer choices that express the most important ideas in the passage. Some sentences do not belong in the summary because they express ideas that are not presented in the passage or are minor ideas in the passage. **This question is worth 2 points.**

Drag your answer choices to the spaces where they belong.
To remove an answer choice, click on it. To review the passage, click on **View Text**.

---

**While plants may seem like they cannot protect themselves, they actually have strong defense systems against predators.**

- 
- 
- 

---

Answer Choices

(A) The bark of a tree works as a deterrent to insects because it is made up of several different layers.

(B) Physical defenses include obvious types like thorns or spines as well as less obvious ones like imitating different things.

(C) Plants that are limited in development, growth, and reproduction need secondary metabolites because they are too weak to protect themselves.

(D) Poison is a type of chemical defense that is used when physical defenses fail.

(E) Almost all plants have some form of physical or chemical defense, but some use more specialized methods against predators.

(F) Plants and insects have a symbiotic relationship that allows each species to be more protected against other animals.

Answer Book p. 17

# Vocabulary Review

Answer Book p. 18

**A. Fill in the blanks with the appropriate words from the box.**

| durable | means | specific |
|---------|-------|----------|
| wonders | exterior | governed |

1 The telegraph was a(n) _____ of communication used in the nineteenth century.

2 The jacket is like new after decades of use because the fabric is quite _____.

3 The recipe identifies _____ brands for some of the ingredients.

4 The Great Wall of China is considered one of the _____ of the ancient world.

5 Most urban centers are _____ by a mayor and a city council.

6 The inside of the house is not as attractive as the _____.

**B. Choose the closest meaning for each highlighted word.**

7 The sailors rebelled against the captain when he refused to change course.
   (A) revolted      (B) voted      (C) fell      (D) navigated

8 The school board elevated the teacher to the position of superintendent.
   (A) transferred      (B) altered      (C) designated      (D) raised

9 Early pyramids were very simple, but later ones were more complex.
   (A) expensive      (B) popular      (C) successful      (D) complicated

10 Deep inside the mountain is a hollow place where the bear sleeps.
   (A) dark      (B) damp      (C) empty      (D) quiet

11 The police placed a barrier in front of the crime scene so nobody could get in.
   (A) sign      (B) obstacle      (C) statue      (D) platform

12 The store clerk arranged the gift boxes on the display case.
   (A) removed      (B) aligned      (C) replaced      (D) updated

13 The formation of labor unions led to significant workplace reforms.
   (A) agreement      (B) duration      (C) creation      (D) change

14 The maze is a challenge for those without a strong sense of direction.
   (A) entertainment      (B) problem      (C) game      (D) mission

# CHAPTER 05

## Negative Fact

# Negative Fact

## About the Question Type

**Negative Fact questions** ask you to identify specific information that is NOT true according to the passage or NOT mentioned in the passage.

These questions usually contain the words *NOT* or *EXCEPT*. Be careful to select the answer choice that includes information that is contradicted by the passage or not mentioned in the passage.

## Question Format

- According to paragraph #, which of the following is NOT true of X?

- According to paragraph #, all of the following are true of X EXCEPT

- The author mentions all of the following EXCEPT

## Key Strategies

- **Step 1** — Read the question and identify the keywords. If the question indicates a specific paragraph, you can ignore the rest of the passage.

- **Step 2** — Scan the passage for the keywords, and locate the relevant information.

- **Step 3** — Verify each answer choice. Select the answer choice that includes information that is contradicted by the passage or not mentioned in the passage.

# Example

## Pax Romana

*Pax Romana* means "Roman peace" in Latin. The term refers to two centuries of peace and prosperity in the Roman Empire from 27 BC to AD 180. During this era, the Roman Empire ranged from Britain in the northwest to Egypt in the southeast. A quarter of the world's population lived under Roman rule.

Following the assassination of Julius Caesar, Augustus brought an end to civil unrest with strong and effective leadership. He removed the threat of rebellion by paying soldiers pensions from the Roman treasury. This increased the empire's military might. Augustus established borders that were easier to defend. He also kept the territories he conquered content by permitting client kings to make their own local and religious decisions.

Later emperors continued the era of stability and prosperity. The empire's wealth expanded through trade with the Far East. The Indians and Chinese exchanged silks and gems for Roman glass and rugs. The Romans invested this wealth in infrastructure. They built roads throughout the empire using the new invention of concrete. They also built impressive domed structures in the capital city. This continued until the wise emperor Marcus Aurelius died, leaving the empire to his incompetent son Commodus.

1 The author mentions all of the following as characteristics of Pax Romana EXCEPT

(A) military strength
(B) territorial conquest
(C) religious conformity
(D) economic prosperity

2 According to paragraph 3, all of the following are true of the Roman Empire EXCEPT:

(A) It built roads with concrete.
(B) It created impressive architecture.
(C) It traded with the Far East.
(D) It exported silks and gems.

## The Florida Everglades

The Everglades, located in South Florida, is the largest subtropical wetland in the United States. During the wet season, Lake Okeechobee overflows and fills the Everglades with fresh water. This creates a vast marshland that supports ⁵ a rich plant and wildlife community. Over 2,000 species of rare plants and animals, including the Florida panther, American crocodile, and mangroves, make their home in the Everglades. Not only does it serve as a vital ecosystem, but it also provides drinking water for people in Florida. ¹⁰

However, it is threatened by human activity. Efforts to prevent flooding in southern Florida have caused great damage to the Everglades. Much of the wetland has been drained so the land could be used to farm sugarcane and other crops. Some of Florida's cities expanded their roads and buildings into the wetland territory, too. Now, less than half of the original wetland remains. Moreover, ¹⁵ invasive species such as exotic plants and insects have been introduced to the region by humans and pose a threat. Habitat loss and the loss of food sources are increasing the risk of extinction of native species. As a result, many animal species are endangered. For example, fewer than 100 panthers are left in the park, and wading bird populations have declined by 90 percent. ²⁰

For two decades, ecologists and politicians have worked together to restore this national treasure. In 2000, the United States Congress devoted the vast sum of $10 billion to the cause with the Comprehensive Everglades Restoration Plan (CERP). Its goal is to restore, protect, and preserve freshwater resources in the Everglades. This will make the ecosystem more like it was before people moved into the ²⁵ region. The local drinking water will be cleaner as well. This restoration project may be expensive, but it will have many benefits to animals and people alike.

1 The word "vital" is closest in meaning to

(A) common

(B) thriving

(C) essential

(D) balanced

2 According to paragraph 1, which of the following is true of the Florida Everglades?

(A) It is the largest wetland in the world.

(B) Its water comes from a lake that floods seasonally.

(C) It drains into a large body of fresh water.

(D) It includes several distinct ecosystems.

3 According to paragraph 2, all of the following are a threat to the Florida Everglades EXCEPT

(A) flood prevention

(B) agricultural activities

(C) endangered species

(D) urban development

4 According to paragraph 3, which of the following is NOT true of CERP?

(A) It aims to conserve freshwater in Everglades.

(B) It will be more beneficial to humans than to animals.

(C) It requires a large amount of money.

(D) Its benefits include improved drinking water.

• Vocabulary Quiz •

The word ⬚ is closest in meaning to

1 vast
  ⓐ extensive
  ⓑ narrow
  ⓒ deep

2 invasive
  ⓐ diverse
  ⓑ intrusive
  ⓒ ancient

3 exotic
  ⓐ non-native
  ⓑ provocative
  ⓒ natural

4 restore
  ⓐ visit
  ⓑ support
  ⓒ renew

# **Reading** Practice 2

## The Taj Mahal

The Taj Mahal is an enormous complex of white marble in Agra, India. It serves as both a tomb and <u>mosque</u>. Shah Jahan, emperor of the Mughal dynasty, commanded that it be constructed in 1632. Four hundred years later, 5 it is as stunning as ever. As a masterpiece of Mughal architecture, it was designated as a UNESCO World Heritage Site in 1983.

The Taj Mahal is regarded by many as a symbol of pure love. According to legend, Shah Jahan's beloved wife, Mumtaz Mahal, died while giving birth to 10 their 14th child. In his grief, Shah Jahan decided to construct a resting place that would honor her forever. He brought together several of the greatest architects of the era. They designed a massive structure that would require more than 20,000 workers and 22 years to complete. Shah Jahan insisted that only the world's finest architecture could be worthy of his late wife. 15

The Taj Mahal has long been recognized for its architectural value. It is constructed with perfect symmetry with many elements mirrored on different sides. For example, its central tomb is surrounded by twin mosques where people can come to worship. Each of the four corners is decorated with an identical tall and narrow tower called a minaret. Unprecedented in earlier Mughal architecture, 20 these minarets show how the Taj Mahal combines different styles. The mosques are red sandstone, traditional in earlier Mughal buildings. But the tomb is made of white marble, popular in other Indian traditions. In addition, the dome of the Taj Mahal is of the Persian style. No wonder the Taj Mahal is regarded as the finest example of the combination of Indian, Persian, and Islamic styles. 25

### Glossary
· mosque: a building used for worship by Muslims

1   According to paragraph 1, which of the following is NOT true of the Taj Mahal?

(A) It functions as a burial site.

(B) It was built by a Mughal ruler.

(C) It was restored in 1983.

(D) Marble was used in its construction.

2   According to paragraph 2, Shah Jahan built the Taj Mahal because he

(A) wanted to demonstrate his power

(B) wished to build a memorial to his wife

(C) needed a place for the people to worship

(D) admired a variety of architectural styles

3   The word "symmetry" in the passage is closest in meaning to

(A) integration

(B) variety

(C) balance

(D) innovation

4   According to paragraph 3, the Taj Mahal is notable for all of the following EXCEPT

(A) mixing various architectural styles

(B) presenting diverse designs on each side

(C) using different construction materials

(D) including four towers of equal size

• Vocabulary Quiz •

The word [        ] is closest in meaning to

1  | enormous |
ⓐ ancient
ⓑ huge
ⓒ comprehensive

2  | stunning |
ⓐ breathtaking
ⓑ old
ⓒ effective

3  | symbol |
ⓐ outgrowth
ⓑ gesture
ⓒ representation

4  | identical |
ⓐ same
ⓑ sacred
ⓒ special

# Reading Practice 3

## Can Animals Predict Earthquakes?

Associations between seismic activity and animal activity have been made for centuries. The Greek philosopher Aristotle witnessed rats, snakes, and centipedes crawl out of their homes several days before a strong earthquake in 373 BC. In 1989, a geologist predicted an earthquake based on numerous reports of missing pets in newspaper ads. Zookeepers reported unusually noisy lemurs 15 minutes 5 before a 2011 quake. These strange animal behaviors before an earthquake could be useful to humans. That's because we do not yet have the ability to make reliable long-term earthquake predictions.

Nobody knows how animals know that earthquakes are coming, but one theory suggests they can sense vibrations in the ground. These vibrations, known as 10 primary and secondary waves (P-waves and S-waves) occur when underground rocks shift. P-waves travel through rock at 1 to 14 kilometers per second. Two minutes later come the violent S-waves that cause the earth to move. Animals may be able to detect the gentler P-waves that humans do not notice. However, that would only provide about two minutes of advance warning. 15

Another possible explanation is that animals may feel ill a few days before an earthquake. Some scientists believe that <u>molecules</u> from the earth's crust become electrically charged when the earth's crust shifts. These ions are released into the air. Animals may sense the ionization with their fur. This may explain the animals' desire to move away from the area. It would also explain why captive 20 animals become restless.

Nevertheless, there is very little solid evidence for animal earthquake prediction. The idea is mostly based on unconfirmed stories. More experiments are necessary before we can use unusual animal activity patterns as an early warning system for earthquakes. 25

### Glossary
·molecule: the smallest physical unit of an element

1 According to paragraph 1, all of the following have occurred before earthquakes EXCEPT

(A) zoo animals making noise

(B) snakes coming out of the ground

(C) pets disappearing

(D) rats gathering in one place


2 According to paragraph 2, which of the following is NOT true about P-waves?

(A) They make the earth shake.

(B) They come before S-waves.

(C) They may be noticed by animals.

(D) They are able to move through rock.


3 The word "restless" in the passage is closest in meaning to

(A) complicated

(B) anxious

(C) motivated

(D) sick


4 According to paragraph 3, ionization of the air prior to earthquakes would explain why animals

(A) are more sensitive to P-waves than humans

(B) feel sick after an earthquake

(C) flee areas with seismic activity

(D) sense the shifting of the earth's crust


• Vocabulary Quiz •

The word ☐ is closest in meaning to

| 1 behaviors | 2 ability | 3 detect | 4 solid |
|---|---|---|---|
| ⓐ appearances | ⓐ foresight | ⓐ notice | ⓐ moral |
| ⓑ actions | ⓑ will | ⓑ perform | ⓑ firm |
| ⓒ experiments | ⓒ capacity | ⓒ direct | ⓒ virtual |

## Totem Poles

Totem poles are tall wooden towers carved in the shapes of animals or humans. They are typically made from cedar trees by the indigenous peoples of the Pacific Northwest of North America. These Native Americans traditionally carved totem poles by hand using sharpened stones, seashells, or 5 bones. However, modern woodcarving tools are used today. When the totem pole is complete, it is raised during a ceremonial festival called potlatch.

These distinctive works of art serve a variety of purposes in Northwestern Native American culture. Most commonly, welcome poles are placed on the 10 village beachfront or at the entryway of a house to greet newcomers. Sometimes the carvings are intended to scare off strangers who might mean to do harm. Shame poles are displayed to ridicule someone who has done something wrong. Certain types of totem poles are designed as a memorial to remember someone who has died. They may serve as a grave marker or even contain the remains of 15 the deceased.

More importantly, totem poles are used to tell the history of a family. Often, different families have different crest animals that occupy a prominent place on the pole. Common animals carved on totem poles include bears, eagles, frogs, killer whales, and even mosquitoes. It is believed that each family's totem has 20 power based on each animal's abilities. For instance, the bear symbolizes physical strength and the eagle represents freedom and courage. Each image carved into a totem pole also represents major events in the lives of the family's ancestors. In this way, the totem pole functions as a sort of textbook, preserving tribal history from generation to generation. 25

### Glossary
·crest: a symbol of a family, a town, or an organization

1 Paragraph 1 answers all of the questions about totem poles EXCEPT:

(A) What are they made from?

(B) Which tools were used to carve them in the past?

(C) How long do they take to produce?

(D) Who builds them?

2 The word "ridicule" in the passage is closest in meaning to

(A) protect

(B) approve

(C) appreciate

(D) mock

3 According to paragraph 2, each of the following is a function of totem poles EXCEPT

(A) celebrating major holidays

(B) welcoming a house guest

(C) honoring a dead person

(D) deterring unwanted visitors

4 According to paragraph 3, the power of a totem pole is derived from

(A) the status of the family that owns it

(B) the prominence of its physical location

(C) the traits of the animals it includes

(D) the abilities of the person who carved it

• Vocabulary Quiz •

The word ☐ is closest in meaning to

1 indigenous
ⓐ native
ⓑ creative
ⓒ evasive

2 purposes
ⓐ uses
ⓑ traits
ⓒ aspects

3 deceased
ⓐ remnants
ⓑ dead
ⓒ victims

4 functions
ⓐ disguises
ⓑ exists
ⓒ serves

## Why We Yawn

➡ We know what a yawn is. It is the action of opening one's mouth and taking in a deep breath. Few actions are as universal as yawning. People of every description yawn. Even animals such as dogs, snakes, and fish yawn. We know when yawning is ⁵ most likely to happen. When we are tired or fatigued, yawns are sure to follow. It is often the very first thing a person does upon waking up. Sometimes yawns are a sign of boredom.

➡ Even so, we do not yet know what biological purpose yawning serves. One common belief is that people yawn to get more oxygen into their bodies. 10 It's true that we inhale more oxygen and exhale more carbon dioxide during a yawn than a regular breath. **A** However, studies have shown that the amount of oxygen available does not bear any relationship to our likelihood to yawn. **B** A more likely explanation is that we yawn to wake ourselves up. **C** Yawning also stimulates muscles in the ear that increase alertness and help us 15 monitor our surroundings. **D** Surprisingly, it's also possible that we yawn in order to cool the brain. The air we breathe in when we yawn lowers the temperature of the blood flowing to the brain.

➡ Yawning also serves a social purpose, creating a bond between individuals. There is a connection between yawning and empathy: the closer you are to 20 someone emotionally, the more likely you are to yawn contagiously. People with higher levels of empathy are more likely to yawn when they notice someone else yawn. Scientists are still studying this phenomenon. It is difficult to think of another behavior that is so common and yet so little understood.

**1** The word "universal" in the passage is closest in meaning to

  Ⓐ complicated

  Ⓑ extraordinary

  Ⓒ widespread

  Ⓓ flexible

**2** Why does the author mention "dogs, snakes, and fish"?

  Ⓐ To provide evidence that yawning is not restricted to humans

  Ⓑ To argue that yawning is a vital bodily function

  Ⓒ To note the difference between humans and animals

  Ⓓ To demonstrate that more research needs to be done

**3** According to paragraph 1, all of the following may cause a person to yawn EXCEPT

  Ⓐ feeling bored

  Ⓑ having stress

  Ⓒ becoming awake

  Ⓓ being tired

Paragraph 1 is marked with an arrow [➡].

**4** Which of the sentences below best expresses the essential information in the highlighted sentence in the passage? *Incorrect* choices change the meaning in important ways or leave out essential information.

  Ⓐ The relationship between oxygen and yawning has been studied.

  Ⓑ Studies have failed to show a connection between yawning and the availability of oxygen.

  Ⓒ According to studies, people yawn because they have access to insufficient oxygen.

  Ⓓ The oxygen in an environment affects the likelihood of a person yawning.

**5** The word "monitor" in the passage is closest in meaning to

(A) observe

(B) locate

(C) navigate

(D) confirm


**6** According to paragraph 2, what effect does yawning have on the brain?

(A) It improves cognitive function.

(B) It lowers the overall temperature.

(C) It stimulates muscle activity.

(D) It increases the flow of blood.

Paragraph 2 is marked with an arrow [➡].


**7** According to paragraph 2, which of the following is true of yawning?

(A) It prevents the absorption of carbon dioxide.

(B) It increases the oxygen supply of the body.

(C) It involves only the muscles in the jaws.

(D) It does not increase alertness.

Paragraph 2 is marked with an arrow [➡].


**8** Which of the following can be inferred from paragraph 3 about contagious yawning?

(A) It happens most frequently among friends and family members.

(B) It is triggered by auditory signals rather than visual ones.

(C) It leads to greater empathy in affected individuals.

(D) It is more commonly observed in children than in adults.

Paragraph 3 is marked with an arrow [➡].

Volume · Review · Help · Back · Next

**9** Look at the four squares [■] that indicate where the following sentence could be added to the passage.

**This is because a yawn accompanies a stretch, and both help to shake off drowsiness.**

Where would the sentence best fit?

Click on a square [■] to add the sentence to the passage.

**10 Directions:** An introductory sentence for a brief summary of the passage is provided below. Complete the summary by selecting the THREE answer choices that express the most important ideas in the passage. Some sentences do not belong in the summary because they express ideas that are not presented in the passage or are minor ideas in the passage. **This question is worth 2 points.**

Drag your answer choices to the spaces where they belong.
To remove an answer choice, click on it. To review the passage, click on **View Text**.

---

**There are a number of possible functions of yawning.**

- 
- 
- 

---

Answer Choices

Ⓐ Yawning is an action that all people and many animals perform.

Ⓑ A yawn involves opening the mouth wide to take in more air.

Ⓒ Scientists believe that yawning is triggered by changes in air temperature.

Ⓓ The exact biological purpose of yawning remains unclear.

Ⓔ A yawn seems to have a social role among humans.

Ⓕ People will often yawn when they see someone else do this.

Answer Book p. 21

# Vocabulary Review

## A. Fill in the blanks with the appropriate words from the box.

| | | |
|---|---|---|
| description | violent | might |
| unrest | extinction | fatigued |

1 The airplane was shaken with _____ bursts of wind as it began to descend.

2 The Bengal tiger has been hunted to the brink of _____.

3 After the marathon, the _____ competitors fell to the ground with exhaustion.

4 The museum's many galleries have art of every possible _____.

5 In battle, the Vikings displayed an overpowering _____ that intimidated their enemies.

6 Claims of election fraud have led to widespread political _____ in the country.

## B. Choose the closest meaning for each highlighted word.

7 It is my mother's desire to visit Paris and climb the Eiffel Tower.
   (A) longing      (B) idea      (C) belief      (D) opportunity

8 If his lawyer were not incompetent, he would be out of prison today.
   (A) stubborn      (B) impersonal      (C) ineffective      (D) overpaid

9 The psychologist's empathy for her patients made them feel understood.
   (A) strategy      (B) pity      (C) criticism      (D) passion

10 Children have an increased likelihood to perform well in school if their home life is stable.
   (A) sensitivity      (B) probability      (C) inevitability      (D) capability

11 After their narrow escape, the two prisoners felt a strong bond between them.
   (A) conflict      (B) grasp      (C) demise      (D) connection

12 All of the world's apes are endangered because of habitat loss.
   (A) protected      (B) isolated      (C) threatened      (D) destroyed

13 The assassination of Abraham Lincoln was committed by a Confederate actor.
   (A) robbery      (B) election      (C) inauguration      (D) murder

14 Publishers that are certain of a book's success will offer the author advance payment.
   (A) immense      (B) grateful      (C) prior      (D) fair

# CHAPTER 06

# Inference

# Inference

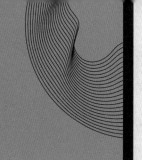

## About the Question Type

**Inference questions** ask you to identify information that is implied but not explicitly stated in the passage.

These questions require you to draw a logical conclusion based on the information in the passage. Be careful to use only the information presented in the passage to select the correct answer choice. Do not draw any conclusions based on what you know about the topic from other sources.

## Question Format

- Which of the following can be inferred from paragraph # about X?

- In paragraph #, what does the author imply about X?

- It can be inferred from paragraph # that

## Key Strategies

- **Step 1** — Read the question and identify the keywords.

- **Step 2** — Scan the passage for the keywords, and locate the relevant information.

- **Step 3** — Select the answer choice that is a logical conclusion based on the information in the passage.

# Example

## Octopus Intelligence

Octopuses have many characteristics that enable them to hunt prey and avoid predators. For example, some can change shape and color to blend into their surroundings. However, the most impressive trait of an octopus is its high intelligence. 5

A common measure of an animal's intelligence is the size of its brain compared to the size of its body. An octopus's brain-to-body ratio is greater than that of any other invertebrate and some vertebrates. However, its comparative brain size does not reach the same level as a mammal's.

The behavior of an octopus also demonstrates that it is intelligent. Some have 10 been observed using tools. For instance, some octopuses observed in Indonesia collect broken coconut shells from the ocean floor and clean the mud from them. They will then find a suitable place to build a protective shelter out of them.

Octopuses also have the ability to solve problems. In an experiment, researchers put an octopus in a maze with a reward at the end. The octopus was not only 15 able to find its way through the maze but was able to do it more quickly in each round of the experiment. This suggests that it remembered the solution to the problem.

---

**1**  Which of the following can be inferred from paragraph 2 about animal intelligence?

(A) The overall size of a brain determines an organism's intellect.

(B) Octopuses have a greater mental capacity than some mammals.

(C) The brain-to-body ratio is usually unrelated to intelligence.

(D) Octopuses are less intelligent than mammals.


**2**  What does the author imply about the experiment involving the maze?

(A) A different octopus was used for every maze.

(B) A more difficult maze was set up for each round.

(C) The first attempt was completed the quickest.

(D) The same route was provided multiple times.

Answer Book p. 23

## Broken Window Theory

The Broken Window Theory states that any visible sign of crime encourages further criminal acts. It also suggests that police should enforce laws against minor crimes to prevent more serious ones. However, the effectiveness of this 5 approach is debatable.

The theory was first proposed in 1982 by the American social scientists James Wilson and George Kelling. They maintained that even a small indication of social disorder, such as a building with a broken window, was a sign that a neighborhood was uncared for. This prompted residents to engage in more 10 disruptive behaviors. Eventually, serious crimes would occur on a regular basis.

Their proposal received a lot of attention from politicians. In particular, Rudolf Giuliani decided to apply the theory when he was elected mayor of New York in 1993. As a result, police officers in this city began to devote a great deal of effort to crack down on minor crimes, such as public drunkenness and subway fare 15 evasion. This strategy continued to be used for approximately 20 years. Studies have suggested that it was successful. During this period, there was a 50 percent reduction in both minor and major crimes throughout the city.

Despite this, some experts have questioned the effectiveness of this method of policing. They agree that New York experienced a drop in crime. However, they 20 argue that it was not caused by applying the Broken Window Theory. During the same period, almost all major cities in the United States experienced a significant decline in crime, regardless of their policing strategies. This was likely due to the expansion of the economy. It led to reduced unemployment and poverty throughout the country. 25

1  The word "debatable" in the passage is closest in meaning to
   (A) appropriate
   (B) provable
   (C) uncertain
   (D) offensive

2  It can be inferred from paragraph 2 that Wilson and Kelling believed that serious crimes
   (A) lead residents to move out of a neighborhood
   (B) are the main cause of social disorder in a city
   (C) affect building owners more than others
   (D) are less likely in well-maintained areas

3  What does the author imply about police officers in New York prior to 1993?
   (A) They did not focus on eliminating minor crimes.
   (B) They were successful in reducing the crime rate.
   (C) They were the subject of an important study.
   (D) They did not support Rudolf Giuliani's strategy.

4  According to paragraph 4, what is the most likely reason for the nationwide drop in crime?
   (A) Economic growth was achieved.
   (B) Penalties for crimes were increased.
   (C) Anti-poverty programs were introduced.
   (D) Policing methods became more advanced.

• Vocabulary Quiz •

The word [          ] is closest in meaning to

| 1 encourages | 2 indication | 3 disruptive | 4 reduction |
|---|---|---|---|
| ⓐ separates | ⓐ chance | ⓐ excessive | ⓐ launch |
| ⓑ punishes | ⓑ hint | ⓑ absurd | ⓑ explanation |
| ⓒ fosters | ⓒ facet | ⓒ unruly | ⓒ decline |

Answer Book p. 24

## Nazca Lines

Located in southern Peru, the Nazca Lines are images carved into the ground of the desert. Most are so large that they can only be viewed from the air. Since they were discovered in 1927, archaeologists have been trying to determine their origin and purpose. 5

The Nazca Lines are the work of the Nazca people, who inhabited the region from 100 BC to AD 700. It is believed that they used stakes with rope attached to plan the images. Then, workers would follow the ropes, removing rocks from the ground. This ensured the visibility of the lines because the surface rocks are red 10 and the sand below is yellow.

These techniques allowed the Nazca people to create various types of images. The most basic are straight lines, some of which are over 40 kilometers long. There are also geometric shapes, such as triangles and spirals. The most complex are the portrayals of animals. For example, a depiction of a condor is approximately 15 130 meters long and includes numerous features such as feet, wings, and a beak.

Researchers have long debated the purpose of the Nazca Lines. A popular early theory was that they were astronomical markers. This is because many ancient monuments from the period indicate where stars will be positioned on certain dates. However, most experts now agree that the Nazca Lines were used for 20 religious rituals. The Nazca people walked along the lines to encourage the gods to provide rain. This theory is supported by the fact that many of the animals portrayed, such as spiders and monkeys, were associated with water in Nazca culture.

1   According to paragraph 2, what made the Nazca Lines more visible?

(A) The length of the carved images

(B) The utilization of colored rope

(C) The placement of massive rocks

(D) The exposure of the underlying sand

2   What does the author imply about the portrayals of animals in paragraph 3?

(A) They are the largest of all of the Nazca Lines.

(B) They are significantly older than first believed.

(C) They tend to include intricate geometric patterns.

(D) They have more details than the other images.

3   The word "rituals" in the passage is closest in meaning to

(A) teachings

(B) sacrifices

(C) preparations

(D) ceremonies

4   It can be inferred from paragraph 4 that the theory about the Nazca Lines functioning as astronomical markers

(A) never had significant support among archaeologists

(B) has been discarded in favor of another explanation

(C) was based on a misunderstanding of Nazca culture

(D) provided insights into other monuments of the period

• Vocabulary Quiz •

The word [          ] is closest in meaning to

| 1  determine | 2  origin | 3  features | 4  positioned |
|---|---|---|---|
| ⓐ sustain | ⓐ function | ⓐ attributes | ⓐ accumulated |
| ⓑ identify | ⓑ source | ⓑ bodies | ⓑ visible |
| ⓒ entertain | ⓒ popularity | ⓒ inspirations | ⓒ located |

# Reading Practice 3

## Praying Mantis

A praying mantis is a large insect that takes its name from its prominent front legs. These are typically positioned in a way that makes it look like the insect is praying. The mantis has a number of evolutionary adaptations that ensure it ₅ is a highly effective predator.

The forelegs of a mantis are its main tool for catching prey. The end of each leg can fold completely over. As a result, the leg can function almost like a pincher. In addition, it is covered in long, pointy spikes. When a mantis stretches its legs rapidly to grab prey, the spines pierce the victim. This makes it easy to kill and ₁₀ eat.

A mantis's neck provides it with another advantage when hunting. The neck is unusually long, and it is very flexible. In fact, a mantis can rotate its head 180 degrees, making it one of the few insects able to look behind itself. This trait enables a mantis to continually scan the vegetation for other insects to eat without ₁₅ having to move its body. As a result, it is often able to find its prey without being noticed.

A mantis's ability to locate prey is further enhanced by its impressive vision. A mantis is unique among insects because it has stereo vision—both of its compound eyes can focus on the same object at the same time. Therefore, a ₂₀ mantis is able to perceive the world in 3D, much in the same way that humans do. This makes it easier for a mantis to detect movement and judge the relative distance of prey.

1 The word "prominent" in the passage is closest in meaning to
   (A) delicate
   (B) sturdy
   (C) noticeable
   (D) curved


2 According to paragraph 2, all of the following are features of a mantis's foreleg EXCEPT
   (A) the capacity to extend quickly
   (B) the existence of sharp spikes
   (C) the presence of a protective covering
   (D) the ability to bend to a great degree


3 What can be inferred from paragraph 3 about the mantis?
   (A) It remains still when searching for food.
   (B) It uses its flexible neck to immobilize prey.
   (C) It consumes both insects and vegetation.
   (D) It lowers its body when a predator approaches.


4 In paragraph 4, the author implies that insects other than mantises
   (A) focus on objects with two eyes at once
   (B) do not have large compound eyes
   (C) detect movement with stereo vision
   (D) do not possess the ability to see in 3D

• Vocabulary Quiz •

The word [        ] is closest in meaning to

| 1 highly | 2 pierce | 3 flexible | 4 enhanced |
|---|---|---|---|
| ⓐ extremely | ⓐ split | ⓐ bendable | ⓐ revealed |
| ⓑ permanently | ⓑ penetrate | ⓑ extensive | ⓑ improved |
| ⓒ relatively | ⓒ defend | ⓒ burdensome | ⓒ provided |

# Reading Practice 4

Answer Book p. 25

## Nikola Tesla

Nikola Tesla was a Serbian inventor and engineer who immigrated to the United States in 1884. Until his death in 1943, Tesla produced a number of patents for inventions that changed our world and are still in use today. Now, Tesla is remembered as one 5 of history's most brilliant inventors whose innovative ideas were ahead of his time.

Perhaps his most significant work was in the field of electricity. Until 1887, the electricity used in the United States was direct current (DC) developed by Thomas Edison. DC allowed electrical current to run in only one direction like 10 in a battery. However, Tesla developed an electrical system known as alternating current, or AC, which could change direction. With AC, the electricity could be delivered to homes and businesses at a much more reasonable price. Now, AC is used for almost all appliances and devices.

Tesla is also credited with making breakthroughs in radio technology. He 15 discovered that he could remotely transmit and receive radio signals without wires. Based on this idea, Tesla developed the first remote-controlled boat. The speed and direction of the boat were controlled using a radio transmitter and receiver. This is considered the world's first wireless remote control.

Another technology that Tesla helped develop was X-rays. While experimenting 20 with some equipment that discharged electrons at a high rate, Tesla noticed that a part of his camera had been damaged. This led him to study what he called "radiant energy." In the process, he is believed to have captured an X-ray image even before Wilhelm Rontgen made his announcement about the discovery of an X-ray in 1895. Unfortunately, his contribution to the discovery of X-rays went unnoticed 25 because much of his work got lost during the fire in his laboratory.

1 The word "immigrated" in the passage is closest in meaning to

(A) defected

(B) visited

(C) traveled

(D) relocated


2 What can be inferred from paragraph 2 about AC?

(A) It was developed before DC.

(B) Its electrical current cannot change direction.

(C) It was widely used in the US prior to 1887.

(D) It is more cost-effective than DC.


3 In paragraph 3, the author implies that Tesla's boat

(A) did not have wires connected to it

(B) had a faster speed than other boats

(C) made advances upon previous wireless technology

(D) could use alternating or direct current


4 According to paragraph 4, what led Tesla to begin studying X-rays?

(A) An image was captured by another inventor.

(B) A device was broken during an experiment.

(C) A fire burned down his lab.

(D) Scientific discovery was announced in a publication.


• Vocabulary Quiz •

The word [        ] is closest in meaning to

1 innovative

ⓐ critical

ⓑ negative

ⓒ groundbreaking

2 reasonable

ⓐ affordable

ⓑ profitable

ⓒ deliberate

3 transmit

ⓐ emerge

ⓑ send

ⓒ observe

4 captured

ⓐ recorded

ⓑ reserved

ⓒ presented

Answer Book p. 26

## Hawaiian Hot Spot

Unlike the other 49 states in the United States, Hawaii is not part of the continent of North America. Instead, it is a chain of islands in the Pacific Ocean: The Big Island, Maui, Lanai, Molokai, Oahu, and Kauai, among others. Geologists have long been fascinated by the volcanic activity that formed the Hawaiian Islands.

➡ To understand the special way that Hawaii was formed, it helps to understand ₅ how volcanoes usually occur. The earth's crust is made up of several tectonic plates that slowly move over the surface of the planet. Traditional volcanoes, like Mount St. Helens in Washington State, arise at the boundaries of tectonic plates. In this model, two neighboring plates collide, with one being forced under the other. As the plate moves down into the earth, it melts. This causes hot magma to erupt to ₁₀ the surface, forming volcanoes.

➡ However, Hawaii's volcanoes formed about 2,000 miles from the boundaries of the Pacific Plate. Between the earth's crust and the core is the mantle, a particularly hot layer at one point in the middle of the plate. **A** Starting about 30 million years ago, the Pacific Plate slid over this hot spot at a pace of three to four inches per ₁₅ year. **B** Molten rock (magma) ascended through the mantle until it erupted on the seafloor forming a volcano. **C** One after another, the Hawaiian Islands formed as the sliding conveyor belt of the Pacific Plate moved over the hot spot. **D**

Hawaii's volcanoes are gradually moving away from the hot spot. As they get further away from the source of their creation, volcanic eruptions of hot magma ₂₀ become less and less common on the islands. Eventually, the volcanoes that formed the islands will die. As a result, the islands will erode and begin to sink into the sea. In millions of years, the part of the Pacific Plate that carries the islands will move under the North American plate. It will cause the Hawaiian Islands to disappear forever. ₂₅

1 The word "fascinated" in the passage is closest in meaning to

   Ⓐ amused

   Ⓑ interested

   Ⓒ shocked

   Ⓓ annoyed

2 According to paragraph 2, traditional volcanoes are formed because

   Ⓐ two tectonic plates crash into each other

   Ⓑ hot magma forms deep under the surface

   Ⓒ a plate slides over a hot portion of the mantle

   Ⓓ the core of the earth melts

Paragraph 2 is marked with an arrow [➡].

3 The word "ascended" in the passage is closest in meaning to

   Ⓐ sank

   Ⓑ destroyed

   Ⓒ rose

   Ⓓ slit

4 The word "it" in the passage refers to

   Ⓐ the Pacific Plate

   Ⓑ hot spot

   Ⓒ molten rock

   Ⓓ mantle

**5** Why does the author mention a "conveyor belt"?

(A) To illustrate how the Pacific Plate moves over the hot spot

(B) To show the speed of the Pacific Plate compared to other plates

(C) To suggest that traditional volcanoes form at regular intervals

(D) To emphasize that the Hawaiian Islands include multiple volcanoes

**6** According to paragraph 3, which of the following is NOT true of the hot spot that formed the Hawaiian Islands?

(A) It caused the volcanic activity under the sea.

(B) It is located between the crust and core of the earth.

(C) It grows cool as the plate absorbs its energy.

(D) It lies in the middle of a tectonic plate.

Paragraph 3 is marked with an arrow [➡].

**7** Which of the sentences below best expresses the essential information in the highlighted sentence in the passage? *Incorrect* choices change the meaning in important ways or leave out essential information.

(A) At the time the volcanoes were over the hot spot, they erupted less often.

(B) Eruptions happen occasionally, but not as often as they used to.

(C) The hot spot will become further and further away from the volcanoes.

(D) The volcanoes erupt less frequently when the hot spot grows more distant.

**8** Which of the following can be inferred about the volcanoes that formed Hawaii?

(A) They will become dormant before the islands they created disappear.

(B) They are still actively erupting on a yearly basis.

(C) They will continue to increase in size after they are no longer able to erupt.

(D) They remain over the hot spot as the Pacific Plate moves.

**9** Look at the four squares [■] that indicate where the following sentence could be added to the passage.

**This rising magma from the volcano cooled and hardened to form an island.**

Where would the sentence best fit?

Click on a square [■] to add the sentence to the passage.

**10 Directions:** An introductory sentence for a brief summary of the passage is provided below. Complete the summary by selecting the THREE answer choices that express the most important ideas in the passage. Some sentences do not belong in the summary because they express ideas that are not presented in the passage or are minor ideas in the passage. **This question is worth 2 points.**

Drag your answer choices to the spaces where they belong.
To remove an answer choice, click on it. To review the passage, click on **View Text**.

**The formation of the Hawaiian Islands is a subject of interest to many geologists.**

- 
- 
- 

Answer Choices

Ⓐ Traditional volcanoes form on the boundaries of tectonic plates.

Ⓑ Hawaii is different from the other states in the United States.

Ⓒ Mount St. Helens is a traditional volcano because magma erupts from it.

Ⓓ The Pacific Plate will eventually move under the North American plate.

Ⓔ Hawaii was formed by volcanic activity over a hot spot in the earth's mantle.

Ⓕ The Hawaiian Islands will move away from the hot spot and sink into the sea.

Answer Book p. 26

# Vocabulary Review

## A. Fill in the blanks with the appropriate words from the box.

| | | |
|---|---|---|
| enabled | sink | erupted |
| disorder | evasion | neighboring |

1 My parents plan to visit Germany and several _____ countries next year.

2 The basketball player's large hands _____ him to hold the ball in one palm.

3 Albert Einstein believed the universe was characterized by chaos and _____.

4 The government will crack down on corporate tax _____ this year.

5 When the volcano _____, it caused extensive damage to the region.

6 As the ship began to _____, the passengers were directed to board the lifeboats.

## B. Choose the closest meaning for each highlighted word.

7 The development of antibiotics such as penicillin was an important breakthrough.
   (A) advance      (B) decision      (C) success      (D) approach

8 The mountain range eroded over millions of years, and it is now a series of small hills.
   (A) mitigated      (B) swallowed      (C) disintegrated      (D) corrected

9 The wise king perceived that the troops were nervous going into battle.
   (A) calculated      (B) sensed      (C) regretted      (D) remembered

10 Looking down from the tree, he judged that he could safely jump to the ground.
   (A) estimated      (B) queried      (C) claimed      (D) hoped

11 The driver slammed on the brakes, but, nonetheless, he collided with the other car.
   (A) interacted      (B) collaborated      (C) crashed      (D) sped

12 Lines were drawn to mark the boundaries of the baseball playing field.
   (A) lanes      (B) drawings      (C) limits      (D) sizes

13 William Shakespeare is beloved for his brilliant verse and mastery of language.
   (A) clever      (B) moderate      (C) familiar      (D) epic

14 At intermission, the lobby lights flickered, which prompted the audience to return.
   (A) discouraged      (B) forced      (C) convinced      (D) caused

# CHAPTER 07

## Rhetorical Purpose

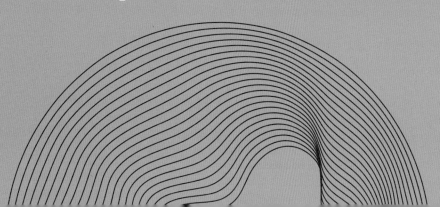

# Rhetorical Purpose

## About the Question Type

**Rhetorical Purpose questions** ask you to identify the function of a particular piece of information presented in the paragraph or the passage. Possible functions include explaining a concept, suggesting an option, illustrating a point, making a comparison, and providing an example.

Rhetoric refers to the writing techniques that an author uses to make his or her point effectively. Make sure to understand why the specified piece of information was presented by the author.

## Question Format

- Why does the author mention "        " in the passage?

- In paragraph #, the author mentions/discusses/includes "        " in order to

- What is the author's primary purpose in paragraph #?

## Key Strategies

- **Step 1** — Read the question and locate the specified piece of information in the passage.

- **Step 2** — Use the surrounding context to determine its purpose.

- **Step 3** — Select the answer choice that best describes the rhetorical function of the piece of information.

# Example

## Egyptian Hieroglyphs

Hieroglyphs are the characters in the writing system first used by the ancient Egyptians some 5,000 years ago. There are more than 2,000 hieroglyphs. Each is an image of a common object that was found in ancient Egypt. Hieroglyphs could stand for the object ₅ itself or a sound based on its name. Therefore, if something did not have a corresponding hieroglyph, it could be spelled out using multiple characters. For example, the name Rob could be represented by three hieroglyphic characters, each matching the sound of one of the English letters.

Because the hieroglyphic system was so complex and detailed, the characters ₁₀ were simplified for people who had no time or patience to draw detailed representations. These simplified forms are known as hieratic and demotic. Hieratic characters are cursive forms of hieroglyphs that were used only for administrative and religious purposes. The demotic was also cursive, and it replaced the hieratic as the script for everyday use for accounting and writing literature. ₁₅

### Glossary
·cursive: written with rounded letters that are joined together

---

1    Why does the author mention "Rob" in paragraph 1?

(A) To contrast the Egyptian and English writing systems

(B) To show how hieroglyphs can represent individual sounds

(C) To explain the influence of hieroglyphs on the English language

(D) To show the similarities between English letters and hieroglyphs


2    In paragraph 2, the author mentions "writing literature" as an example of the

(A) function of the demotic script

(B) complexity of the hieroglyph system

(C) superiority of hieratic forms over demotic ones

(D) way that hieroglyphs became simpler over time

Answer Book p. 27

## Ant Communication

Ants are considered social insects because they function in groups rather than operating independently. These groups are called colonies. In order to live and work successfully in a colony, ants must communicate with one another. 5

Antennae are one method ants use to send and receive information. When a worker ant meets up with another member of its colony, they often touch antennae. This sends a message about what can be expected along the trail the worker has explored. Although ants are deaf to sounds that humans can hear, their antennae also function like ears. Antennae have hair-like sensors at the tips 10 that can pick up sound frequencies around one kilohertz.

Other signals that antennae can detect are created by chemicals known as pheromones. These pheromones are a key method of communication for ants. When ants move, they leave pheromones on the ground. Each ant colony uses a different pheromone, so its members can recognize each other. These chemicals 15 can also signal where food is or an intention to mate. When an ant is crushed, its pheromones serve as a warning to other members of the colony.

Ants also make chirping sounds called stridulations. These are produced by rubbing two hard parts of their abdomens together. Stridulations are sometimes heard and sometimes felt as vibrations. Queen ants stridulate to signal that 20 they are ready to nest. Individuals stridulate to signal that an emergency is taking place. In fact, researchers believe that this is the most important role of stridulations. An ant that produces these vibrations often serves as an emergency beacon, summoning others when a predator tries to enter the colony's nest.

1 The author describes ants as "social insects" in order to

(A) introduce a discussion of ant mating practices

(B) explain why ants need to communicate

(C) compare the behavior of ants to that of humans

(D) show that ants have individual personalities


2 The word "independently" in the passage is closest in meaning to

(A) originally

(B) individually

(C) virtually

(D) immediately


3 According to paragraph 3, pheromones are NOT used to

(A) give directions to a food source

(B) attract a mate

(C) signal a danger to a colony

(D) lead others to a new nest


4 Why does the author mention "an emergency beacon" in paragraph 4?

(A) To emphasize the control that queen ants have over others

(B) To identify a common threat to the home of a colony

(C) To specify a key function of an interaction method

(D) To indicate the importance of a well-organized nest defense


• Vocabulary Quiz •

The word _____ is closest in meaning to

1 explored
  ⓐ exhausted
  ⓑ investigated
  ⓒ abandoned

2 intention
  ⓐ aim
  ⓑ opportunity
  ⓒ reward

3 role
  ⓐ emphasis
  ⓑ function
  ⓒ drawback

4 summoning
  ⓐ excluding
  ⓑ fearing
  ⓒ calling

# Reading Practice 2

## Doctors Without Borders

Doctors Without Borders is an international <u>humanitarian</u> organization. It was founded in 1971 by a group of physicians and journalists. They wanted to provide medical treatment to populations that lack access to health care. Today, 5 the group's staff has expanded to nearly 30,000 in 60 countries around the world.

These brave aid workers help victims of natural disasters, wars, famines, and epidemics. The organization's first project was to provide supplies and health care after a 1972 earthquake in Nicaragua. That legacy continues today. Doctors 10 Without Borders treated patients within minutes of a 2010 earthquake in Haiti. It also serves endangered populations in war zones around the world. Aid workers have jeopardized their lives to assist the wounded in countries like Lebanon, Chechnya, and Yemen. In addition to offering personal medical attention, the group provides basic necessities, such as food, clean water, and shelter. 15

Along with these services, Doctors Without Borders speaks out against injustice on behalf of people who seek help. For example, the organization protests when fair access to medication is denied. They challenged American drug companies to make COVID-19 vaccines available cheaply throughout the world. Sometimes these actions put aid workers in danger of becoming the targets of political 20 violence. Doctors Without Borders staff have even been killed in Afghanistan and Somalia. Nevertheless, Doctors Without Borders continues to fulfill its mission of providing a helping hand and a voice for those in need. In recognition of its efforts, it was awarded the Nobel Peace Prize in 1999.

### Glossary

· humanitarian: helping to improve the welfare of people

1 Why does the author mention "60 countries around the world" in paragraph 1?

(A) To show how the organization has grown over the years

(B) To suggest that the organization needs more volunteers

(C) To contrast the organization with local humanitarian groups

(D) To emphasize the bravery of the organization's employees


2 The word "jeopardized" in the passage is closest in meaning to

(A) delayed

(B) complicated

(C) risked

(D) limited


3 According to paragraph 2, which of the following is true of Doctors Without Borders?

(A) It develops medications to help victims of disease.

(B) It provides medical assistance to people affected by wars.

(C) It focuses primarily on shipping medical supplies.

(D) It recruits aid workers from only a few countries.


4 In paragraph 3, the author discusses "Afghanistan and Somalia" in order to

(A) argue in favor of hiring workers from conflict regions

(B) show the risks its workers face on a mission

(C) illustrate the ability of Doctors Without Borders to negotiate peace

(D) list countries that Doctors Without Borders recently worked in


• Vocabulary Quiz •

The word ☐ is closest in meaning to

1 assist
ⓐ evacuate
ⓑ alert
ⓒ help

2 injustice
ⓐ virtue
ⓑ unfairness
ⓒ scarcity

3 fair
ⓐ equal
ⓑ faithful
ⓒ creative

4 recognition
ⓐ substitution
ⓑ explanation
ⓒ acknowledgement

# Reading Practice 3

## Charles Darwin and the Galapagos Islands

The Galapagos Islands are a biologist's treasure chest. Consisting of 19 islands about 1,000 kilometers away from the South American coast, the Galapagos and surrounding waters are inhabited by some 9,000 species. Many of those species are unique to the islands, including some of its iguanas, lizards, and giant tortoises.

This remarkable biological diversity was studied in 1835 by the famous British biologist Charles Darwin. He was 22 years old at the time, working as a naturalist on a five-year journey aboard the *HMS Beagle*. His job was to collect plants and animal specimens from the Galapagos. Among his discoveries were 14 species of finch, with differently shaped beaks. He realized that these birds' beaks were different for a reason. A pointed beak helped some finches nibble seeds from cactus fruits without getting hurt. A sharp beak helped others catch insects. He returned to Europe and consulted a bird specialist to see if his observations were correct.

While Darwin already believed that animal species evolved over time, his discoveries in the Galapagos gave him a new idea: natural selection. He decided that the species he had encountered must have developed traits that helped them survive in the islands. The animals with the most advantageous qualities survived. Those that were poorly suited to their habitat died off. In 1859, he recorded these observations in his groundbreaking book *The Origin of Species*. Today, the theory of evolution and natural selection is the foundation of modern biology. Scientists still visit the Galapagos to study how its remarkable creatures have evolved.

1 Why does the author mention a "treasure chest"?

(A) To suggest that valuable natural resources can be found on the islands

(B) To imply that the islands are significant to the species that inhabit them

(C) To stress the popularity of the islands with biologists

(D) To emphasize the richness of the islands' biodiversity


2 Which of the following is true about Darwin when he made his journey to the Galapagos?

(A) He was hired to study plants and animals.

(B) He was the first human to visit the islands.

(C) His crew members were also trained biologists.

(D) His purpose was to find new species of finch.


3 The word "advantageous" in the passage is closest in meaning to

(A) beneficial

(B) impressive

(C) influential

(D) distinctive


4 The author mentions "*The Origin of Species*" in paragraph 3 in order to

(A) provide an example of a book that Darwin studied

(B) introduce an important influence on Darwin's work

(C) identify the source of a principle of modern biology

(D) establish that Darwin was a highly successful author


• Vocabulary Quiz •

The word ☐ is closest in meaning to

| 1 remarkable | 2 consulted | 3 encountered | 4 modern |
|---|---|---|---|
| ⓐ exceptional | ⓐ fascinated by | ⓐ counted | ⓐ contemporary |
| ⓑ artistic | ⓑ conferred with | ⓑ survived | ⓑ experimental |
| ⓒ insignificant | ⓒ appointed to | ⓒ found | ⓒ theoretical |

Answer Book p. 29

# The California Gold Rush

In 1848, a <u>sawmill</u> worker at Sutter's Mill found bits of precious metal in the soil of the American River. Word spread that gold glittered in the streams of California. The prospect of life-changing wealth launched the Gold Rush, which attracted people from all over the world.

This mass migration sped up California's admission to the United States. When gold was first struck, California was Mexican territory, which was at war with the US. Within a month, a peace treaty was signed. Mexico turned control of California over to the Americans. The flood of gold-seeking "forty-niners" who came to the region in 1849 required a strong government. That made statehood an urgent priority. By 1850, California was admitted as the 31st state.

During this time, the demographics of the territory changed dramatically. At the start of the Gold Rush, there were 700 individuals (other than Native Americans) in California. By 1859, that number had soared to 380,000. Prospectors came not only from the United States but from Europe, Australia, Asia, and Latin America. Local Native Americans also looked for gold, though hundreds were forced to do so as slaves. These prospectors quickly learned that searching for gold in rocks, dirt, and freezing water was hard and dangerous work. Many died of disease or accidents. Some struck it rich, but most were not as lucky.

The Gold Rush also permanently altered the California landscape. Soon, most of the gold that could be found by individuals was gone, but industrial companies dug deeper with <u>hydraulic</u> mining technology. The industrial mining filled dams with sediment and redirected rivers from farmers who needed it. Wood was required for these projects, so logging stripped the land of more natural resources. California was forever changed by the Gold Rush, giving the state its nickname: The Golden State.

### Glossary

· sawmill: a factory in which trees are sawn into flat pieces
· hydraulic: operated by the pressure created by water

1 Why does the author discuss the "forty-niners"?

(A) To describe how a foreign territory was acquired

(B) To emphasize the need for a peace treaty

(C) To explain why statehood was achieved quickly

(D) To compare different types of state governments

2 The word "soared" in the passage is closest in meaning to

(A) registered

(B) calculated

(C) escalated

(D) related

3 According to paragraph 3, migrant prospectors endured all of the following EXCEPT

(A) cold water

(B) accidents

(C) slavery

(D) illness

4 The author mentions "The Golden State" in paragraph 4 in order to

(A) stress that the Gold Rush made a lasting impact on California

(B) imply that California is a beautiful state despite the environmental destruction

(C) reinforce the idea that the Gold Rush resulted in California's statehood

(D) provide evidence that gold made California a wealthy state

• Vocabulary Quiz •

The word [        ] is closest in meaning to

| 1 precious | 2 treaty | 3 urgent | 4 permanently |
|---|---|---|---|
| ⓐ rusted | ⓐ agreement | ⓐ pressing | ⓐ eternally |
| ⓑ valuable | ⓑ doctrine | ⓑ opposite | ⓑ carefully |
| ⓒ shiny | ⓒ marker | ⓒ shallow | ⓒ thoroughly |

Answer Book p. 30

## Theater Lighting Techniques through History

➡ Throughout the 2,000-year history of the dramatic arts, theaters have struggled to find the best way to light the stage. **A** The ancient Greeks staged their plays in outdoor theaters with only the sun to provide light. **B** The sun would illuminate the stage ₅ from behind the audience. **C** Additionally, the Greeks would pause the performance to take advantage of the changing position of the sun. **D** They also directed the sunlight to where they wanted it using large mirrors.

➡ The next major stage lighting innovation happened during the Italian ₁₀ Renaissance. In the late 1500s, candles would be hung from the ceiling in chandeliers or placed at the edge of the stage as footlights. Thousands of candles were required to provide adequate lighting. Of course, this made it more costly to put on a play, as candles were quite expensive at this time. Another problem was that there was a significant danger that the theater would catch on fire. Also, the ₁₅ candles would consume so much oxygen that the cast and audience could be left gasping for air. Sometimes people would faint.

➡ In 1783, France introduced the kerosene oil lamp, which was superior to the candle because it could be adjusted to provide a higher or lower flame. For 100 years, oil was the preferred way to light the stage. However, oil lamps were ₂₀ expensive. Gaslight, introduced in the early 1800s, was cheaper. It also provided control. Using valves to release gas into a system of pipes, light could be directed onto the stage at different angles and levels of brightness.

Electric lamps were introduced in 1873. A year after they were invented, the Paris Opera began using them. In the early twentieth century, electric lighting began to ₂₅ be colored by placing a gel in front of a lamp. This was made of plastic and gave designers the ability to build complex lighting plots that set the mood of a scene. Different colors could be blended for effect. Lighting became as important to the emotional impact of a play as the actors' performances.

**1** Which of the following can be inferred from paragraph 1 about Greek plays?

(A) They were not performed at night.

(B) They were not staged with spectators.

(C) They were lit using open flames.

(D) They were performed without breaks.

Paragraph 1 is marked with an arrow [➡].

**2** The word "adequate" in the passage is closest in meaning to

(A) sufficient

(B) effective

(C) harmless

(D) affordable

**3** The word "consume" in the passage is closest in meaning to

(A) transform

(B) give off

(C) use up

(D) combine

**4** According to paragraph 2, all of the following are presented as a disadvantage of using candles EXCEPT

(A) longer preparation times

(B) higher production costs

(C) a decline in air quality

(D) the threat of fire

Paragraph 2 is marked with an arrow [➡].

**5** Which of the sentences below best expresses the essential information in the highlighted sentence in the passage? *Incorrect* choices change the meaning in important ways or leave out essential information.

    Ⓐ Gaslight provided the ability to shine bright light on the stage from different angles.

    Ⓑ The angle and brightness of stage lighting could be controlled by releasing gas.

    Ⓒ With gas, a large system of pipes had to be installed and controlled with valves.

    Ⓓ Although oil light was brighter, gas was easier to control using a network of pipes.

**6** According to paragraph 3, oil lamps were considered an improvement over candles because

    Ⓐ their flames could be adjusted

    Ⓑ they were easy to install

    Ⓒ their fuel was widely available

    Ⓓ they were difficult to damage

Paragraph 3 is marked with an arrow [➡].

**7** The word "This" in the passage refers to

    Ⓐ the Paris Opera

    Ⓑ electric lighting

    Ⓒ a gel

    Ⓓ a lamp

**8** The author mentions "the actors' performances" in order to

    Ⓐ refute the idea that colored lights were needed in a play

    Ⓑ emphasize the increased significance of lighting in a production

    Ⓒ argue that lighting designers should be paid more than performers

    Ⓓ identify how emotion is conveyed to audience members

**9** Look at the four squares [■] that indicate where the following sentence could be added to the passage.

**This would also keep sunlight out of the audience's eyes.**

Where would the sentence best fit?

Click on a square [■] to add the sentence to the passage.

**10 Directions:** An introductory sentence for a brief summary of the passage is provided below. Complete the summary by selecting the THREE answer choices that express the most important ideas in the passage. Some sentences do not belong in the summary because they express ideas that are not presented in the passage or are minor ideas in the passage. **This question is worth 2 points.**

Drag your answer choices to the spaces where they belong.
To remove an answer choice, click on it. To review the passage, click on **View Text**.

---

**For centuries, theaters looked for a good way to light the stage during a performance.**

- 
- 
- 

---

Answer Choices

Ⓐ People sometimes fainted when attending plays lit with candles.

Ⓑ The flame of an oil lamp could be increased or decreased in size.

Ⓒ Gels are plastic filters that change the color of a light.

Ⓓ Electric lamps give lighting designers more control over the mood of a play.

Ⓔ Candles proved a hazardous way to light the stage.

Ⓕ Gas provided an improvement over oil as a lighting method.

Answer Book p. 30

# Vocabulary Review

**A. Fill in the blanks with the appropriate words from the box.**

| | | |
|---|---|---|
| corresponding | colony | admission |
| illuminated | superior | disaster |

1 Ford's Model T sold very well since it was _____ to other vehicles at the time.

2 When researchers inspected the leaf, they found a(n) _____ of bacteria.

3 _____ to the EU requires unanimous approval by all current member states.

4 She struck a match, which briefly _____ her face in the dark room.

5 We assembled the chair by inserting the legs of the chair into _____ holes.

6 The drought was a(n) _____ that caused many crops to fail.

**B. Choose the closest meaning for each highlighted word.**

7 A fundraiser was held to provide support to the victims of the recent flood.
  (A) casualties      (B) weapons      (C) suspects      (D) reporters

8 Her statement was so controversial that she was stripped of her authority.
  (A) fond      (B) ashamed      (C) deprived      (D) questioned

9 The astronomer detailed several observations regarding the planet he'd discovered.
  (A) findings      (B) motions      (C) questions      (D) miracles

10 Parents must have great patience when dealing with the questions of a curious child.
  (A) talent      (B) perseverance      (C) mood      (D) will

11 About 1.4 billion people inhabit China now, although this number will likely decline.
  (A) relocate      (B) populate      (C) leave      (D) consider

12 The promise of free land attracted settlers to the US in the nineteenth century.
  (A) enticed      (B) improved      (C) declared      (D) adjusted

13 As a country with many immigrants, Canada has a high degree of cultural diversity.
  (A) heritage      (B) severity      (C) minority      (D) variety

14 A public transportation system is a necessity for people who do not own a vehicle.
  (A) advantage      (B) combination      (C) complication      (D) requirement

# CHAPTER 08

## Sentence Insertion

# Sentence Insertion

## About the Question Type

**Sentence Insertion questions** ask you to identify the best place within a paragraph to insert the given sentence.

Pay attention to words or phrases that indicate the logical relationships between the sentences before and after the squares. These include, among others, conjunctive adverbs such as *however, therefore, nevertheless, yet,* and *moreover,* as well as pronouns like *it, they, this,* and *that.*

## Question Format

Look at the four squares [■] that indicate where the following sentence could be added to the passage.

**[A given sentence]**

Where would the sentence best fit?

Click on a square [■] to add the sentence to the passage.

## Key Strategies

- **Step 1** — Read the given sentence and look for transitional words or phrases. Use these to determine the logical relationships between the given sentence and the rest of the paragraph.

- **Step 2** — Determine the location the sentence should be placed in the paragraph.

- **Step 3** — Confirm that the paragraph has a logical flow with the sentence inserted.

# Example

## The Marshmallow Test

In the 1960s, psychologist Walter Mischel wondered how his children, then toddlers, learned to exercise self-control. **A** He devised an experiment in which a group of four-year-old children were offered marshmallows. **B** They could either eat one marshmallow now or wait 15 minutes and then eat two marshmallows. **C** About a third of the children ate the first treat right away. **D** Another third waited patiently for the double reward. The others waited a few minutes before giving in to temptation. Mischel tried the experiment, now known as the marshmallow test, under various conditions to learn what enabled the toddlers to delay gratification.

What really made the marshmallow test famous, though, was Mischel's follow-up study in the late 1980s. Returning to the same individuals, who were then in their 30s, Mischel investigated the importance of self-control in their lives. **A** The children who had been able to wait longer as toddlers had higher SAT scores and performed better in their jobs. **B** They also had a greater sense of self-worth and better relationships. **C** They were even less likely to have chronic diseases. **D** This demonstrates that those who can resist temptation as children are more likely to do well in life.

#### Glossary
· SAT (=Scholastic Aptitude Test): a standardized test used for college admissions in the United States

---

1   Look at the four squares [■] in paragraph 1 that indicate where the following sentence could be added to the passage.

**They were given the following two options.**

Where would the sentence best fit?

2   Look at the four squares [■] in paragraph 2 that indicate where the following sentence could be added to the passage.

**However, the ones who had poor impulse control were less successful, happy, and healthy as adults.**

Where would the sentence best fit?

Answer Book p. 32

## Mangrove Trees

Mangroves are a type of tree that grows along coastlines. There are anywhere from 50 to 100 different species. In the United States, they grow mostly in Florida. They are also found in many other tropical regions, such as Central America and Southeast Asia. Mangroves may seem like a typical plant, but they have a very special feature. They are the only species of tree that tolerates saltwater.

There are two different ways they are able to live in salty conditions. **A** Some mangrove species have a filter that almost completely excludes the salt from entering their system. **B** With this filter, they can block over 90 percent of the salt from seawater, preventing a process called osmosis. **C** If this were allowed to occur, the saltwater would completely dehydrate the trees and kill them. **D**

Another method is to manage the salt after it has entered the plant. Mangrove species that use this approach are called secretors. They are capable of pushing the salt out through special pores and glands. As the moisture from the salt evaporates, small salt crystals are left behind on the surface of the leaves.

In addition to their unique ability, mangroves play a critical role in ecosystems. They help stabilize the coastline and reduce erosion from storm surges, waves, and tides. Moreover, the tangle of thick roots sticking out from the water slows moving tidal waters, causing sediment to settle on the muddy bottom. This creates a habitat that traps organic materials and important nutrients. It is an ideal environment for many fish and other animals seeking food or shelter from predators.

1 The word "tolerates" in the passage is closest in meaning to

(A) endures
(B) receives
(C) recycles
(D) eliminates

2 Look at the four squares [■] that indicate where the following sentence could be added to the passage.

**In this process, water moves from areas low in salt concentration to areas high in salt concentration.**

Where would the sentence best fit?

3 According to paragraph 3, which of the following is true about secretors?

(A) They deal with the salt by blocking its entry.
(B) Their special pores absorb the salt.
(C) Saltwater evaporates more quickly on them.
(D) Salt crystals remain on their leaves.

4 According to paragraph 4, which of the following is NOT a reason why mangrove trees are important?

(A) They reduce storm surges and waves on the coastline.
(B) Their roots cause water from tides to slow down.
(C) They make surroundings that confine sources of nourishment.
(D) They provide a good home for animals that need protection.

• Vocabulary Quiz •

The word _____ is closest in meaning to

1 excludes
ⓐ rewards
ⓑ prevents
ⓒ obtains

2 approach
ⓐ method
ⓑ secret
ⓒ conclusion

3 stabilize
ⓐ formalize
ⓑ inhibit
ⓒ preserve

4 ideal
ⓐ perfect
ⓑ satisfactory
ⓒ pleasant

Answer Book p. 32

## Stealth Technology

Invented in World War II, radar is used to detect a moving object such as an airplane. Its widespread utilization has led to research into stealth technology. The purpose of this technology is to make military aircraft 5 undetectable to the enemy.

**A** One key to making an aircraft invisible to radar is its shape. **B** Radar identifies objects by sending and receiving radio waves. **C** A radio antenna sends out these waves, and objects like airplanes reflect them back. **D** But if a plane has no wide or rounded surfaces for the radio waves to bounce off easily, it can hide 10 from radar. That is why stealth planes are often flat with sharp edges. The waves are deflected at an angle that ensures they will not return to their source.

The other way to defeat radar is to absorb it into the body of the plane. Metallic surfaces reflect radar waves easily. The F-117 Nighthawk, a stealth aircraft developed in the 1980s, is made from absorbent glass fibers and plastic. Other 15 planes are coated in an absorbent black substance called iron ball paint. This paint turns radio waves into heat that cannot bounce back to the source.

Stealth technology is not without its disadvantages. For one thing, planes that use stealth technology are very costly to produce. Due to the special materials that are required, the F-117 costs $45 million. Stealthy B-2 bombers are even 20 more expensive at $2.2 billion each. Also, the unusual designs are not as efficient for flying. For example, the F-117 has unusually positioned tails, which make it unstable. But in dangerous military operations, invisibility is priceless.

1 The word "Its" in the passage refers to

(A) World War II

(B) radar

(C) object

(D) airplane

2 Look at the four squares [■] that indicate where the following sentence could be added to the passage.

**Then the waves return to the radio antenna, providing information about the objects.**

Where would the sentence best fit?

3 According to the passage, which of the following is NOT a way of preventing radar waves from returning to their source?

(A) Building planes with sharp points

(B) Turning radar waves into heat

(C) Making planes out of metal

(D) Absorbing radar waves into the plane

4 According to the passage, what is a disadvantage of the F-117?

(A) It costs more than the B-2 bomber.

(B) It has tails that make it unsteady.

(C) It is detectable by radar waves.

(D) It is a recent and untested invention.

• Vocabulary Quiz •

The word [          ] is closest in meaning to

| 1 widespread | 2 undetectable | 3 identifies | 4 unusual |
|---|---|---|---|
| ⓐ careful | ⓐ invisible | ⓐ prepares | ⓐ meticulous |
| ⓑ generous | ⓑ valuable | ⓑ spots | ⓑ hilarious |
| ⓒ prevalent | ⓒ hazardous | ⓒ implements | ⓒ peculiar |

## Seahorse Reproduction

Every day before dawn, male and female seahorses come together to perform a beautiful courtship ritual. The couples begin to dance. Their monkey-like tails loop around each other. They change color several times, from one vivid hue to ⁵ another. Sometimes they swim around each other for hours or even days. What evolutionary purpose does this remarkable ballet serve? Scientists do not know for sure. However, they suspect that the mating dance is to synchronize the movement of the couple before the male seahorse gets pregnant. ₁₀

Seahorses are unusual in the animal world because the males become pregnant and give birth. The female generates eggs and then deposits them into a pouch in the male's stomach. The male fertilizes the eggs inside the pouch and carries the embryos. He provides them with oxygen and nutrients, and he removes carbon dioxide and waste. After about two weeks, the eggs hatch inside their father's ₁₅ pouch. Then the male expels as many as 1,000 tiny seahorses into the surrounding water.

Once in the wild, the seahorse babies are on their own. **A** The mother and father provide no care or instruction to the newborns. **B** The tiny seahorses can be caught up in ocean currents, eaten by predators, and even (if they wait too ₂₀ long in the site of their birth) consumed by their own father. **C** Consequently, fewer than five in a thousand seahorses survive and grow up to perform their own beautiful mating dances. **D**

1 According to paragraph 1, which of the following is NOT true of seahorses during their mating dances?

(A) They wrap their tails around each other.
(B) They change colors as they dance.
(C) They begin dancing late at night.
(D) They dance for hours or days.

2 The word "expels" in the passage is closest in meaning to

(A) pulls
(B) protects
(C) controls
(D) releases

3 According to paragraph 2, female seahorses are responsible for which action?

(A) Fertilizing the eggs
(B) Producing the eggs
(C) Nourishing the eggs
(D) Hatching the eggs

4 Look at the four squares [■] that indicate where the following sentence could be added to the passage.

**They do not even attempt to provide any protection to their offspring.**

Where would the sentence best fit?

• Vocabulary Quiz •

The word [ ] is closest in meaning to

1 vivid
ⓐ bright
ⓑ accurate
ⓒ fictional

2 suspect
ⓐ prefer
ⓑ assume
ⓒ learn

3 instruction
ⓐ structure
ⓑ affection
ⓒ guidance

4 consequently
ⓐ therefore
ⓑ moreover
ⓒ reversely

Answer Book p. 33

## Martha Graham

Most young women of Martha Graham's generation were introduced to dance through the traditional ballet. **A** The pink lacey skirts and graceful twirling were irresistible to many young ladies. **B** But even as a youth, Graham was different. **C** Her youthful enthusiasm for dance was sparked by a more modern style of ballet in 1911 when she saw a performance by Ruth St. Denis, who was dressed as a Hindu goddess. **D** Much to the dismay of her affluent Pennsylvania parents, the 16-year-old Graham knew then what she wanted to do with her life. They wanted her to go to college and do something practical. Instead, she created a new form of dance.

Graham's distinctive modern dance style provided the dance world with an alternative to ballet. Ballet emphasized grace and technique, built around five classic movements. It was formal and precise. In contrast, Graham's style valued deep emotional expression. Sometimes violent and sometimes sensual, her dance was always passionate. It was based on the principle of "contraction and release." This meant alternately tensing and releasing her muscles while breathing rhythmically and utilizing the center of her body. In this way, she created movements that expressed human emotions directly and powerfully. Tradition meant little to her. She wanted her dance to be shocking and new.

Today, Graham is recognized as the greatest dancer of the 20th century. From the 1920s to the early 1990s, she was as important to the art of modern dance as Picasso was to modern painting. She founded the Martha Graham Dance Company in 1926. Although she retired from dancing in 1969 and died in 1991, her company continues to present groundbreaking dance. The company has trained many of the great dancers and choreographers of our time.

1  Look at the four squares [■] that indicate where the following sentence could be added to the passage.

**She was inspired by the exotic dancing.**

Where would the sentence best fit?

2  The word "It" in the passage refers to

(A) modern dance style

(B) ballet

(C) grace

(D) technique

3  According to paragraph 2, which of the following was NOT true of Graham's style of dance?

(A) It was based on the tension and release of muscles.

(B) It valued emotional expression.

(C) It was precise and formal.

(D) It was passionate and sensual.

4  Which of the sentences below best expresses the essential information in the highlighted sentence in the passage?

(A) Her impact on modern dance was comparable to that of Picasso's on modern painting.

(B) She collaborated with Picasso to create her dance from the 1920s to the early 1990s.

(C) She incorporated important elements from Picasso's art in her dance.

(D) Her dance inspired modern artists such as Picasso to create unique paintings.

• Vocabulary Quiz •

The word [       ] is closest in meaning to

1 | irresistible
ⓐ hateful
ⓑ deceptive
ⓒ tempting

2 | precise
ⓐ exact
ⓑ unclear
ⓒ sensational

3 | passionate
ⓐ enthusiastic
ⓑ mindful
ⓒ practical

4 | retired
ⓐ learned
ⓑ refrained
ⓒ resigned

Answer Book p. 34

## Neanderthals in the Ice Age

➡ During the earth's most recent ice age, glaciers covered much of the northern Eurasian mainland. Modern humans were beginning to appear in the relative warmth of Africa. The territory to the north, from England to Siberia, was occupied by Neanderthals. This hardy species was the closest genetically to ours. But the Neanderthals had to endure much harsher conditions. How did they survive for 5 350,000 years?

➡ The Neanderthals had physical advantages that helped them live in the cold. Their short and bulky bodies were efficient at conserving heat. They had short arms and legs, leaving them with minimally exposed skin. They also had extremely wide noses. This feature enabled them to warm and humidify the cold, dry air in their 10 expansive nasal cavities.

➡ **A** The Neanderthals' large brains also provided intelligence and skill to help them survive. **B** For example, innovative stone-shaping techniques gave them the ability to make effective weapons. **C** They were also masters of fire, lived in shelters, and were the first early humans to wear clothing. **D** 15

➡ In the end, however, an especially cold and dry period of the ice age may have extinguished the species. Some 44,000 years ago, average temperatures in Europe dropped below zero degrees Celsius, and the Neanderthals began to disappear. Some scientists think that large mammals were dying off at the time, leaving the Neanderthals with little food. Other scientists disagree, believing that the 20 Neanderthals were simply unable to compete with our own species. Regardless, the Neanderthals' remarkable survival story ended, and the territories where they once dwelled were soon the home of Homo sapiens.

**1** Why does the author mention "Africa"?

   (A) To establish the relative locations of modern humans and Neanderthals

   (B) To explain how the Neanderthals were able to escape the cold

   (C) To show where the Neanderthals experienced the harshest conditions

   (D) To discuss the climate in the southern hemisphere during the ice age

**2** The word "hardy" in the passage is closest in meaning to

   (A) exotic

   (B) strong

   (C) invasive

   (D) ancient

**3** Which of the following can be inferred from paragraph 1 about the earth's climate?

   (A) Global temperatures were less stable in the past.

   (B) Siberia was once warmer than the rest of Eurasia.

   (C) England was covered by glaciers previously.

   (D) Multiple ice ages have occurred before.

Paragraph 1 is marked with an arrow [➡].

**4** According to paragraph 2, the Neanderthals had wide noses that helped them

   (A) warm the air they breathed

   (B) smell prey from long distances

   (C) compensate the small size of their bodies

   (D) heat their bodies with their breath

Paragraph 2 is marked with an arrow [➡].

**5** In paragraph 3, the author's description of Neanderthals mentions all of the following EXCEPT

Ⓐ their ability to control fire

Ⓑ the fact that they wore clothing

Ⓒ their ability to make tools

Ⓓ their innovative hunting techniques

Paragraph 3 is marked with an arrow [➡].

**6** The word "extinguished" in the passage is closest in meaning to

Ⓐ distinguished

Ⓑ frozen

Ⓒ ended

Ⓓ exhibited

**7** Which of the sentences below best expresses the essential information in the highlighted sentence in the passage? *Incorrect* choices change the meaning in important ways or leave out essential information.

Ⓐ The long survival of the Neanderthals slowed the spread of Homo sapiens.

Ⓑ Once the Neanderthals died off, Homo sapiens occupied their former lands.

Ⓒ The territories of Neanderthals and Homo sapiens often overlapped.

Ⓓ After Homo sapiens moved into an area, the Neanderthals would leave.

**8** According to paragraph 4, which of the following is NOT a potential explanation for the extinction of the Neanderthals?

Ⓐ Insufficient nutrition

Ⓑ harsh climate

Ⓒ Interspecies competition

Ⓓ Infectious disease

Paragraph 4 is marked with an arrow [➡].

**9** Look at the four squares [■] that indicate where the following sentence could be added to the passage.

**This allowed them to hunt large animals such as mammoths, reindeer, and bison.**

Where would the sentence best fit?

Click on a square [■] to add the sentence to the passage.

**10 Directions:** An introductory sentence for a brief summary of the passage is provided below. Complete the summary by selecting the THREE answer choices that express the most important ideas in the passage. Some sentences do not belong in the summary because they express ideas that are not presented in the passage or are minor ideas in the passage. **This question is worth 2 points.**

Drag your answer choices to the spaces where they belong.
To remove an answer choice, click on it. To review the passage, click on **View Text**.

---

**Neanderthals survived for a long time even though they lived in an extremely cold climate.**

- 
- 
- 

---

Answer Choices

Ⓐ The Neanderthals had unusually large brains.

Ⓑ The Neanderthals had adaptations that made them well suited for cold climates.

Ⓒ The Neanderthals lived in Eurasia, in between glaciers and Africa.

Ⓓ The Neanderthals were clever, which helped them to survive cold conditions.

Ⓔ The Neanderthals began to die off approximately 44,000 years ago.

Ⓕ The Neanderthals interbred with modern humans.

Answer Book p. 34

# Vocabulary Review

**A. Fill in the blanks with the appropriate words from the box.**

| | | |
|---|---|---|
| evaporated | enthusiasm | temptation |
| endured | alternatives | seek |

1 She lived every day of her life with _____, enjoying everything she did.

2 There is no water left in the dog's dish because it has _____.

3 Dessert is a nightly _____ that must be avoided by people trying to lose weight.

4 The website helps students who _____ information about studying abroad.

5 The natives _____ discrimination from colonists who viewed them as savages.

6 Most restaurants offer meatless _____ for customers who are vegetarian.

**B. Choose the closest meaning for each highlighted word.**

7 The performer operating the puppet was invisible to the audience.
   (A) interesting      (B) delightful      (C) undetectable      (D) crucial

8 The German scientist visited Copenhagen while the Nazis occupied Denmark.
   (A) resented      (B) seized      (C) fought      (D) resisted

9 Some people endure chronic headaches, making daily life very difficult.
   (A) persistent      (B) mild      (C) potential      (D) possible

10 The restaurant catered to affluent diners who were used to expensive and exotic dishes.
   (A) discerning      (B) wealthy      (C) hungry      (D) busy

11 The townspeople recognized the mayor from a distance due to his distinctive walk.
   (A) authoritative      (B) distant      (C) unique      (D) friendly

12 For a lawyer, the ability to make a convincing argument is priceless.
   (A) invaluable      (B) expensive      (C) attractive      (D) contrary

13 The student was given a light punishment because he was only minimally disruptive.
   (A) extremely      (B) contrarily      (C) decreasingly      (D) slightly

14 The government emphasized that the strict rules were necessary.
   (A) mentioned      (B) stressed      (C) uttered      (D) insisted

# CHAPTER 09

## Summary

# Summary

## About the Question Type

**Summary questions** ask you to complete a summary of the passage by selecting three out of six sentences that best express the major ideas in the passage.

Correct answer choices are restatements of the main idea of one or more paragraphs in the passage. Incorrect answer choices often express inaccurate information, minor points (examples, supporting ideas, etc.), or details that are not mentioned in the passage.

## Question Format

**Directions:** An introductory sentence for a brief summary of the passage is provided below. Complete the summary by selecting the THREE answer choices that express the most important ideas in the passage. Some sentences do not belong in the summary because they express ideas that are not presented in the passage or are minor ideas in the passage. **This question is worth 2 points.**

> Drag your answer choices to the spaces where they belong.
> To remove an answer choice, click on it. To review the passage, click on **View Text**.

**[An introductory sentence]**
- 
- 
- 

Answer Choices

## Key Strategies

- **Step 1** — Read the introductory sentence that represents the main idea of the passage.

- **Step 2** — Scan the passage to see if each answer choice is supported by the passage.

- **Step 3** — Select the three answer choices that express the major ideas in the passage.

# Example

Answer Book p. 35

## The King of Instruments

The piano is known as the king of instruments. It is the largest of all orchestral instruments, weighing in at 300 to 1,000 pounds. It has an unmatched musical range, spanning seven octaves. It can produce the lowest note of the deep-voiced double bassoon and the highest note of the high-pitched piccolo. And it is unusually expressive, capable of playing the same note as a soft whisper or as a    5 thunderous boom. How did this special instrument come to be?

The piano is the culmination of centuries of musical innovation. Keyboard instruments have been around since the Greeks built the Hydraulis in 220 BC. Also known as the water organ, it made sound by pushing air from a pool of water into a set of pipes not unlike a modern organ's. In the eleventh century,  10 the hammered dulcimer was invented in the Middle East. The dulcimer works by striking strings with a small hammer. During the Renaissance, the clavichord and harpsichord emerged. Neither could be played with much emotion. No matter how hard the keys were pushed, the sound was the same.

In 1700, Bartolomeo di Francesco improved upon those earlier models by  15 using a hammer to play the strings with a greater variety of intonations. An Italian harpsichord craftsman, Cristofori gave his invention a lengthy name that emphasized this capacity for variety. The name translated to "a harpsichord that can play loud and soft noises." The original name was later shortened to "piano." The king of instruments had been born.    20

---

1   **Directions:** An introductory sentence for a brief summary of the passage is provided below. Complete the summary by selecting the THREE answer choices that express the most important ideas in the passage.

**The piano was invented at the opening of the eighteenth century.**

(A) The piano was influenced by several earlier instruments that also had keyboards.

(B) The hammered dulcimer is like the piano in that it was invented in the Middle East.

(C) The piano improved upon its predecessors by allowing musicians to play with more emotion.

(D) The clavichord and harpsichord were important ancestors of the piano.

(E) The first piano was invented in Greece in 220 BC.

(F) Musicians are able to create a wide range of sounds using the piano.

Answer Book p. 36

## Carbon Footprints

A carbon footprint is a way of measuring the amount of greenhouse gases produced. These gases prevent heat from escaping Earth's atmosphere. As a result, the planet's average temperature increases. Glaciers melt, sea levels rise, and severe weather 5 becomes more prevalent. The carbon footprint is sometimes expressed as the amount of land required to produce the amount of carbon emitted by an activity. For example, it would take the equivalent of four Earths to sustain the world's population if everyone lived a typical American lifestyle. 10

Each nation in the world has its own carbon footprint. China and the United States have the largest footprints. These countries account for a combined 43 percent of the world's carbon emissions. Yet, they have only 24 percent of its people. Most of these gases are generated by burning fossil fuels. These include both coal and oil. Therefore, environmentalists advocate transitioning to energy 15 sources that do not produce greenhouse gases, like wind and solar. They also demand that the world's forests be preserved. Trees absorb 1.4 tons of carbon dioxide per acre. In 2015, about 200 countries committed to these goals by signing the Paris Agreement.

There are numerous ways that an individual's carbon footprint can be lowered. 20 For example, this can be accomplished by using trains and bicycles instead of cars. A serving of beef adds six pounds of greenhouse gases to the atmosphere because cows emit methane. Therefore, replacing meat with vegetables is an effective strategy for lowering a carbon footprint. Locally produced food is better, too, because transporting food puts carbon dioxide in the air. 25

1 The word "prevalent" in the passage is closest in meaning to

(A) common
(B) important
(C) damaging
(D) predictable

2 The word "its" in the passage refers to

(A) China
(B) the United States
(C) the world
(D) carbon

3 According to paragraph 3, each of the following helps to reduce a person's carbon footprint EXCEPT

(A) taking public transportation
(B) eating a diet with more vegetables
(C) finding better sources of meat
(D) buying locally made products

4 **Directions:** An introductory sentence for a brief summary of the passage is provided below. Complete the summary by selecting the THREE answer choices that express the most important ideas in the passage.

**The carbon footprint provides a way to measure how much greenhouse gas is emitted.**

(A) Each individual can play a role in averting the dangers of climate change.
(B) Cows produce greenhouse gases by naturally emitting methane, a powerful greenhouse gas.
(C) People can prevent climate change on a national level by reducing fossil fuel usage.
(D) China and the United States are two largest contributor of greenhouse gases.
(E) For each acre of forest, more than a ton of carbon dioxide is removed from the atmosphere.
(F) Greenhouse gases cause the planet to become warmer, which endangers its survival.

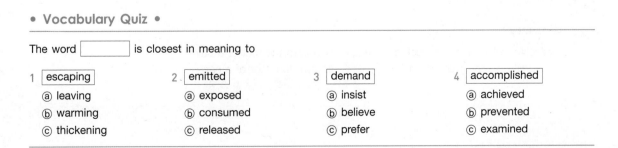

• Vocabulary Quiz •

The word ☐ is closest in meaning to

1 escaping
ⓐ leaving
ⓑ warming
ⓒ thickening

2 emitted
ⓐ exposed
ⓑ consumed
ⓒ released

3 demand
ⓐ insist
ⓑ believe
ⓒ prefer

4 accomplished
ⓐ achieved
ⓑ prevented
ⓒ examined

Answer Book p. 36

## How Drought Ended the Maya Empire

For twelve centuries, the Maya Empire was the most advanced civilization in the Americas. The Maya people built glorious stone cities and developed their own system of writing. They also made important discoveries in mathematics and astronomy. By AD 900, however, their society had collapsed. Their cities, once home to millions of people, were empty. Their limestone palaces and temples were abandoned. Historians have long struggled to understand the cause of this sudden decline. Armed with the tools of modern science, researchers are finally beginning to put the pieces of the puzzle together.

Numerous studies indicate that the Maya civilization was devastated by a severe drought. Scientists examined mineral deposits at the bottom of a lake. They found evidence that the amount of rainfall dropped off steeply between AD 750 and 1000. They also dated the formation of stalactites and stalagmites in caves. These showed that conditions were dry during the same period. The Maya had large stone reservoirs to store rainwater during the dry seasons. However, this drought was likely so prolonged that the reservoirs were emptied. Drinking water was hard to find.

The Maya apparently made the drought worse by burning and chopping down trees. They were victims of their own success. Because they had to feed their large population, forests were replaced with cornfields. Additionally, their impressive architecture fueled deforestation. For each square meter of limestone, the Maya had to burn 20 trees. With fewer trees to absorb solar radiation, fewer rainclouds formed above the Maya territory. According to computer simulations, deforestation was responsible for as much as 60 percent of the drought. Despite their cleverness, the Maya did not yet understand the devastating impact their activities would have on their survival.

### Glossary
· stalactite: a long piece of rock that hangs down from the roof of a cave
· stalagmite: a long piece of rock that sticks up from the floor of a cave

1 Why does the author mention the "pieces of the puzzle"?

(A) To show that researchers derive enjoyment studying Maya history

(B) To emphasize that the reason for the Maya decline is not obvious

(C) To illustrate that there were many components to the construction of Maya buildings

(D) To refute the idea that the collapse of the Maya Empire is easy to understand


2 According to paragraph 2, the Maya population dwindled because

(A) reservoirs could not store enough water to support the population

(B) rain fell in insufficient quantities for an extended period

(C) the construction of stone buildings occurred on farmlands

(D) harmful minerals accumulated in many bodies of water


3 The word "fueled" in the passage is closest in meaning to

(A) drove

(B) began

(C) allocated

(D) postponed


4 **Directions:** An introductory sentence for a brief summary of the passage is provided below. Complete the summary by selecting the THREE answer choices that express the most important ideas in the passage.

**Science is uncovering the reason for the sudden decline of the Maya civilization.**

(A) The Maya people made important mathematical discoveries.

(B) Stalactites and stalagmites are columns of water and minerals.

(C) The Maya civilization was advanced for its time, making many important contributions.

(D) The Maya built reservoirs to store rainwater during periods of low rainfall.

(E) Deforestation made the dry conditions even worse.

(F) A terrible drought made water hard to come by during the last 200 years of the Maya Empire.


• Vocabulary Quiz •

The word ☐ is closest in meaning to

| 1 advanced | 2 collapsed | 3 steeply | 4 apparently |
|---|---|---|---|
| ⓐ steady | ⓐ oppressed | ⓐ sharply | ⓐ fortunately |
| ⓑ developed | ⓑ delivered | ⓑ arguably | ⓑ quietly |
| ⓒ curious | ⓒ ended | ⓒ impressively | ⓒ evidently |

## The History of Medicine

For much of history, many illnesses were attributed to witchcraft and the gods. Minor problems such as the common cold were considered natural events that could be treated with herbs. More serious illnesses were believed to 5 be caused by supernatural beings. Spells, potions, and incantations were common approaches to healing.

Humanity's understanding of the body has changed significantly over the centuries. The ancient Egyptians had little interest in anatomy. Nevertheless, their spiritual beliefs led them to preserve bodies through the process of 10 mummification. As a result, we know that the illnesses they faced were similar to those that we face today. The Greeks developed their own medical system. Treatment was aimed at restoring the balance of body fluids. In India, the Hindus believed health depended on a balance of spirit, phlegm, and bile. The Chinese, too, focused on balance with their concept of yin and yang. 15

By the 1800s, experimental investigation had taken root in Europe. Advances in chemistry and laboratory equipment aided in the production of medicine. However, there were few effective drugs beyond opium and quinine. Hence, useless folklore cures such as poisonous, metal-based compounds were popular treatments. Research on bacteriology by Robert Koch, Edward Jenner, and Louis 20 Pasteur led to actual cures of certain infectious diseases. However, the decline in lethal diseases was due more to improvements in public health and nutrition. It was not until the twentieth century that there were true breakthroughs in medicine. This is when great advances in pharmacology and surgery occurred.

### Glossary
·phlegm: the thick yellowish mucus that develops in the throat during a cold
·bile: a liquid produced by the liver that aids in the digestion of fats

1 The phrase "attributed to" in the passage is closest in meaning to

   (A) blamed on

   (B) referred to

   (C) allowed for

   (D) delayed by


2 Why does the author mention "metal-based compounds"?

   (A) To provide an example of a useless folk cure

   (B) To explain the difference between new and old medicine

   (C) To show how scientific developments improved medicine

   (D) To illustrate the uses of metal in modern medicine


3 According to paragraph 3, experiments in bacteriology had which effect?

   (A) They restored the balance of bodily fluids.

   (B) They increased the use of drugs such as opium.

   (C) They made traditional treatments more effective.

   (D) They gave scientists a way to treat diseases.


4 **Directions:** An introductory sentence for a brief summary of the passage is provided below. Complete the summary by selecting the THREE answer choices that express the most important ideas in the passage.

**Illness was once believed to be caused by supernatural forces.**

   (A) Our understanding of human bodies has evolved greatly over the centuries.

   (B) The common cold was treated with herbs in ancient times.

   (C) Experimentation was an important element of medicine in the nineteenth century.

   (D) The Hindus believed that phlegm was a key factor in maintaining health.

   (E) Medical breakthroughs did not begin until the twentieth century.

   (F) Opium and quinine were among the earliest drugs used by doctors.


• **Vocabulary Quiz** •

The word [      ] is closest in meaning to

1 [ beings ]
  ⓐ powers
  ⓑ creatures
  ⓒ factors

2 [ aided ]
  ⓐ ailed
  ⓑ assisted
  ⓒ resulted

3 [ infectious ]
  ⓐ contagious
  ⓑ deadly
  ⓒ effective

4 [ lethal ]
  ⓐ unpleasant
  ⓑ effective
  ⓒ fatal

Answer Book p. 38

## Origin of the Pacific Islanders

The origins of the first settlers of the Pacific Islands are only gradually being pieced together by scientists. DNA technology has given them a better understanding of the current and previous island inhabitants. The stories of Melanesia and Polynesia, two regions of the Pacific Islands, are just beginning to be told as a result of genetic studies.

The evidence indicates that Melanesia was the first region to be inhabited. Some 70,000 years ago, people from present-day Indonesia arrived in Papua New Guinea. Many of these Papuans spread out into the islands to the east of New Guinea starting around 4,000 years ago. They were generally dark-skinned. As a result, European explorers named the region Melanesia, or "black islands."

Scholars have long debated about whether the first Polynesians came from Melanesia. Linguists noted that Polynesian languages are more like those of East Asians than those of the Papuans. Early DNA studies suggested that Polynesians had mingled with Melanesians. These two facts seemed to conflict with each other. However, this conflict was recently resolved. Scientists analyzed the DNA of four ancient Polynesian women. It revealed that the women likely had ancestors from Taiwan and the Philippines, not Melanesia. In addition, the analysis showed that the Polynesians acquired the Papuan genes much more recently than the East Asian ones.

From DNA analysis, a fascinating new picture emerged. About 3,000 years ago, people from East Asia began making perilous canoe journeys in the Pacific. They passed the Melanesian Islands and proceeded to Polynesia. Thousands of years later, Melanesians arrived in Polynesia. They intermarried with the people who were already there. Without genetic science, this story would remain a mystery.

1  According to paragraph 2, there is evidence for all of the following claims about the Papuans EXCEPT

(A) they originated from an area that is now part of Indonesia
(B) they moved eastward from New Guinea to settle on other islands
(C) they came into contact with explorers from Europe
(D) they left Melanesia approximately 70,000 years ago


2  The word "those" in the passage refers to

(A) Polynesians
(B) linguists
(C) languages
(D) East Asians


3  The word "perilous" in the passage is closest in meaning to

(A) costly
(B) nautical
(C) tiring
(D) dangerous


4  **Directions:** An introductory sentence for a brief summary of the passage is provided below. Complete the summary by selecting the THREE answer choices that express the most important ideas in the passage.

**The history of the Pacific Islanders is just beginning to be understood.**

(A) The first Melanesians came from Indonesia to New Guinea.
(B) Scientists disagreed about the origins of the Polynesians.
(C) The earliest settlers of Polynesia arrived from East Asia.
(D) The term Melanesia refers to the skin color of the Melanesians.
(E) The first Papuans came to Melanesia in canoes.
(F) DNA technology shows scientists how the early Pacific Islanders traveled.


• Vocabulary Quiz •

The word [        ] is closest in meaning to

| 1 current | 2 mingled | 3 conflict | 4 analyzed |
|-----------|-----------|------------|------------|
| ⓐ modern | ⓐ blended | ⓐ agree | ⓐ prepared |
| ⓑ enduring | ⓑ achieved | ⓑ clash | ⓑ examined |
| ⓒ present | ⓒ defeated | ⓒ doubt | ⓒ distributed |

# iBT Reading Test

Answer Book p. 38

## Cosmic Rays

   Cosmic rays are <u>subatomic</u> particles that travel through space slightly slower than the speed of light. Some are emitted in solar flares from the Sun, and some originate from deeper in the galaxy or even outside the Milky Way. Every second, Earth is bombarded by roughly 10,000 cosmic rays per square meter. Much of this cosmic radiation is deflected by the planet's magnetic shield, but some makes it ₅ into the upper atmosphere and to the surface.

   Studying cosmic rays is not always easy. Because they can be deflected by magnetic shields in space, cosmic rays cannot be traced directly back to their source. Instead, scientists deduce the origins of cosmic rays by examining their abundance and composition. Austrian physicist Victor Hess first discovered cosmic ₁₀ rays in 1912 by measuring radiation as he ascended into the upper atmosphere in a hot air balloon. He was testing the hypothesis that radiation came from Earth's core, but it turned out that the amount of radiation increased as he got higher due to the presence of cosmic rays. Since then, scientists have learned that about 89 percent of cosmic rays are lightweight hydrogen protons, 10 percent are helium, ₁₅ and 1 percent are heavier nuclei like uranium.

   ➡ **A** Scientists make the effort to study the cosmic rays that reach Earth in the hope that these tiny particles will reveal the secrets of massive stellar events deep in space, like the birth or death of a star. **B** They have long suspected that higher energy cosmic rays are produced when <u>supernova</u> remnants explode in space. **C** In ₂₀ 2017, researchers confirmed this when they detected waves from the merger of two neutron stars. **D** This has made scientists believe that they will be able to research similar phenomena in the future by identifying the cosmic rays they produce.

---

| Glossary | ☒ |
|---|---|

**subatomic:** of particles smaller than atoms
**supernova:** a star experiencing an explosion

**1** The word "bombarded" in the passage is closest in meaning to

  (A) hosted

  (B) reflected

  (C) impacted

  (D) intercepted

**2** The author's description of cosmic rays mentions all of the following EXCEPT their

  (A) speed while traveling through space

  (B) reaction when colliding with a magnetic shield

  (C) origin in eruptions on the Sun's surface

  (D) ability to penetrate Earth's core

**3** Which of the sentences below best expresses the essential information in the highlighted sentence in the passage? *Incorrect* choices change the meaning in important ways or leave out essential information.

  (A) It is possible to detect cosmic rays by studying the various magnetic fields that they interact with.

  (B) Tracking cosmic rays is impossible as their course is changed by interaction with magnetic fields.

  (C) Cosmic rays bounce from magnetic field to magnetic field, so finding them is challenging.

  (D) Since cosmic rays often bypass magnetic fields, it is difficult to trace the course they follow.

**4** The word "their" in the passage refers to

  (A) magnetic shields

  (B) scientists

  (C) origins

  (D) cosmic rays

**5** The word "composition" in the passage is closest in meaning to

   Ⓐ makeup

   Ⓑ documentation

   Ⓒ creativity

   Ⓓ decay

**6** Which of the following can be inferred about Victor Hess?

   Ⓐ He wanted to confirm that radiation comes from stellar events.

   Ⓑ He expected radiation to decrease as his balloon rose into the sky.

   Ⓒ He tested the chemical components of cosmic rays on his journey.

   Ⓓ His hypothesis was supported by the hot air balloon experiment.

**7** According to the passage, which of the following is NOT true of scientists studying cosmic rays?

   Ⓐ They use particles that reach Earth to learn about distant space events.

   Ⓑ They are unable to determine the origin of the cosmic rays that reach Earth.

   Ⓒ They have been studying cosmic rays for more than a century.

   Ⓓ They can estimate the number of cosmic rays hitting Earth.

**8** According to paragraph 3, cosmic rays produced by supernovas

   Ⓐ constitute a threat to people

   Ⓑ cause violent space collisions

   Ⓒ travel in a straight line

   Ⓓ are especially energetic

Paragraph 3 is marked with an arrow [➡].

**9** Look at the four squares [■] that indicate where the following sentence could be added to the passage.

**Neutron stars are the relatively small but dense remains of a supergiant star.**

Where would the sentence best fit?

Click on a square [■] to add the sentence to the passage.

**10 Directions:** An introductory sentence for a brief summary of the passage is provided below. Complete the summary by selecting the THREE answer choices that express the most important ideas in the passage. Some sentences do not belong in the summary because they express ideas that are not presented in the passage or are minor ideas in the passage. **This question is worth 2 points.**

Drag your answer choices to the spaces where they belong.
To remove an answer choice, click on it. To review the passage, click on **View Text**.

---

**Cosmic rays are particles from outer space.**

- 
- 
- 

---

Answer Choices

Ⓐ It can be difficult to collect data about cosmic rays.

Ⓑ Most cosmic rays that reach Earth come from other galaxies.

Ⓒ Cosmic rays were discovered in a hot air balloon journey.

Ⓓ Scientists study subatomic particles to find out about massive celestial events.

Ⓔ A merger of neutron stars produced cosmic rays.

Ⓕ Our planet is continually exposed to large quantities of cosmic rays.

Answer Book p. 38

# Vocabulary Review

Answer Book p. 40

## A. Fill in the blanks with the appropriate words from the box.

| | | |
|---|---|---|
| presence | previous | store |
| remnants | explodes | unmatched |

1 As a portrait artist, Rembrandt is _____ by any other painter in skill.

2 After the earthquake, volunteers searched the _____ of the buildings.

3 My _____ car was much less fuel efficient than my current one.

4 Squirrels collect nuts throughout the fall in order to _____ food for the winter.

5 Walking into the room, my father cleared his throat to announce his _____.

6 A meteor that _____ in Earth's atmosphere sometimes creates a fireball in the sky.

## B. Choose the closest meaning for each highlighted word.

7 The choir lifted their voices together into one glorious sound of praise.
   (A) magnificent      (B) audible      (C) varied      (D) merged

8 The prolonged snowfall over the weekend resulted in numerous road closures.
   (A) sudden      (B) abrupt      (C) predicted      (D) extended

9 The new space telescope is the culmination of years of research.
   (A) sum      (B) minimum      (C) reduction      (D) basis

10 Looking at the crumbs on the boy's shirt, I deduced that he had eaten the cookies.
   (A) concluded      (B) grasped      (C) reported      (D) joked

11 The author's popular novel has been translated into over 30 different languages.
   (A) converted      (B) written      (C) blessed      (D) burned

12 After the murderer confessed to the detective, the mystery was resolved.
   (A) inspired      (B) executed      (C) solved      (D) burdened

13 The lost hiker traced the old trail through the woods until he reached a farm.
   (A) observed      (B) followed      (C) dropped      (D) piled

14 The magician refused to reveal his secrets to anyone in the audience.
   (A) approach      (B) disclose      (C) reject      (D) possess

# CHAPTER 10

## Category Chart

# Category Chart

■ **About the Question Type**

**Category Chart questions** ask you to complete a table by placing the relevant information in the appropriate categories.

When reading the passage, try to identify what is being compared or contrasted, and recognize the important information for each category.

■ **Question Format**

**Directions:** Select the appropriate phrases from the answer choices and match them to the type to which they relate. **This question is worth 3 points.**

| Drag your answer choices to the spaces where they belong. To remove an answer choice, click on it. To review the passage, click on **View Text**. | |
|---|---|

| Answer Choices | Category 1 |
|---|---|
| | • |
| | • |
| | • |
| | **Category 2** |
| | • |
| | • |

■ **Key Strategies**

- **Step 1** — Check the categories in the table.

- **Step 2** — Scan the passage and identify the important information for each category.

- **Step 3** — Select the answer choices that best paraphrase the important information in the passage for each category. Answer choices that include information from the passage that is unrelated to the categories or inaccurate information can be eliminated.

# Example

## DNA and RNA

There are two nucleic acids containing genetic information in every cell of an organism: deoxyribonucleic acid (DNA) and ribonucleic acid (RNA). They have a lot in common, but there are important functional and structural differences between the two.

While DNA is essentially the blueprint for life, RNA plays a more active role. DNA includes the instructions for the production of proteins, which are the basic unit of the cells that all living creatures are composed of. Therefore, an organism's DNA determines its traits. The primary role of RNA is to transport the information from the DNA to the ribosome, which is the part of the cell where proteins are produced.

Structurally, RNA looks a little like an incomplete DNA. DNA consists of two strands of sugar phosphate wound around each other like a spiral staircase. Crossing the staircase are the paired "steps" (called bases) of the staircase: adenine, thymine, cytosine, and guanine. In contrast, RNA has only one twisty strand of sugar phosphate, and its bases are unpaired. The chemical composition of the bases is the same as in DNA, except that thymine is replaced with uracil.

The two nucleic acids are found in different locations in the cell. DNA resides in the nucleus, or center, of the cell. There is also a small amount of DNA in the cell's mitochondria, which transfers energy from food into the cells. RNA is found mainly in the cell's cytoplasm, a thick solution between the outer membrane and the nucleus.

1  **Directions:** Select the appropriate phrases from the answer choices and match them to the type of nucleic acid with which they are associated.

| Answer Choices | DNA |
|---|---|
| (A) Produces a special cell called a ribosome | • |
| (B) Looks like a spiral staircase | |
| (C) Transports information to another part of the cell | • |
| | • |
| (D) Has one strand of sugar phosphate | RNA |
| (E) Determines the characteristics of an organism | |
| (F) Is located in the nucleus of the cell | • |
| (G) Contains pairs of thymine and uracil | • |

Answer Book p. 40

## American Comics

Comics are forms of media that feature panels with both images and text. These panels are usually arranged in <u>chronological</u> order to create a linear narrative. In the United States, the two main forms of comics are comic strips and comic books.

Comic strips are typically published in newspapers daily and have up to eight ⁵ panels. They are the oldest of the two comic formats—the first comic strip was *The Yellow Kid*, which ran from 1895 to 1898. Comic strips often focus on humor, with each individual strip developing a single joke or funny situation. The reason for this is that the limited number of panels makes it difficult to present complex storylines. In addition, the inclusion of comic strips in newspapers means that ¹⁰ they cannot have controversial content.

Comic books provide much more freedom. Individual issues with over twenty pages of panels are published once a month, so writers can develop more elaborate stories with a greater range of themes. The first comic book was released in 1933, and the format experienced a boom over the next two decades with the debut ¹⁵ of popular superheroes such as Superman and Captain America. During World War II, stories involving these characters fighting German and Japanese soldiers were actively encouraged by the US government to boost the morale of American military personnel. However, in the 1950s, there was growing concern about the negative influence of comic books on children. In order to avoid government ²⁰ regulation, the major comic book publishers created and agreed to follow the Comics Code Authority (CCA). This collection of rules limits depictions of excessive violence and references to socially inappropriate topics.

### Glossary

· chronological: arranged in the order of time

1 Why does the author mention "*The Yellow Kid*"?

(A) To suggest that comic strips were better liked than books

(B) To explain why comics were included in newspapers

(C) To identify the earliest known example of a type of comic

(D) To provide a description of a controversial comic strip

2 The word "boost" in the passage is closest in meaning to

(A) improve

(B) distribute

(C) impact

(D) recover

3 According to paragraph 3, which of the following is true about the CCA?

(A) It is limited to banning violent images.

(B) It was a response to a wartime issue.

(C) It was imposed by the government.

(D) It is a set of voluntary guidelines.

4 **Directions:** Select the appropriate phrases from the answer choices and match them to the type of comics with which they are associated.

| Answer Choices | Comic strips |
| --- | --- |
| (A) First appeared in the nineteenth century | • |
| (B) Introduced famous super-powered characters | • |
| (C) Avoid including a chronological narrative | Comic books |
| (D) Published on a monthly basis | • |
| (E) Promoted by the government initially | • |
| (F) Based on stories that appeared in newspapers | • |
| (G) Tend to focus on comedic content | • |

• Vocabulary Quiz •

The word [          ] is closest in meaning to

1 controversial
ⓐ intellectual
ⓑ conservative
ⓒ contentious

2 elaborate
ⓐ exciting
ⓑ inspiring
ⓒ complicated

3 morale
ⓐ spirits
ⓑ ethics
ⓒ strength

4 excessive
ⓐ extreme
ⓑ humorous
ⓒ personal

## Chimpanzees and Bonobos

No species in the animal kingdom is closer genetically to humans than chimpanzees and bonobos. The three species share about 98.8 percent of their DNA. They also likely have a single common ancestor species. However, chimpanzees and bonobos are much more closely related. They diverged genetically only about two million years ago, approximately five million years after  5
humans had become a distinct species.

The two ape species remain remarkably similar physically, but there are a few key differences. For example, chimps are stronger, but bonobos are more graceful. Also, chimps have shorter legs whereas bonobos have bigger heads. In addition, chimps begin life with a light-colored face that darkens as they age. Bonobos are  10
dark-skinned for life.

Still, the physical differences are not nearly as striking as the behavioral differences. Although both species are highly social, chimpanzees experience a great deal more violence and conflict with other group members than bonobos. Much of the chimp's energy is directed toward competition for food and mates.  15
The males are dominant and often aggressive with the females. In contrast, bonobo society is dominated by the females. It is perhaps consequently more peaceful. Infanticide, which occurs often in chimp society, is unheard of with bonobos.

These behavioral differences may be explained by geography. Bonobos are  20
found only in a small territory south of the Congo River. A drought about two million years ago led to the gorillas that once lived in this region dying off. As a result, bonobos evolved in an environment without significant competition for resources. This made them relatively peaceful. In contrast, chimpanzees inhabit a larger area north of the river that they share with gorillas. The need to constantly  25
compete for food and territory is likely what has made them so aggressive.

### Glossary

· infanticide: killing of infants or offspring

1 The word "diverged" in the passage is closest in meaning to

    (A) evolved         (B) increased         (C) separated         (D) merged

2 Which of the sentences below best expresses the essential information in the highlighted sentence in the passage?

    (A) Chimpanzees frequently fight with each other, and sometimes the conflicts cause injuries.

    (B) Bonobos are friendly creatures who rarely get into physical fights with other bonobos.

    (C) While chimpanzees are more violent than bonobos, bonobos have more non-physical conflicts.

    (D) Chimpanzees clash with one another more than bonobos do, but both species are social.

3 According to paragraph 4, bonobos are more peaceful than chimpanzees because bonobos

    (A) are dominated by males

    (B) had less competition for food

    (C) are more graceful physically

    (D) live north of the Congo River

4 **Directions:** Select the appropriate phrases from the answer choices and match them to the species with which they are associated.

| Answer Choices | Chimpanzees |
| --- | --- |
| (A) Share their territory with gorillas | ● |
| (B) Live in female-dominated groups | ● |
| (C) Diverged from humans two million years ago | ● |
| (D) Have shorter legs | Bonobos |
| (E) Are aggressive with humans | ● |
| (F) Are more graceful | ● |
| (G) Often kill their offspring | |

• **Vocabulary Quiz** •

The word ☐ is closest in meaning to

1 ancestor
   ⓐ professional
   ⓑ precursor
   ⓒ primate

2 perhaps
   ⓐ possibly
   ⓑ rarely
   ⓒ reversely

3 relatively
   ⓐ comparatively
   ⓑ completely
   ⓒ seemingly

4 compete
   ⓐ perform
   ⓑ hunt
   ⓒ contend

Answer Book p. 42

## The Industrial Revolution

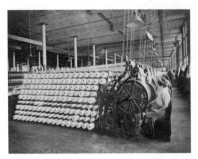

The Industrial Revolution brought massive change at an unprecedented pace to both sides of the Atlantic Ocean. However, it began much earlier in the United Kingdom than in the United States. Technological change swept through Britain  5 as early as 1701 when Jethro Tull invented the seed drill and transformed the seed planting process. Not until 1793, when English immigrant Samuel Slater opened a textile mill in Rhode Island, did these changes truly begin to revolutionize America.

The textile industry was among the first to be transformed by the Industrial  10 Revolution. By the mid-1700s, Britain's cottage industry of individual weavers and spinners was being replaced by textile factories. The spinning jenny, which connected eight spindles to a single wheel, sped thread production. The power loom automated the weaving process, allowing clothing items to be made very cheaply. These innovations began to make their way to the United States by the  15 end of the eighteenth century. American inventor Eli Whitney developed the cotton gin, which strengthened the slave-powered cotton industry.

As similar technological improvements swept through every industry, transportation was required to shuttle goods and raw materials over long distances. Britain improved its primitive road network and dug canals to allow  20 boats to traverse the country. The steam engine, the defining energy source of the Industrial Revolution, powered steamboats and locomotives with coal and water by the late eighteenth century. In America, these innovations facilitated the settlement of the west.

There were costs to the rapid development. In Britain, urbanization brought  25 overcrowding, pollution, and disease. While the middle and upper classes thrived, the lower classes were subjected to terrible working conditions. In the United States, millionaire factory owners profited while the poor, especially immigrants, suffered. Reforms like child labor law and environmental regulation were required to mitigate the dark side of the Industrial Revolution.  30

1 Why does the author mention "Eli Whitney"?

(A) To demonstrate that technological changes occurred in the US
(B) To show that slaves were commonly used in American industry
(C) To contrast a textile industry in the UK with one in the US
(D) To suggest that American inventors were superior to British ones

2 According to the passage, which of the following was NOT transformed by technology in the Industrial Revolution?

(A) Producing inexpensive clothing items
(B) Making threads from raw materials
(C) Planting seeds on a farm
(D) Cleaning the air and water

3 The word "mitigate" in the passage is closest in meaning to

(A) darken          (B) lessen          (C) keep          (D) end

4 **Directions:** Select the appropriate phrases from the answer choices and match them to the country with which they are associated.

| Answer Choices | The United Kingdom |
|---|---|
| (A) Began the industrialization process with the invention of the seed drill | ● |
| (B) Used the cotton gin to strengthen the textile industry | ● |
| (C) Powered settlement in the east with the steam engine | ● |
| (D) Transported raw materials to continental Europe through canals | **The United States** |
| (E) Enriched millionaire factory owners | ● |
| (F) Created new systems of roads | |
| (G) Replaced its cottage industry of weavers | ● |

• **Vocabulary Quiz** •

The word [          ] is closest in meaning to

1 pace
ⓐ amount
ⓑ speed
ⓒ detail

2 shuttle
ⓐ move
ⓑ steal
ⓒ grab

3 primitive
ⓐ impressive
ⓑ defective
ⓒ basic

4 thrived
ⓐ suffered
ⓑ prospered
ⓒ labored

Answer Book p. 42

## Gothic and Renaissance Stained Glass

Stained glass windows were a dominant art form of the Middle Ages. **A** The glass in these colorful windows was constructed from sand and wood ash mixed with powdered metals. **B** The term "stained glass" comes from a silver stain that ₅ was applied to one side of the window. **C** From the tenth to sixteenth centuries, the history of stained glass can be divided into two stylistic periods: Gothic and Renaissance. **D**

Until the early 1400s, there was great demand for colorful windows depicting Biblical stories. This provided craftspeople and painters with a medium that was ₁₀ featured in the most ambitious architecture of the period. The dizzying vertical height of Gothic churches and cathedrals made tall stained glass displays possible. Religious scholars were usually responsible for the designs. This presented them with a lasting opportunity to deliver theological messages to the illiterate masses. As national identities formed throughout Europe, distinct national styles of stained ₁₅ glass developed. The German style was dark and heavy. The English preferred highly detailed images that tended toward the grotesque. The French showcased the rapid sketching ability of their artists.

By the 1430s, the Gothic style of stained glass began to be replaced with the more realistic approach of the great Renaissance painters. Although stained glass ₂₀ was less prominent in architecture, it also became more ornate. Lead lines were deemphasized to enhance the realism of the artwork. Humor crept into the designs. Secular subjects were more common. Glass was also less expensive during this period. As a result, stained glass became increasingly popular in houses. However, the medium lost its appeal to many artists. The reason was that the ₂₅ amount of paint used increased, preventing light from shining through the glass.

1 Look at the four squares [■] that indicate where the following sentence could be added to the passage.

**Then it was painted, and pieces of it were held together with lead lines.**

Where would the sentence best fit?

2 The word "ornate" in the passage is closest in meaning to

(A) notorious      (B) important      (C) optimistic      (D) elaborate

3 According to paragraph 3, stained glass lost popularity among artists because

(A) religious disputes resulted in a dislike of religious art

(B) the public reacted poorly to the use of humor in a sacred setting

(C) glass became a prohibitively expensive material

(D) the amount of paint used began to block natural light

4 **Directions:** Select the appropriate statements from the answer choices and match them to the style with which they are associated.

| Answer Choices | Gothic |
|---|---|
| (A) Religious themes were not the only subject for stained glass windows. | ● |
| (B) Different nations developed their own distinctive styles. | ● |
| (C) Religious scholars created the designs to serve a theological purpose. | ● |
| (D) The process of making stained glass was dangerous for many craftspeople. | |
| (E) A realistic illustration style became more prevalent. | Renaissance |
| (F) The prevailing architectural style provided a showcase for stained glass. | ● |
| (G) A rapid sketching style became a hallmark of this period. | ● |

• Vocabulary Quiz •

The word ☐ is closest in meaning to

1 ambitious
ⓐ dramatic
ⓑ aspiring
ⓒ economical

2 lasting
ⓐ enduring
ⓑ sudden
ⓒ outstanding

3 showcased
ⓐ celebrated
ⓑ hid
ⓒ displayed

4 secular
ⓐ fictional
ⓑ historical
ⓒ nonreligious

## How Migrating Birds Find Their Way

➡ Every spring, millions of birds migrate north to territories that are not oppressively hot. These temperate regions provide more opportunities for food. Then, in autumn, the birds return to warmer regions in the south to avoid harsh winters. These 5 miraculous journeys can be as long as 16,000 miles. Scientists are still experimenting in an effort to learn how they do it, and the answer lies in the birds' ability to both orient and navigate.

➡ To orient is to determine one's magnetic compass direction. Scientists have identified a region in the front of some birds' brains that they call "Cluster N." 10 This part of the brain seems to interact with the birds' eyes when flying at night, pointing them toward north. But even when Cluster N is not active, birds can still use the setting sun or the position of the stars to find north, just as humans do. Researchers have confirmed this by conducting experiments in planetariums, which are large, dome-like theaters that present visual representations of the night 15 sky. The birds normally use Polaris, the North Star, to head in the right direction. However, when the planetarium stars revolved around the star Betelgeuse instead of Polaris, the birds used Betelgeuse to orient.

➡ The second ability a bird must have is to navigate, which means to assess its position mid-flight. **A** One of the ways birds achieve this feat is to rely on their 20 sense of smell. **B** Their beaks develop an olfactory map of the odors along their path. **C** Another avian trick may be to use the trigeminal nerve in their beaks to determine how strong the earth's magnetic fields are at a given location. **D** In this way, they can tell how close they are to the earth's poles or to the equator. It seems that birds have multiple methods for orienting and navigating so that they 25 can find their way under any circumstances.

| Glossary | ☒ |
|---|---|
| **olfactory:** of the sense of smell | |
| **trigeminal nerve:** a nerve responsible for sensation in the face | |

Volume Review Help Back Next

**1** The word "oppressively" in the passage is closest in meaning to

Ⓐ unbearably

Ⓑ mildly

Ⓒ unusually

Ⓓ decidedly

**2** According to paragraph 1, birds migrate north because

Ⓐ their bodies are unable to cope with extremely harsh weather

Ⓑ they naturally seek out warm weather in the spring

Ⓒ the journey is not as long in that direction as it is to the south

Ⓓ more food is available in areas with temperate climates

Paragraph 1 is marked with an arrow [➡].

**3** The word "them" in the passage refers to

Ⓐ scientists

Ⓑ brains

Ⓒ birds

Ⓓ eyes

**4** Which of the sentences below best expresses the essential information in the highlighted sentence in the passage? *Incorrect* choices change the meaning in important ways or leave out essential information.

Ⓐ If Cluster N is not available to a bird, it behaves like a human would by checking out where the sun is.

Ⓑ In addition to Cluster N and the setting sun, the birds look up at the night sky to figure out what humans would do to find north.

Ⓒ Birds navigate by the sun or the stars like humans when their brains cannot use Cluster N.

Ⓓ The location of the stars helps birds to activate Cluster N and figure out, like a human, where north is.

**5** Why does the author mention "the star Betelgeuse"?

   Ⓐ To argue that Polaris is not the only star birds use to orient

   Ⓑ To explain that birds need to be able to see the stars to orient

   Ⓒ To provide evidence that birds rely on stars to orient

   Ⓓ To criticize scientists for misrepresenting the stars to orienting birds

**6** According to paragraph 2, Cluster N is a

   Ⓐ flying technique used by birds

   Ⓑ method of memorizing the night sky

   Ⓒ section of a bird's brain

   Ⓓ connection between the eyes and the beak

Paragraph 2 is marked with an arrow [➡].

**7** The word "assess" in the passage is closest in meaning to

   Ⓐ observe

   Ⓑ evaluate

   Ⓒ change

   Ⓓ lower

**8** According to paragraph 3, a bird's trigeminal nerve serves to

   Ⓐ find the magnetic compass direction north

   Ⓑ verify the strength of the earth's magnetic fields

   Ⓒ smell different landmarks on the bird's journey

   Ⓓ interact with the eyes to help the bird evaluate its position

Paragraph 3 is marked with an arrow [➡].

Volume  Review  Help  Back  Next

**9** Look at the four squares [■] that indicate where the following sentence could be added to the passage.

**For example, they might build a map of sea odors in one location, or of swamp smells in another.**

Click on a square [■] to add the sentence to the passage.

**10 Directions:** Select the appropriate statements from the answer choices and match them to the type of ability with which they are associated. **This question is worth 3 points.**

Drag your answer choices to the spaces where they belong.
To remove an answer choice, click on it. To review the passage, click on **View Text**.

| Answer Choices | Orientation |
|---|---|
| ⒶBirds can sense their position using the earth's magnetic fields. | • |
| ⒷBirds use Polaris to determine the direction of their travels. | • |
| ⒸBirds observe the position of the setting sun. | • |
| ⒹBirds communicate with birdsongs to determine their migratory direction. | |
| | Navigation |
| ⒺA bird's sense of smell helps it to find its exact location. | • |
| ⒻA bird's wings respond to magnetic fields as they flap. | |
| ⒼA bird's brain has a mechanism that points it toward north. | • |

Answer Book p. 43

# Vocabulary Review

**A. Fill in the blanks with the appropriate words from the box.**

| | | |
|---|---|---|
| conducting | feat | typically |
| unprecedented | transformed | related |

1 Though the members of the royal family are _____ to one another, they fight a lot.

2 The 2004 Indian Ocean Tsunami was a(n) _____ natural disaster.

3 The city is _____ a survey to determine whether to construct new bike paths.

4 On a Friday night, the library is _____ almost empty.

5 The emergence of rock and roll in the 1950s _____ popular music forever.

6 In an impressive _____ of engineering, the bridge was constructed in 1869.

**B. Choose the closest meaning for each highlighted word.**

7 She wore a striking yellow dress that attracted a lot of attention.
   (A) colorful      (B) astonishing      (C) pretty      (D) skimpy

8 The science fiction movie had appeal for both children and adults.
   (A) action      (B) truth      (C) attraction      (D) scenes

9 Some were offended that the newspaper profited from its coverage of the tragedy.
   (A) gained      (B) advertised      (C) converted      (D) bought

10 During World War II, military submarines traversed the Pacific on a regular basis.
   (A) approached      (B) crossed      (C) shipped      (D) sank

11 After watching the violent movie, the child played in an aggressive manner.
   (A) uncomfortable      (B) threatening      (C) patronizing      (D) foolish

12 The government hopes to facilitate economic growth by supporting local companies.
   (A) evade      (B) draft      (C) admire      (D) ease

13 He was truly moved by the gifts his friends sent him; he was not pretending.
   (A) mainly      (B) hilariously      (C) inevitably      (D) actually

14 Students are encouraged to actively participate in class by asking questions.
   (A) eagerly      (B) decisively      (C) frankly      (D) quietly

# Actual Test

Actual Test **1**

Actual Test **2**

Answer Book p. 45

## Minerals

   Whether they are sprinkling salt on their food, wearing diamond rings, or brushing their teeth with fluoride, most people interact with minerals every day of their lives without understanding what they are. There are four essential characteristics that all minerals share.

➡ To begin with, minerals are naturally formed. There are many materials made ₅ in laboratories that mimic mineral properties, but these are not technically minerals. For example, a synthetic emerald may have a green sparkle similar to the real thing and may even be made from the same chemicals. But if an emerald was not naturally formed from beryllium that has escaped from magma deep in the earth's crust, it is not truly a mineral and, consequently, does not have the same value. ₁₀ Many minerals are formed from cooled magma; others crystallize in water.

   While some minerals form in water, a substance must be solid in order to be classified as a mineral. In fact, minerals can be among the hardest solids on the planet. **A** Geologists measure the hardness of minerals using the Mohs scale, which determines how easy it is to scratch a mineral. **B** Diamond rates a score of ₁₅ 10 out of 10 on the Mohs scale because it is virtually impossible to scratch. **C** On the other hand, the mineral talc can be easily crushed into talcum powder (which is found in makeup or baby powder), so it rates a 1 on the Mohs scale. **D**

➡ The third characteristic of minerals is that they have a consistent chemical composition, right down to the atomic level. In other words, the atoms that ₂₀ constitute the mineral must be in a specific chemical ratio. For instance, the earth's most common mineral, quartz, is one part silicon and two parts oxygen. Some minerals, like gold, consist of a single element.

➡ Finally, every mineral has a crystalline structure, which means that the atoms are organized in a geometric pattern. For that reason, minerals are among the most ₂₅ beautiful substances on the earth. The Romans thought opal had mystical powers because its crystals can flash every color in the spectrum.

| Glossary | ☒ |
| --- | --- |
| **fluoride:** a chemical that is added to toothpaste to keep teeth healthy | |

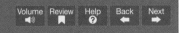

Actual Test 1

HACKERS APEX READING for the TOEFL iBT Basic

**1** Why does the author mention people "sprinkling salt on their food"?

    Ⓐ To provide evidence that minerals are edible

    Ⓑ To illustrate that people use minerals on a daily basis

    Ⓒ To criticize people who use too much salt in their food

    Ⓓ To show that minerals can be ground into small particles

**2** The word "these" in the passage refers to

    Ⓐ minerals

    Ⓑ materials

    Ⓒ laboratories

    Ⓓ properties

**3** Which of the sentences below best expresses the essential information in the highlighted sentence in the passage? *Incorrect* choices change the meaning in important ways or leave out essential information.

    Ⓐ Nothing is as valuable as an emerald formed from molten fluids at the earth's core.

    Ⓑ Emeralds that are formed in the earth's core are neither minerals nor valuable.

    Ⓒ Emeralds that are not created by a natural process are less valuable because they are not real minerals.

    Ⓓ When an emerald contains beryllium, it is always considered a mineral.

**4** According to paragraph 2, which of the following is NOT true of synthetic emerald?

    Ⓐ It is manufactured in a laboratory.

    Ⓑ It is easily distinguished from natural ones.

    Ⓒ It exhibits mineral properties.

    Ⓓ It may contain the chemical beryllium.

Paragraph 2 is marked with an arrow [➡].

**5** The word "classified" in the passage is closest in meaning to

- Ⓐ concealed
- Ⓑ imagined
- Ⓒ featured
- Ⓓ categorized


**6** According to paragraph 4, the chemicals that make up minerals are

- Ⓐ among the most valuable elements on the planet
- Ⓑ present in different ratios for each instance of the same mineral type
- Ⓒ in the same proportions for all specimens of a particular mineral
- Ⓓ more common than the chemicals used in laboratories

Paragraph 4 is marked with an arrow [➡].


**7** The word "substances" in the passage is closest in meaning to

- Ⓐ materials
- Ⓑ examples
- Ⓒ structures
- Ⓓ varieties


**8** According to paragraph 5, the Romans believed opal had special powers because of its

- Ⓐ chemical uniformity
- Ⓑ indestructible hardness
- Ⓒ ability to refract colors
- Ⓓ underground origins

Paragraph 5 is marked with an arrow [➡].

**9** Look at the four squares [■] that indicate where the following sentence could be added to the passage.

**That score makes talc the softest among all minerals.**

Where would the sentence best fit?

Click on a square [■] to add the sentence to the passage.

**10 Directions:** An introductory sentence for a brief summary of the passage is provided below. Complete the summary by selecting the THREE answer choices that express the most important ideas in the passage. Some sentences do not belong in the summary because they express ideas that are not presented in the passage or are minor ideas in the passage. **This question is worth 2 points.**

Drag your answer choices to the spaces where they belong.
To remove an answer choice, click on it. To review the passage, click on **View Text**.

**Minerals are defined by clear criteria.**

- 
- 
- 

Answer Choices

(A) Minerals have crystalline structures.

(B) Minerals can be created in laboratories.

(C) Minerals can sometimes be ground into powder.

(D) Minerals are naturally occurring.

(E) Minerals are believed to have mystical powers.

(F) Minerals have definite chemical compositions.

Answer Book p. 45

# Anasazi Cliff Dwellings

➡ The cliff dwellings of ancient Native Americans known as the Anasazi have attracted tourists from all over the world. The structures are exceptional in size, design, and durability. They are made of stone and were built on the cliffs of Mesa Verde, Colorado. ₅ At first glance, the dwellings appear to be very large multi-storied apartment complexes with square windows but no doors. The Anasazi entered the buildings by climbing a ladder and going through a hole in the roof. Historians speculate that it may have taken the Anasazi eighty years to construct the dwellings and that only a century after they were completed, the Anasazi ₁₀ abandoned these beautiful, sturdy homes.

➡ These cliff dwellings are an archaeological goldmine that reveals much about the people who lived there. Climatic conditions could be brutal in the ancient Colorado Desert, including extended periods of drought. But the dwellings were constructed at a point in history (around AD 1190) when they were fairly stable. ₁₅ The Anasazi population was at a high point. This prompted their move from simple pit houses, partially underground, to the elaborate homes in the cliffs. They hunted deer and bighorn sheep and feasted on domesticated turkeys. They could easily slip up and down the narrow ladders because they were a small people, ranging from 5'1" to 5'5" in height. ₂₀

Why did the Anasazi leave these architectural wonders so abruptly? There appear to be several reasons. **A** The more they hunted big game for food, the less abundant those animals became. **B** Deforestation also contributed to the lack of available resources. **C** In 1276, a drought struck that lasted for 23 long years. **D** In addition to these unfavorable environmental conditions, the Anasazi may have been ₂₅ attacked in their homes. Archaeologists uncovered the remains of some 34 people that were never formally buried. At least eight of those skeletons bore evidence of violent causes of death. Whatever the reasons, the surviving Anasazi made their way south toward sites in Arizona and New Mexico. The ruins of the cliff dwellings remained empty for centuries until they were discovered by cowboys in the 1880s. ₃₀ Today, they are preserved in a national park.

11 The word "durability" in the passage is closest in meaning to

(A) complexity

(B) construction

(C) appeal

(D) sturdiness

12 The word "speculate" in the passage is closest in meaning to

(A) conclude

(B) guess

(C) raise

(D) urge

13 Which of the following is NOT mentioned in paragraph 1 about the cliff dwellings?

(A) The identity of the people who built them

(B) The method residents used to enter them

(C) The number of people who occupied them

(D) The materials used to construct them

Paragraph 1 is marked with an arrow [➡].

14 Why does the author mention an "archaeological goldmine"?

(A) To describe the Anasazi's method of subsistence

(B) To explain how information about the Anasazi was gained

(C) To refute misconceptions about the Anasazi's poverty

(D) To argue that more research is required to understand the Anasazi

**15** The word "they" in the passage refers to

(A) cliff dwellings

(B) people

(C) climatic conditions

(D) periods

**16** Which of the sentences below best expresses the essential information in the highlighted sentence in the passage? *Incorrect* choices change the meaning in important ways or leave out essential information.

(A) The height of the Anasazi enabled them to enter and exit the cliff dwellings in large numbers.

(B) The Anasazi were little, so they had no difficulty using the small ladders in the dwellings.

(C) Up and down the Anasazi went, leaving and returning to their homes in the cliffs.

(D) Some Anasazi were as short as 5'1", making it easy to leave their homes.

**17** According to paragraph 2, the Anasazi left their pit houses because they

(A) had a larger population to accommodate

(B) found big game in the mountains

(C) were too large for the small residences

(D) experienced warmer conditions in the cliffs

Paragraph 2 is marked with an arrow [➡].

**18** The author's explanation of the Anasazi's departure from the cliffs mentions all of the following EXCEPT

(A) an unusually long dry spell

(B) the scarcity of meat during that period

(C) evidence of a battle in the cliffs

(D) the deterioration of the architecture

**19** Look at the four squares [■] that indicate where the following sentence could be added to the passage.

**Wood was a major source of fuel during the brutal Colorado winters.**

Where would the sentence best fit?

Click on a square [■] to add the sentence to the passage.

**20 Directions:** An introductory sentence for a brief summary of the passage is provided below. Complete the summary by selecting the THREE answer choices that express the most important ideas in the passage. Some sentences do not belong in the summary because they express ideas that are not presented in the passage or are minor ideas in the passage. **This question is worth 2 points.**

Drag your answer choices to the spaces where they belong.
To remove an answer choice, click on it. To review the passage, click on **View Text**.

---

**The Anasazi built an extraordinary network of homes on mountain cliffs.**

- 
- 
- 

---

Answer Choices

(A) The cliff dwellings were deserted mysteriously a short time after they were built.

(B) The Anasazi lived in apartment-like homes that were too small for large families.

(C) Archeologists learned much about the Anasazi from studying their homes.

(D) The people who lived in the cliff dwellings could not read or write.

(E) Several factors contributed to the early departure of the Anasazi from the cliff dwellings.

(F) A major battle took place in the cliff dwellings, killing most of the Anasazi.

Answer Book p. 46

# Edison's Phonograph

➡ The history of recorded sound began when Thomas Edison invented the phonograph. Edison envisioned that his "talking machine" would ultimately be in every American home. In his era, in-home music was a luxury that was mainly enjoyed by the rich. With the mass production of the phonograph, he hoped to make it affordable for everyone to listen to music in their homes. However, his primary ₅ motivation was to create a system to record telephone messages. He believed that businesspeople would be the first to buy the device, thinking that sound recordings could offer an alternative to written messages in business communication. In this sense, Edison's phonograph was a precursor of contemporary voicemail.

One night in July of 1877, Edison and his staff worked out a sound-recording ₁₀ technique in his laboratory. He knew that sound waves could generate vibrations on a thin membrane, called a *diaphragm*. He wondered if the vibrations could be used to create marks by attaching something like a needle with a hard point to the diaphragm. So he asked an employee to connect one to a diaphragm, which itself was attached to a telephone speaker. As Edison shouted into the speaker, ₁₅ the diaphragm vibrated, causing the needle to move and etch the sound marks into a piece of wax-covered paper below. When the pattern on the piece of paper was guided back under the needle, to everyone's amazement, Edison's voice was played back.

➡ Edison soon made a technical drawing of his phonograph design, and, by ₂₀ December of 1877, his engineering team had created the first working model. **A** It was publicly demonstrated at the publishing office of the magazine *Scientific American*. **B** Huge crowds of people assembled to listen to the talking machine. **C** Yet the original design was mainly just a curiosity as it had limited commercial value and was only suitable for exhibits. **D** Because it could only record one or two ₂₅ minutes of sound, it was not practical for extensive use. Moreover, the sound quality was poor, so some listeners could not understand the words coming from the speaker. Therefore, Edison had to make modifications. In 1887 and 1888, he manufactured an improved phonograph and a perfected phonograph, which he marketed under the Edison Phonograph Company. Although Edison's phonographs were commercially ₃₀ successful, their cost never actually became affordable for everyone.

**21** The word "envisioned" in the passage is closest in meaning to

   Ⓐ realized

   Ⓑ anticipated

   Ⓒ characterized

   Ⓓ proved

**22** Why does the author mention "contemporary voicemail" in the passage?

   Ⓐ To argue that technology has not changed much since Edison's time

   Ⓑ To give a recent example that is similar to Edison's invention

   Ⓒ To identify a modern technology that was based on Edison's designs

   Ⓓ To suggest that Edison's invention was not very sophisticated

**23** According to paragraph 1, what was Edison's main inspiration for making the phonograph?

   Ⓐ He intended to market it to rich people.

   Ⓑ He hoped to make music production less expensive.

   Ⓒ He sought to eliminate written communication.

   Ⓓ He wanted to create a telephone recording method.

Paragraph 1 is marked with an arrow [➡].

**24** The word "one" in the passage refers to

   Ⓐ needle

   Ⓑ point

   Ⓒ diaphragm

   Ⓓ employee

**25** Which of the sentences below best expresses the essential information in the highlighted sentence in the passage? *Incorrect* choices change the meaning in important ways or leave out essential information.

(A) Everyone was amazed because the pattern on the piece of paper was successfully reproduced.

(B) A recording of Edison's voice was played by directing the pattern under the needle a second time.

(C) At the moment when everyone heard Edison's voice repeated, they reacted with amazement.

(D) The needle created a pattern on the paper that recorded Edison's voice.

**26** The word "modifications" in the passage is closest in meaning to

(A) restrictions

(B) adjustments

(C) suggestions

(D) investments

**27** According to paragraph 3, what was the response to Edison's first phonograph?

(A) It was advertised in scientific publications.

(B) It was generally ignored by the press.

(C) Large numbers of people gathered to hear it.

(D) Critics complained about its high price.

Paragraph 3 is marked with an arrow [➡].

**28** Which of the following can be inferred about the 1887 and 1888 phonographs?

(A) They could record no more than two minutes of sound.

(B) They had higher sound quality than the original.

(C) They were not suitable for commercial production.

(D) They were manufactured in two different locations.

**29** Look at the four squares [■] that indicate where the following sentence could be added to the passage.

**At the time, this publication was the most popular source of information about new technologies in the country.**

Where would the sentence best fit?

Click on a square [■] to add the sentence to the passage.

**30 Directions:** An introductory sentence for a brief summary of the passage is provided below. Complete the summary by selecting the THREE answer choices that express the most important ideas in the passage. Some sentences do not belong in the summary because they express ideas that are not presented in the passage or are minor ideas in the passage. **This question is worth 2 points.**

Drag your answer choices to the spaces where they belong.
To remove an answer choice, click on it. To review the passage, click on **View Text**.

**Edison's invention of the phonograph initiated the history of sound recording.**

- 
- 
- 

Answer Choices

(A) Edison and his staff discovered a method of recording sound while working in his laboratory.

(B) Edison thought that his phonograph would be useful both for homes and businesses.

(C) The phonographs that Edison produced were inexpensive enough for anyone to afford.

(D) After designing and producing a model, Edison made additional phonographs for commercial use.

(E) Edison's first phonograph was useful for exhibits but not for commercial distribution.

(F) When Edison announced his invention to the press, few people seemed interested in it.

Answer Book p. 47

# A Tree's Changing Leaves

➡ The changing colors of tree leaves are partly due to the changing of the seasons. As the seasons change, plants produce different pigments. There are three main pigment classes that are produced in a leaf: <u>chlorophyll</u>, carotenoids, and flavonoids. During the spring and summer, leaves serve as factories where much of the food a tree needs is manufactured. This process requires chlorophyll, which 5 gives a leaf its green color. However, as the seasons become colder, the chemical processes that take place in a tree result in leaves that are a mixture of red, purple, orange, and yellow. Changes in temperature and the length of daylight cause the leaves to stop their food-making process. With this stoppage, the chlorophyll breaks down, and the green color disappears, to be replaced with the colors of autumn. 10

➡ The amount and type of pigment present as well as chemical interactions within the plant can also determine the color of a leaf. Because chlorophyll is abundant during the spring and summer seasons, the other pigments in a leaf are masked. During the fall, the decomposition rate of chlorophyll remains constant even during the time that its production slows down. Therefore, the green color of a leaf 15 fades gradually rather than abruptly. A greater amount of the carotenoid pigment in a leaf will produce yellow, while a larger proportion of flavonoids will produce red, blue, purple, and magenta. If a leaf has equal proportions of carotenoids and flavonoids, the color orange often results. In the absence of pigments, other plant chemicals can affect leaf color. For example, tannin often produces the brownish 20 color of oak leaves.

➡ As temperatures decrease, the process of abscission (detachment) begins. **A** At the beginning of autumn, a special layer called the abscission zone develops at the point where the leaf is attached to the stem. **B** Eventually, the stem can no longer support the leaf, and it falls in the breeze. **C** The tree then seals the cut, 25 and a scar develops where the leaf was once attached. **D** The tree is ready for a long winter's nap.

| Glossary | ☒ |
|---|---|
| **chlorophyll:** the green pigment in plants that helps plants make food from carbon dioxide | |

**1** Which of the sentences below best expresses the essential information in the highlighted sentence in the passage? *Incorrect* choices change the meaning in important ways or leave out essential information.

Ⓐ Various parts of a tree produce the nutrients it needs, including the leaves.

Ⓑ Leaves are the primary source of the food a tree consumes throughout the year.

Ⓒ In summer, as in spring, growing leaves consume much of a tree's nutrients.

Ⓓ Leaves produce most of the nutrition for trees in the spring and summer.

**2** The phrase "take place" in the passage is closest in meaning to

Ⓐ occur

Ⓑ produce

Ⓒ change

Ⓓ continue

**3** According to paragraph 1, which of the following is NOT true of chlorophyll?

Ⓐ It makes a tree's leaves green.

Ⓑ It is necessary for making nutrients for plants.

Ⓒ It is the only pigment in a leaf.

Ⓓ It decomposes in autumn.

Paragraph 1 is marked with an arrow [➡].

**4** The word "its" in the passage refers to

Ⓐ fall

Ⓑ decomposition rate

Ⓒ chlorophyll

Ⓓ time

**5** The word "abruptly" in the passage is closest in meaning to

  Ⓐ precisely

  Ⓑ immediately

  Ⓒ suddenly

  Ⓓ repeatedly

**6** Why does the author mention "tannin"?

  Ⓐ To state what substance is most responsible for tree leaf color

  Ⓑ To give an example of a non-pigment that can affect leaf color

  Ⓒ To compare pigments with other chemicals produced by trees

  Ⓓ To describe how the leaves of an oak tree change color

**7** According to paragraph 2, red-colored leaves result from

  Ⓐ an increase in carotenoid production

  Ⓑ a pigment that is freshly produced in autumn

  Ⓒ a greater amount of flavonoids

  Ⓓ a plant chemical that is not a pigment

Paragraph 2 is marked with an arrow [➡].

**8** Which of the following questions about abscission is answered in paragraph 3?

  Ⓐ How strong is the wind that blows leaves off trees?

  Ⓑ Where does the abscission zone develop?

  Ⓒ What function does the scar left by abscission have?

  Ⓓ How long does it take for the leaves to fall off a tree?

Paragraph 3 is marked with an arrow [➡].

**9** Look at the four squares [■] that indicate where the following sentence could be added to the passage.

**This layer prevents water and nutrients from passing from the main part of the tree to the leaves.**

Where would the sentence best fit?

Click on a square [■] to add the sentence to the passage.

**10 Directions:** An introductory sentence for a brief summary of the passage is provided below. Complete the summary by selecting the THREE answer choices that express the most important ideas in the passage. Some sentences do not belong in the summary because they express ideas that are not presented in the passage or are minor ideas in the passage. **This question is worth 2 points.**

Drag your answer choices to the spaces where they belong.
To remove an answer choice, click on it. To review the passage, click on **View Text**.

---

**Tree leaves go through seasonal changes.**

- 
- 
- 

---

Answer Choices

(A) Chlorophyll provides leaves with their green color in the warm months.

(B) Orange leaves result from the fusion of two different pigments.

(C) Leaves stop producing food when sunlight becomes less available.

(D) The type and amount of pigment present determine what colors the leaves are likely to be.

(E) Leaves fall off due to a layer that forms between the leaf and the stem.

(F) When leaves fall, a scar develops on the tree that prevents it from forming leaves again.

Answer Book p. 48

# Meteorite from Mars

Many meteorites are found in the polar regions, buried deep under the ice. This is not because there is a higher incidence of their falling at Earth's poles. Rather, the cold and dry conditions preserve the meteorites for many years, and they are easier to distinguish against the icy, white environment. On December 27, 1984, Roberta Stone discovered a Martian meteorite called ALH84001 on the Allan Hills in 5 Antarctica.

➡ At first, the meteorite was classified as a diogenite, believed to have come from the asteroid belt. It was put away for ten years until an American scientist studying diogenites requested a sample for study. He noticed it was unlike other diogenites he had studied and requested an isotope analysis. Oxygen isotopic 10 composition refers to the relative amounts of the three stable isotopes of oxygen $^{16}O$, $^{17}O$, and $^{18}O$ present in a rock. Samples with similar isotopic compositions belong to the same family and presumably come from the same parent. **A** Since the oxygen isotopic composition of the meteorite was different from that of Earth's rocks, it could not have come from our home planet. **B** Another meteorite found 15 in India is believed to have come from Mars because it, too, contained ratios of oxygen and nitrogen isotopes not found on Earth. **C** Analysis of carbonates in these two meteorites indicated that they were formed from fluids in contact with the atmosphere of Mars. **D**

➡ ALH84001 sparked worldwide headlines when further analysis suggested that 20 life might have existed on Mars. Many theories have been put forward regarding the meteorite. Although scientists agree on the data, they disagree on the interpretations of these experimental results. Some believe that the 4.5-billion-year-old meteorite was formed under wet conditions, suggesting water and life existed on Mars before they did on Earth. Others suggest that the meteorite may even have 25 transported Martian life here. They further propose that we may all be descendants of Martian life forms. Later experiments revealed that the salty ice of Antarctica might have contaminated the meteorites. Scientists now agree that the evidence of life on Mars from ALH84001, although compelling, is inconclusive. Nevertheless, ALH84001 is one of the oldest meteorites discovered to date and continues to yield 30 new information about meteorites and Mars.

**11** The word "incidence" in the passage is closest in meaning to

(A) abundance

(B) error

(C) chance

(D) occurrence

**12** The word "it" in the passage refers to

(A) diogenite

(B) the asteroid belt

(C) sample

(D) study

**13** According to paragraph 2, what is a common feature of ALH84001 and the meteorite found in India?

(A) They were both initially classified as diogenites.

(B) They both had an isotopic composition similar to Earth's.

(C) They contained carbonates suggesting they were from Mars.

(D) They contained isotopes that were difficult to identify.

Paragraph 2 is marked with an arrow [➡].

**14** The phrase "put forward" in the passage is closest in meaning to

(A) proposed

(B) confirmed

(C) demanded

(D) examined

**15** Why does the author mention "salty ice" in the passage?

(A) To prove that the meteorite is from Mars

(B) To suggest that some theories about ALH84001 may be incorrect

(C) To give an example of a claim about Martian life

(D) To identify the distinguishing characteristics of meteorites

**16** The word "compelling" in the passage is closest in meaning to

(A) persuasive

(B) confident

(C) deliberate

(D) extensive

**17** It can be inferred from paragraph 3 that the majority of meteorites are

(A) classified as diogenites

(B) mainly composed of nitrogen

(C) believed to be from Mars

(D) younger than 4.5 billion years

Paragraph 3 is marked with an arrow [➡].

**18** In paragraph 3, the author of the passage implies that ALH84001

(A) transported water between planets

(B) proves that life exists on Mars today

(C) was formed before life developed on Earth

(D) raises questions about the age of meteorites

Paragraph 3 is marked with an arrow [➡].

**19** Look at the four squares [■] that indicate where the following sentence could be added to the passage.

**The Moon was also ruled out as a possibility.**

Where would the sentence best fit?

Click on a square [■] to add the sentence to the passage.

**20 Directions:** An introductory sentence for a brief summary of the passage is provided below. Complete the summary by selecting the THREE answer choices that express the most important ideas in the passage. Some sentences do not belong in the summary because they express ideas that are not presented in the passage or are minor ideas in the passage. **This question is worth 2 points.**

Drag your answer choices to the spaces where they belong.
To remove an answer choice, click on it. To review the passage, click on **View Text**.

---

**One of many meteorites found at the poles was of Martian origins.**

- 
- 
- 

---

Answer Choices

(A) Meteorites contain isotopes that can be used to calculate how long a sample has been on Earth.

(B) ALH84001 was identified as a Martian meteorite after its chemical composition was analyzed.

(C) The meteorite discovered by Roberta Stone was covered by media all over the world.

(D) Scientists speculated that ALH84001 may have carried Martian life to Earth.

(E) A meteorite from India was formed in a collision between Mars and a large asteroid.

(F) Initial conclusions about life on Mars from ALH84001 were found to be improbable.

# Development of the Printing Press

The modern printing press emerged in the fifteenth century in Germany. In contrast to previous printing technologies in the West, this press contained movable type, so it could easily produce many different letter and word combinations. Although many people worked on developing the modern printing press, Johannes Gutenberg is usually acknowledged as its creator.                                                    5

➡ At first, Gutenberg worked on a way to reproduce printed materials more efficiently. He experienced many failures, particularly because the materials he required were expensive and he was always in need of investors. Some investors knew the economic value of his printing technology and tried to take it for themselves through legal action. Thus, Gutenberg spent much time and money on  10 lawyers and court fees, and his project's advancement was slow.

➡ However, he succeeded in making efficient printing presses in the 1450s. These presses had frames that were designed to produce forty-two lines of type in two columns, for a total of eighty-four lines. **A** Each frame could be fitted with a tray that holds the metal type. **B** Within each tray, the metal type—which  15 represented letters of the alphabet—was assembled into words and lines. **C** Once the entire frame was filled, a piece of paper was firmly pressed against the rows of type, which were covered in ink. **D** Because the metal type could be altered to represent any text, workers could conveniently reposition it for printing each page in a book or manuscript without much wasted time or effort.                              20

➡ Gutenberg's method of publication led to dramatic and far-reaching effects on society and knowledge. Initially, it was used to print the Gutenberg Bible. This Bible was more than 1,200 pages long, and Gutenberg's press could produce thousands of copies in the same amount of time it would have taken scribes to make just one copy in the conventional way. Later, the press was used by Martin Luther to  25 print 300,000 copies of his Ninety-Five Theses, which divided the Catholic Church and started the Protestant Reformation. In addition, the press allowed for wider distribution of the classical Roman, Greek, and Arabic literature that inspired the Renaissance. It also helped natural philosophers to more freely share their scientific and mathematical ideas. Indeed, without the printing press, the Scientific Revolution  30 of the sixteenth and seventeenth centuries would not have been possible.

**21** The word "acknowledged" in the passage is closest in meaning to

(A) required

(B) criticized

(C) recognized

(D) admired

**22** Which of the following can be inferred about printing prior to the fifteenth century in Europe?

(A) It relied upon a single press.

(B) It did not use movable type.

(C) It lacked a standard procedure.

(D) It did not exist in Germany.

**23** What are TWO reasons given in paragraph 2 for Gutenberg's failures? Choose TWO answers.

(A) The high cost of materials

(B) The lack of available technology

(C) The inability to hire lawyers

(D) The constant demand for investors

Paragraph 2 is marked with an arrow [➡].

**24** Which of the sentences below best expresses the essential information in the highlighted sentence in the passage? *Incorrect* choices change the meaning in important ways or leave out essential information.

(A) The metal type was convenient to reposition, but workers still could not print multiple pages of a text at the same time.

(B) Printing each page in a book or manuscript took much time and effort due to the continual need to alter the metal type.

(C) Changing the metal type was convenient, so workers could quickly and easily alter its position for each page in a printed work.

(D) Workers saved time and effort because they could reposition the metal type for the next page while printing the current page.

**25** According to paragraph 3, which of the following is true of the printing presses Gutenberg developed in the 1450s?

- (A) They produced a maximum of forty-two columns.
- (B) Their frames used a tray for metal type.
- (C) Their lines contained exactly one word each.
- (D) They imprinted paper without the need for ink.

Paragraph 3 is marked with an arrow [➡].

**26** The word "conventional" in the passage is closest in meaning to

- (A) admissible
- (B) traditional
- (C) predictable
- (D) exceptional

**27** Why does the author mention "the Scientific Revolution" in the passage?

- (A) To highlight why the Catholic Church was divided
- (B) To explain how Gutenberg's press became efficient
- (C) To give a reason for the success of the printing press
- (D) To emphasize the long-term impact of the printing press

**28** Which of the following is NOT mentioned as an effect of the Gutenberg press in paragraph 4?

- (A) It allowed quicker production of the Bible.
- (B) It merged Catholic and Protestant thought.
- (C) It facilitated the spread of classical literature.
- (D) It enabled the sharing of scientific knowledge.

Paragraph 4 is marked with an arrow [➡].

**29** Look at the four squares [■] that indicate where the following sentence could be added to the passage.

**Then, after it was peeled back from the press, it revealed the completed text neatly arranged in rows and columns.**

Where would the sentence best fit?

Click on a square [■] to add the sentence to the passage.

**30 Directions:** An introductory sentence for a brief summary of the passage is provided below. Complete the summary by selecting the THREE answer choices that express the most important ideas in the passage. Some sentences do not belong in the summary because they express ideas that are not presented in the passage or are minor ideas in the passage. **This question is worth 2 points.**

Drag your answer choices to the spaces where they belong.
To remove an answer choice, click on it. To review the passage, click on **View Text**.

---

**The modern printing press of Gutenberg revolutionized the printing process.**

- 
- 
- 

---

Answer Choices

(A) Gutenberg's press and style of printing affected society in significant and lasting ways.

(B) In the beginning, Gutenberg faced challenges in developing a better press.

(C) The modern printing press was the first machine capable of printing on paper.

(D) Gutenberg faced legal problems when he tried to file for a patent for his printing press.

(E) Printers used the Gutenberg press to introduce classical literature during the Renaissance.

(F) By the middle of the fifteenth century, Gutenberg had success in creating productive presses.

Answer Book p. 50

MEMO

|H|A|C|K|E|R|S|

# APEX
# READING
## for the
# TOEFL iBT® Basic

COPYRIGHT © 2022, by Hackers Language Research Institute

**April 7, 2022**

**Hackers Language Research Institute**
**23, Gangnam-daero 61-gil, Seocho-gu, Seoul, Korea**
**Inquiries** publishing@hackers.com

**ISBN** 978-89-6542-469-7 (53740)

**Printed in South Korea**

3 4 5 6 7 8 9 10   28 27 26 25 24

**The Most Preferred Education Brand in Korea,**
**HACKERS BOOK(www.HackersBook.com)**
• Free supplementary study materials

No. 1 in Hankyung Business' Most Preferred Brand Rankings 2019, Education Group category

# HACKERS

# APEX
# READING
## for the
# TOEFL iBT
### Basic

## Answer Book

HACKERS

# APEX
# READING
## for the
# TOEFL iBT® Basic

# Answer Book

HACKERS

# CHAPTER 01

# Vocabulary

## Example

1 (D)  2 (B)

### 동물의 위장술

동물들은 보통 그들의 자연환경과 비슷한 색을 만들어 냄으로써 자연 배경에 뒤섞인다. 이 기술은 위장술로 알려져 있다. 그것은 포식자들에 대항하여 동물들을 보호하기 위해서 뿐만 아니라 먹이를 사냥하는 동물들을 위장하기 위해서도 사용될 수 있다. 동물들의 색이 그들의 환경의 그것과 일치하기 때문에 위장술은 야생에서 동물들을 식별하는 것을 어렵게 한다.

몇몇 동물들은 다수의 아주 작은 신체구조들을 통해 색을 바꾼다. 마치 프리즘이 가시광선을 흩뿌려 무지개의 색들을 반사하는 것처럼, 이 구조들은 자연광을 특정한 혼합색으로 전환한다. 예를 들어, 북극곰은 사실 검은 피부와 투명한 털을 가지고 있다. 그러나 빛이 북극곰을 비추면, 북극곰의 털 하나하나가 빛을 굴절시키고, 이리저리 튀게 하여 그 동물이 하얗게 보이게 한다.

다른 동물들은 사실 생물 색소라고 불리는 색소를 만들어내어 그들의 피부색을 바꾼다. 이 색소들은 일부 빛의 파장은 흡수하고 다른 것들은 반사한다. 문어는 피부색뿐만 아니라 무늬를 바꾸기 위해서도 생물색소를 이용한다. 문어가 위협당한다고 느낄 때, 그것은 겉으로 보기에는 주변의 지형 속으로 사라질 수 있다.

blend into ~에 뒤섞이다   camouflage 몡위장술
predator 몡포식자   disguise 됭위장하다
distinguish 됭식별하다   match 됭일치하다   multiple 혱다수의
scatter 됭흩뿌리다   visible light 가시광선   reflect 됭반사하다
convert 됭전환하다   particular 혱특정한   bounce 됭반사하다
pigment 몡색소   biochrome 몡생물 색소   absorb 됭흡수하다
threatened 혱위협당한   seemingly 윈겉으로 보기에는
disappear 됭사라지다   terrain 몡지형

**1** 지문의 단어 "distinguish"와 의미가 가장 비슷한 것은?

  (A) 기억하다

  (B) 보호하다

  (C) 맞닥뜨리다

  (D) 알아보다

**2** 지문의 단어 "convert"와 의미가 가장 비슷한 것은?

  (A) 무시하다

  (B) 변형시키다

  (C) 지우다

  (D) 이용하다

## Reading Practice 1

1 (C)   2 (B)   3 (B)   4 (A)

**Vocabulary Quiz**

1 ⓐ   2 ⓑ   3 ⓐ   4 ⓑ

### 팝 아트

제2차 세계대전 이후, 미국은 평화와 번영의 시기를 누리기 시작했고, 이 시기 동안에 미국인들은 그들이 더 많은 돈과 여가 시간을 가지고 있다는 것을 알게 되었다. 상점을 가득 채운 대량 생산된 소비재가 다채로운 선전으로 광고되었다. 이것은 새로운 문화 유형의 출현으로 이어졌다. 로큰롤 음악이 인기를 얻었고 텔레비전 쇼가 오락거리로 라디오 쇼를 대체하기 시작했다. 예술계에서는 팝 아트 운동이 이러한 변화들에 반응했다.

그때까지, 지배적인 미술 양식은 추상표현주의였는데, 그것은 주로 엘리트 계층에 의해 감상되었다. 그러나 팝 아트는 철학적인 관념 대신 일상용품에 기초했다. 팝 아트 작가들은 광고를 본떠 만든 사실적인 이미지로 그것들을 묘사했고, 상업적인 대량 생산 도구들을 이용하여 그들의 예술 작품을 대량으로 복제했다. 그 목표는 독창성에 대한 관념을 파괴하고 "고급" 예술과 "저급" 예술 간의 경계를 모호하게 만드는 것이었다.

만화책에서 영감을 받은 작품들로 유명한 로이 리히텐슈타인과 재스퍼 존스는 그 운동의 몇몇 선구자들이었다. 그러나 아마도 앤디 워홀이 가장 잘 알려졌을 것이다. 캠벨 수프 통조림 그림을 창작한 것에 더해, 그는 마릴린 먼로, 엘비스 프레슬리, 마이클 잭슨과 같은 유명한 인물들의 이미지를 초상화에 이용했다. 그뿐만 아니라, 그는 전통적인 그림들과 인쇄된 이미지들을 결합하여 미술품을 만드는 자신만의 기법을 개발했다. 오래된 방식과 새로운 방식의 혼합은 독특한 작품들을 만들어냈다.

예술이 부자들뿐만 아니라 모두에게 접근 가능하게 되었기 때문에 팝 아트 운동은 중요했다. ⁴팝 아트가 대중 매체와 일상용품의 요소들을 포함했기 때문에, 그것은 일반 대중에게 인기가 있었다. 실제로, 많은 사람들이 그것을 "모두를 위한 예술"로 여겼다.

prosperity 몡번영   mass-produced 혱대량 생산된
consumer goods (식품·의류 등의) 소비재   lead to ~으로 이어지다
emergence 몡출현, 발생   dominant 혱지배적인
abstract expressionism 추상표현주의
appreciate 됭감상하다, 가치를 인정하다   based on ~에 기초한
philosophical 혱철학적인   depict 됭묘사하다
commercial 혱상업적인   originality 몡독창성
blur 됭모호하게 만들다   renowned for ~으로 유명한
pioneer 몡선구자   prominent 혱유명한
accessible 혱접근 가능한   incorporate 됭포함하다
regard 됭여기다

**1** 지문의 단어 "prosperity"와 의미가 가장 비슷한 것은?

  (A) 변화

  (B) 갈등

  (C) 부유함

  (D) 정의

**2** 지문의 단어 "them"이 가리키는 것은?

  (A) 엘리트 계층

(B) 일상용품
(C) 철학적인 관념
(D) 팝 아트 작가들

**3** 지문의 단어 "accessible"과 의미가 가장 비슷한 것은?

(A) 논란의 여지가 있는
(B) 접근 가능한
(C) 합리적인
(D) 가치 있는

**4** 지문에 따르면, 팝 아트는 평범한 사람들에게 왜 인기가 있었는가?

(A) 사람들이 자주 보거나 사용하는 것에 기초했다.
(B) 엘리트 계층에 의해 "고급" 예술로 여겨졌다.
(C) 유명 인사들 사이에서 유행하게 되었다.
(D) 전통적인 미술 기법과 새로운 미술 기법을 혼합했다.

## Reading Practice 2 본문 p.16

**1** (B)  **2** (C)  **3** (D)  **4** (D)

**Vocabulary Quiz**

**1** ⓑ  **2** ⓐ  **3** ⓑ  **4** ⓒ

### 아보카도의 환경 위협

지난 십 년간, 전 세계의 아보카도 생산량은 두 배 이상이 되었다. 더 많은 소비자들이 아보카도의 건강상의 이점을 잘 알게 됨에 따라 이 추세는 지속될 가능성이 높은데, 아보카도는 비타민과 건강에 좋은 지방의 훌륭한 공급원이다. 유감스럽게도, 아보카도의 높아진 인기는 환경에 부정적인 영향을 미쳐왔다.

한 가지 문제는 아보카도의 재배가 삼림 파괴의 원인이 된다는 것이다. 이 과일의 재배는 매우 수익성이 있어서, 점점 더 많은 토지가 그것을 재배하기 위해 개간되고 있다. ²예를 들어, 멕시코에서는 새로운 아보카도 농장을 만들기 위해 매년 대략 30,000에이커의 숲이 사라지는데, 숲의 파괴는 지구 온난화로 연결되기 때문에 이것은 걱정거리이다. 그것은 또한 점점 더 많은 수의 토종 식물과 동물 종을 서식지 상실로 인해 위험에 처하게 한다.

아보카도는 이 과일을 생산하는 나무들이 다량의 물을 필요로 하기 때문에 추가적인 문제들을 야기한다. 평균적으로, 한 개의 아보카도를 생산하기 위해 70리터의 물이 필요하다. 그에 비해, 오렌지 한 개를 재배하기 위해서는 오직 22리터의 물만 사용된다. 아보카도 재배는 세계 많은 지역의 수자원을 고갈시켰고, 어떤 경우에는, 그 지역 주민들에게 상당한 물 부족을 초래하기도 했다.

아보카도를 수송하기 위해 사용되는 에너지의 양 또한 걱정거리이다. 아보카도는 주로 중남미에서 재배되지만, 이 과일의 최대 시장은 유럽과 미국에 있다. ⁴아보카도는 수송 중에 반드시 섭씨 13도 이하로 보관되어야 하는데, 그것들이 더 높은 온도에 노출되면 빨리 익어버리기 때문이다. 따라서, 아보카도를 생산자로부터 소비자에게 수송하기 위해서는 많은 양의 에너지가 필요하다.

negative 휑부정적인   cultivation 몡재배, 경작
contribute to ~의 원인이 되다   deforestation 몡삼림 파괴
profitable 휑수익성이 있는   approximately 뤈대략

concern 몡걱정거리   destruction 몡파괴
global warming 지구 온난화   put ~ at risk ~을 위험에 처하게 하다
habitat 몡서식지   intensive 휑다량의 ~을 필요로 하는
by comparison 그에 비해   deplete 동고갈시키다
significant 휑상당한   shortage 몡부족   transport 동수송하다
primarily 뤈주로   ripen 동익다   expose 동노출시키다

**1** 지문의 어구 "contributes to"와 의미가 가장 비슷한 것은?

(A) 유지하다
(B) 야기하다
(C) 해치다
(D) 방지하다

**2** 2단락에 따르면, 다음 중 멕시코에 관해 사실인 것은?

(A) 삼림 파괴를 방지하기 위해 법률을 통과시키려고 한다.
(B) 아보카도의 최대 생산국이 되었다.
(C) 매년 새로운 땅을 경작한다.
(D) 멸종 위기종을 보호하기 위한 지역을 남겨둔다.

**3** 지문의 단어 "depleted"와 의미가 가장 비슷한 것은?

(A) 상처를 입었다
(B) 대체했다
(C) 수정했다
(D) 줄였다

**4** 4단락에 따르면, 아보카도를 수송하기 위해서는 많은 양의 에너지가 필요한데, 왜냐하면 그것들이

(A) 익은 후에 이동되어야 하기 때문이다
(B) 대량으로 수송되어야 하기 때문이다
(C) 배송 전에 가공되어야 하기 때문이다
(D) 수송 중에 차게 유지되어야 하기 때문이다

## Reading Practice 3 본문 p.18

**1** (D)  **2** (B)  **3** (B)  **4** (D)

**Vocabulary Quiz**

**1** ⓑ  **2** ⓐ  **3** ⓒ  **4** ⓐ

### 인류의 오른손 사용

잘 쓰는 손은 오른손 또는 왼손을 쓰는 것에 대한 선호이다. 어떤 추정치에 따르면, 90퍼센트가 넘는 사람들이 오른손잡이이다. 이것은 인류를 특별하게 만든다. 침팬지와 같은 다른 영장류 집단들은 거의 동일한 수의 오른손잡이와 왼손잡이 개체들을 포함한다.

인류의 오른손 사용에 대한 경향은 새로운 현상이 아니다. 우리의 초기 조상들을 연구하는 고고학자들은 과거에 많은 사람들이 이 특징을 공유했다는 증거를 발견했다. 예를 들어, 그들은 190만 년 전부터 140만 년 전까지 만들어진 다수의 석기를 조사했다. 오른손잡이인 사람들이 절반이 약간 넘는 도구들을 만들었다. 60만 년 전의 보존된 치아에 대한 연구는 이 경향이 시간이 지나면서 더 강해졌다는 것을 보여준다. 그 치아의 마모는 대부분의 사람들이 음식을 입에 넣기 위해 오른손을 사용했다는 것을 보여준다.

오랜 시간 동안 오른손 사용이 인류의 흔한 특징이었다는 많은 증거가 있지만, 과학자들은 여전히 그 이유에 대해 확실하게 알지 못한다. 한 가지 이론은 그것이 사회적 협동과 관련이 있다는 것이다. 초기 인류는 도구들을 공유했고 함께 작업했다. 만약 한 집단 내 대다수의 구성원이 같은 쪽 손을 사용한다면 이것은 더 수월하다. 따라서, 인류가 많은 세대에 걸쳐 집단으로 거주했고 서로 협동했기 때문에 그들이 주로 오른손잡이가 되었을 가능성이 있다.

또 다른 가능성 있는 설명은 뇌가 두 개의 반구로 나뉜 방식에 기반한 것이다. 왼쪽은 신체의 오른쪽 부분을 통제하고 그 반대의 경우도 마찬가지이다. ⁴인류의 경우, 좌반구는 언어도 처리한다. 인류가 언어를 자주 사용하기 시작하면서, 좌뇌가 지배적이게 되었을 가능성이 있다. 이것이 신체의 오른쪽을 사용하는 것에 대한 선호를 야기했을 수 있다.

handedness 명(왼손·오른손 중) 잘 쓰는 손    preference 명선호
estimate 명추정치    primate 명영장류    roughly 부거의
tendency 명경향    phenomenon 명현상
archaeologist 명고고학자    characteristic 명특징
slightly 부약간    preserved 형보존된    wear 명마모
indicate 동보여주다    trait 명특징    cooperation 명협동
reside 동거주하다    potential 형가능성 있는    split 동나누다
handle 동처리하다    dominant 형지배적인

**1** 지문의 단어 "tendency"와 의미가 가장 비슷한 것은?

(A) 태도
(B) 지지
(C) 진전
(D) 성향

**2** 지문의 단어 "they"가 가리키는 것은?

(A) 인류
(B) 고고학자들
(C) 조상들
(D) 사람들

**3** 지문의 단어 "resided"와 의미가 가장 비슷한 것은?

(A) 형성했다
(B) 살았다
(C) 일했다
(D) 저항했다

**4** 4단락에 따르면, 다음 중 인류의 뇌에 관해 사실인 것은?

(A) 오른쪽 부분이 신체의 오른쪽을 통제한다.
(B) 각 반구가 따로따로 발달했다.
(C) 시간이 지나면서 두 반구 모두 새로운 기능을 발달시켰다.
(D) 한쪽이 언어 사용을 담당한다.

## Reading Practice 4
본문 p. 20

1 (D)    2 (C)    3 (A)    4 (B)

**Vocabulary Quiz**

1 ⓐ    2 ⓒ    3 ⓑ    4 ⓑ

### 사막에서 낙타가 살아남는 방법

사막은 물이 거의 없는 지역이다. 대부분은 일 년 내내 극심한 더위로 특징지어진다. 따라서, 사막 동물들은 수분의 부족과 높은 기온에 대처할 수 있어야 한다. 사막 생태계에 성공적으로 적응한 동물의 한 가지 예는 낙타이다.

낙타는 물을 매우 효율적으로 사용하기 때문에 사막에서 살아남을 수 있다. 사실, 대부분의 낙타는 물을 마시지 않고 7~10일을 지낼 수 있다. 이것에 대한 한 가지 이유는 낙타의 콧속이 극도로 차갑고 건조하기 때문이다. 그 결과, 낙타의 숨 속에 있는 수증기가 공기 중으로 빠져나가기 전에 액체로 바뀐다. 그런 다음 이것은 낙타의 몸으로 돌아간다. 낙타는 또한 체온이 섭씨 41도에 도달할 때까지 땀을 흘리지 않기 때문에 물을 보존할 수 있다. 대부분의 동물들은 이보다 훨씬 낮은 체온에서 땀을 흘리기 시작한다.

더위를 견디는 능력은 낙타가 사막 환경에 아주 적합하게 해주는 또 다른 요소이다. ⁴ᴬ가장 중요하게는, 낙타의 지방은 주로 그것의 등에 있는 혹에 저장된다. 신체의 나머지 부분의 지방 부족은 열이 아주 빠르게 발산될 수 있다는 것을 의미한다. ⁴ᶜ게다가, 밤에 낙타의 체온은 크게 떨어진다. 하루를 낮은 체온으로 시작하는 것은 낙타가 오랜 시간 동안 더위를 견딜 수 있게 해준다. ⁴ᴰ마지막으로, 낙타는 그것의 발에 두꺼운 발바닥을 가지고 있다. 이것들은 낙타가 걸을 때 뜨거운 사막 모래로부터의 보호를 제공한다.

be characterized by ~으로 특징지어지다    extreme 형극심한
cope with ~에 대처하다    adapt to ~에 적응하다
ecosystem 명생태계    efficiently 부효율적으로
extremely 부극도로, 극히    water vapor 수증기
liquid 명액체    conserve 동보존하다    sweat 동땀을 흘리다
reach 동도달하다, 이르다    tolerate 동견디다, 참다
factor 명요소, 요인    suited 형적합한, 적당한
primarily 부주로    hump 명혹    release 동발산하다, 방출하다
drop 동떨어지다    significantly 부크게, 상당히
endure 동견디다    thick 형두꺼운    pad 명(동물의) 발바닥
offer 동제공하다    protection 명보호

**1** 지문의 단어 "adapted"와 의미가 가장 비슷한 것은?

(A) 보호했다
(B) 견뎠다
(C) 의존했다
(D) 적응했다

**2** 지문의 단어 "This"가 가리키는 것은?

(A) 낙타
(B) 숨
(C) 액체
(D) 공기

**3** 지문의 단어 "conserve"와 의미상 가장 유사한 것은?

(A) 아끼다
(B) 잃다
(C) 증가시키다
(D) 제공하다

**4** 낙타가 높은 기온을 견딜 수 있는 이유로 언급되지 않은 것은?

(A) 그것은 대부분의 지방을 혹에 저장한다.
(B) 그것의 코는 낮 동안 축축하다.

(C) 그것의 몸은 밤에 급격히 식는다.

(D) 그것의 발은 뜨거운 모래로부터 보호된다.

## iBT Reading Test
본문 p.22

| 1 (A) | 2 (C) | 3 (D) | 4 (D) |
|-------|-------|-------|-------|
| 5 (C) | 6 (C) | 7 (C) | 8 (A) |
| 9 (D) | 10 (A), (C), (D) | | |

### 기자의 대피라미드

기자의 대피라미드는 세계 7대 불가사의 중 여전히 존재하는 유일한 것이다. 건축은 기원전 2560년경에 완료되었다. 약 3,800년 동안, 서기 1311년에 링컨 대성당이 건립될 때까지 그 피라미드는 가장 높은 인공 건축물이었다.

고고학자들은 고대 이집트인들이 어떻게 그렇게 거대한 건축물을 지었는지 확실히 알지 못한다. 특히, 피라미드를 구성하는 230만 개의 돌덩어리들을 운반하기 위해 사용된 방법은 알려지지 않았다. ⁴이것들 중 가장 작은 것은 1.3톤의 무게가 나가고 가장 큰 것은 거의 80톤이다. 하나의 이론은, 그 덩어리들이 썰매 위에 놓인 다음 피라미드의 건설 현장으로 끌려왔다는 것이다. 피라미드가 더 높아짐에 따라, 그것 주위에 경사로들이 놓였다. 이는 덩어리들이 위층에 추가될 수 있게 했다. ⁵고대 이집트인들은 황소나 말을 노동에 이용하지 않았기 때문에 그 노동은 전적으로 사람들에 의해 이루어졌을 것이다. 3만 명의 노동자들이 대피라미드를 건설하는 데 20년이 걸렸다고 여겨진다. **이는 인력 측면에서 큰 투자를 의미했다.** 또한 그렇게 많은 노동자들을 먹이고 수용하기 위해 상당한 자원이 필요했다.

명백한 의문점은 이 건축물을 짓는 데 왜 그렇게 많은 노력을 들였는가 하는 것이다. 대 피라미드는 이집트의 통치자인 쿠푸를 위한 무덤의 역할을 했다. 고대 이집트인들은 파라오라고 알려진 그들의 왕들이 인간이라기보다는 신이라고 믿었다. 그러므로, 그들은 인상적인 무덤들을 가져야만 했다. 이 묘지들은 시신뿐만 아니라 내세를 즐기는 데 필요한 물건들을 포함했다. ⁸ᴮ/⁸ᶜ/⁸ᴰ예를 들어, 파라오들은 보통 아름다운 예복, 값비싼 포도주, 반지와 목걸이 같은 보물들과 함께 묻혔다. 또한, 내부의 벽에는 고인의 삶과 관련된 그림들이 그려졌다. 사실상, 피라미드는 파라오들을 위한 기념비였다.

construction 명 건축   manmade 형 인공의
cathedral 명 대성당   erect 통 건립하다
archaeologist 명 고고학자   massive 형 거대한
comprise 통 구성하다   weigh 통 무게가 나가다
ramp 명 경사로   entirely 부 전적으로   significant 형 상당한
feed 통 먹이다   accommodate 통 수용하다
obvious 형 명백한   serve 통 역할을 하다   mortal 명 인간
afterlife 명 내세   interior 형 내부의   in effect 사실상
monument 명 기념비

**1** 1단락에서, 글쓴이는 왜 "the Lincoln Cathedral"을 언급하는가?

(A) 피라미드의 규모를 강조하기 위해

(B) 두 건축물의 차이를 설명하기 위해

(C) 또 다른 건축학적 불가사의의 예시를 들기 위해

(D) 그것이 여전히 세계에서 가장 높은 인공 건축물임을 주장하기 위해

**2** 아래 문장 중 지문 속의 음영된 문장의 핵심 정보를 가장 잘 표현한 것은? 오답은 문장의 의미를 크게 바꾸거나 핵심 정보를 생략한다.

(A) 고고학자들은 이집트 피라미드의 목적에 대해 궁금해한다.

(B) 이집트인들은 그 거대한 건축물을 특별한 이유 없이 건설했다.

(C) 이집트인들이 피라미드를 건설하기 위해 사용한 방법들은 알려지지 않았다.

(D) 고고학자들은 대피라미드의 수수께끼를 풀기 위해 노력한다.

**3** 지문의 단어 "comprise"와 의미가 가장 비슷한 것은?

(A) 둘러싸다

(B) 완성하다

(C) 포함하다

(D) 구성하다

**4** 2단락에 따르면, 다음 중 돌덩어리들에 관해 사실인 것은?

(A) 정사각형 모양으로 잘렸다.

(B) 같은 장소에서 온다.

(C) 운송 중 받은 손상을 보여준다.

(D) 무게 측면에서 상당히 다양하다.

**5** 2단락에 따르면, 대피라미드의 건설은

(A) 10년 이상 지속되지 않았다

(B) 많은 노동자들의 죽음을 초래했다

(C) 동물의 이용을 수반하지 않았다

(D) 다른 나라들의 자원을 필요로 했다

**6** 지문의 단어 "served"와 의미가 가장 비슷한 것은?

(A) 준비했다

(B) 배달했다

(C) 기능했다

(D) 도움을 주었다

**7** 지문의 단어 "they"가 가리키는 것은?

(A) 노동자들

(B) 이집트인들

(C) 왕들

(D) 인간들

**8** 3단락에 따르면, 다음 중 일반적으로 파라오와 함께 매장된 것이 아닌 것은?

(A) 그림책

(B) 값비싼 보석류

(C) 알코올성 음료

(D) 의복

**9** 네 개의 네모[■]는 다음 문장이 삽입될 수 있는 곳을 나타내고 있다.

**이는 인력 측면에서 큰 투자를 의미했다.**

이 문장은 어디에 들어가는 것이 가장 적절한가?

**10 지시:** 지문 요약을 위한 도입 문장이 아래에 주어져 있다. 지문의 가장 중요한 내용을 나타내는 보기 3개를 골라 요약을 완성하라. 어떤 문장은 지문에 언급되지 않은 내용이나 사소한 정보를 나타내므로 요약에 포함되지 않는다. **이 문제는 2점이다.**

기자의 대피라미드는 독특한 건축물이다.
· (A) 과학자들은 사용된 건축 방법에 대해 정확히 알지 못한다.
· (C) 이집트인들은 대피라미드를 묘지로 건설했다.
· (D) 대피라미드는 수천 년 전에 지어졌다.

(B) 이후의 건물들은 대피라미드를 본떠서 만들어졌다.
(E) 해마다 노동자의 수가 달라졌다.
(F) 파라오의 보물들이 무덤 안에 포함되었다.

## Vocabulary Review
본문 p.26

| 1 preference | 2 transport | 3 disguise |
| 4 absorb | 5 impressive | 6 seemingly |

7 (C)  8 (B)  9 (B)  10 (D)
11 (D)  12 (B)  13 (D)  14 (B)

---

## CHAPTER 02
# Reference

## Example
본문 p.29

1 (C)  2 (D)

### 위약 효과

위약은 실제 의학적 속성이 없는 알약과 같은 의학적 치료제이다. 위약은 새로운 약물이 시험될 때 종종 사용된다. 일부 환자들에게는 위약이 주어지고 다른 이들에게는 유효한 약물이 주어지며, 각각의 효력이 비교된다. 위약을 복용한 후 한 사람의 신체적인 상태나 정신적인 상태가 개선될 때, 이것은 위약 효과라고 불린다. 어떤 경우에는, 위약이 실제 약과 같은 좋은 결과를 낳을 수 있다. 연구들은 이 가능성을 입증했다. 몇몇 연구들은 위약을 복용한 사람들 중 약 절반이 상태의 호전을 보고했다고 밝혔다.

그렇다면, 무엇이 위약 효과를 일으키는가? 최근의 한 연구는 치료제에 대한 기대가 이 현상의 이유라는 것을 보여준다. 어떤 사람이 그것이 효과적일 것이라고 믿으면, 긍정적인 결과가 나올 가능성이 더 높다. 다시 말해서, 정신은 신체에 강력한 영향을 미치고, 심지어 그것을 낫게 하는 데 도움을 줄 수 있다.

물론, 위약은 실제로 종양을 줄어들게 하거나 콜레스테롤을 낮출 수 없다. 그것들은 전통적인 의미로는 환자들을 치료하지 못할 것이다. 대신, 위약은 뇌에 의해 통제되는 증상들에 작용한다. 그것들은 통증, 스트레스, 피로를 완화시킬 가능성이 가장 크다.

placebo 몡위약, 속임약    treatment 몡치료제, 치료
property 몡속성, 특성    medication 몡약물    active 혱유효한
effectiveness 몡효력, 유효성    compare 동비교하다
condition 몡상태    improve 동개선되다    report 동보고하다
expectation 몡기대    phenomenon 몡현상    outcome 몡결과

---

influence 몡영향    shrink 동줄어들게 하다    tumor 몡종양
symptom 몡증상    alleviate 동완화시키다    fatigue 몡피로

1  지문의 어구 "this possibility"가 가리키는 것은?
  (A) 약물을 시험하는 것
  (B) 누군가의 상태가 호전되는 것
  (C) 이로운 결과를 낳는 것
  (D) 실제 약을 복용하는 것

2  지문의 단어 "it"이 가리키는 것은?
  (A) 결과
  (B) 정신
  (C) 영향
  (D) 신체

## Reading Practice 1
본문 p.30

1 (A)  2 (B)  3 (B)  4 (C)

### Vocabulary Quiz

1 ⓑ  2 ⓑ  3 ⓐ  4 ⓐ

### 미국의 냉동식품 산업의 성장

미국의 냉동식품 산업은 1929년에 발명가 클라렌스 버즈아이가 어떤 음식이든 즉시 냉동하는 기술을 개발했을 때 시작됐다. 그러나, 그것은 초창기 몇 년 동안에는 그렇게 빠르게 확장되지 않았다. ²ᴬ/²ᶜ냉동식품에 대한 대중의 무관심은 구할 수 있는 제품의 선택 제한—주로 생선과 몇 가지 채소—에 더하여, 이 제품들을 장기간 저장하기 위한 가정 내 냉동고의 부족에서 부분적으로 기인했다. ²ᴰ하지만, 주된 원인은 사람들이 저렴하고 편리한 통조림 식품을 선호한다는 것이었다.

제2차 세계대전은 냉동식품이 미국 소비자들에게 더욱 받아들여지는 것에 있어 중요한 역할을 했다. 통조림 식품의 용기에 사용되는 금속인 양철은 공급이 부족했고, 그래서 미국 정부는 이 자원을 절약하기 위해 엄격한 통제를 시행했다. 게다가, 생산되는 통조림 제품의 대부분이 군대에 의해 그것의 인력에 공급하기 위해 사용되었다. 결과적으로, 미국의 식품 회사들은 훨씬 더 다양한 종류의 냉동 제품을 만들기 시작했고, 그 나라 모든 지역들의 주요 식료품점 체인들은 이것들을 공격적으로 대중에 광고했다.

냉동식품은 전후 여러 해 동안 훨씬 더 받아들여졌다. 1940년대에, 주로 냉장고의 구성 요소로서 가정용 냉동고가 도입된 것은 사람들이 냉동식품을 주택에 무기한으로 보관할 수 있게 해주었다. 그 산업은 TV 디너의 발명과 함께 1950년대에 또 한 번의 상승을 경험했다. 이것들은 이미 조리되어 단순히 오븐에서 다시 데워지기만 하면 되는 주요리, 채소, 디저트를 포함한 완전한 냉동 식사였다. 구매와 요리 모두를 매우 쉽게 만듦으로써, 그것들은 빠르게 미국 대중의 인기를 얻었다. 얼마 지나지 않아, 식품 제조사들은, 피자에서부터 닭고기 커틀릿까지, 다양한 미리 조리된 냉동식품을 제공하고 있었다.

instantly 뿐즉시    freeze 동냉동하다    expand 동확장되다
disinterest 몡무관심    partially 뿐부분적으로
be attributable to ~에서 기인하다    selection 몡선택; 종류
convenient 혱편리한    acceptable 혱받아들여지는
personnel 몡인력    aggressively 뿐공격적으로

advertise 동광고하다　residential use 가정용
component 명구성 요소　refrigerator 명냉장고
indefinitely 부무기한으로　boost 명상승　extremely 부매우
catch on with ~의 인기를 얻다　precooked 형미리 조리된

1 지문의 단어 "it"이 가리키는 것은?

(A) 산업
(B) 발명가
(C) 기술
(D) 식품

2 1단락에 따르면, 다음 중 냉동식품이 처음에 인기가 없었던 이유가 아닌 것은?

(A) 회사들은 다양한 선택지를 제공하지 않았다.
(B) 냉동고는 장기간 가동하기에 비용이 많이 들었다.
(C) 주택들은 적당한 저장 공간을 포함하지 않았다.
(D) 소비자들은 다른 종류의 제품을 선호했다.

3 지문의 단어 "these"가 가리키는 것은?

(A) 회사들
(B) 제품들
(C) 체인들
(D) 지역들

4 지문의 단어 "indefinitely"와 의미가 가장 비슷한 것은?

(A) 대단히
(B) 자주
(C) 끝없이
(D) 일반적으로

## Reading Practice 2
본문 p.32

1 (C)　　2 (B)　　3 (B)　　4 (C)

### Vocabulary Quiz

1 ⓒ　　2 ⓐ　　3 ⓐ　　4 ⓑ

### 오티스의 엘리베이터

현대의 엘리베이터는 1800년대에 개발되었다. 최초의 형태들은 승강대를 위아래로 움직이기 위해 증기나 수압을 이용했다. 이 엘리베이터들은 화물을 수송하기 위해서만 사용되었는데, 그것들이 사람을 나르기엔 너무 위험했기 때문이었다.

이후 1852년에, 미국인 발명가 엘리샤 오티스가 최초의 승객용 엘리베이터를 고안했다. ²오티스는 가구 제조사에 고용되어 있었고, 노동자들은 무거운 자재들을 더 높은 층들로 들어 올릴 방법이 필요했다. 화물용 엘리베이터는 밧줄이 자주 끊어졌기 때문에 그것들을 옮기기에 그다지 신뢰할 수 없었다. 장비가 손상될 수 있었고 노동자들 또한 다칠 수 있었다. 그래서, 오티스는 금속 막대기와 스프링을 이용하여 안전장치를 고안했다. 만약 케이블이 끊어지면, 그 장치가 엘리베이터가 떨어져 땅과 충돌하는 것을 막아줄 것이었다.

오티스는 그의 새로운 발명품을 1853년 국제 박람회에서 극적인 시범 설명과 함께 선보였다. 군중 앞에서, 오티스는 승강대에 탑승해서

공중으로 높이 올랐다. 그는 도르래 위의 밧줄을 자르라고 명령했다. 구경꾼들이 기겁했지만, 그의 발명품 덕분에, 통로 위의 엘리베이터는 그것이 멈출 때까지 불과 몇 인치 정도 떨어졌을 뿐이었다.

그 후, 엘리베이터는 사람들을 운반할 정도로 충분히 안전해졌다. 하지만 그보다 더, 오티스의 발명품은 건축 양식에 혁신을 일으켰다. 매우 높은 건물들은 사람들이 많은 층의 계단을 자주 오르내릴 수 없었기 때문에 실용적이지 않았다. 그러나, 엘리베이터가 안전해지면서, 건물들은 점점 더 높게 지어질 수 있었다. 오늘날, 우리의 현대 도시들은 모두 한 세기도 더 전에 발명된 안전 장치와 동일한 형태를 사용하는 엘리베이터들이 있는 고층 건물들로 가득 차 있다.

platform 명승강대　cargo 명화물　employ 동고용하다
manufacturer 명제조사　lift 동들어 올리다
unreliable 형신뢰할 수 없는　injure 동부상을 입히다
dramatic 형극적인　demonstration 명시범 설명　pulley 명도르래
onlooker 명구경꾼　shaft 명(엘리베이터의) 통로　secure 형안전한
revolutionize 동혁신을 일으키다　architecture 명건축 양식
practical 형실용적인　regularly 부자주　filled with ~으로 가득 찬
skyscraper 명고층 건물

1 지문의 단어 "them"이 가리키는 것은?

(A) 사람들
(B) 노동자들
(C) 자재들
(D) 층들

2 2단락에 따르면, 다음 중 오티스의 엘리베이터에 관해 사실인 것은?

(A) 이전의 엘리베이터들보다 더 빠르게 움직였다.
(B) 오티스는 물자를 옮길 방법을 찾기 위해 그것을 고안했다.
(C) 1853년 국제 박람회에서 가장 인기 있는 발명품이었다.
(D) 좀처럼 끊어지지 않는 케이블을 가지고 있었다.

3 지문의 어구 "his new invention"이 가리키는 것은?

(A) 장비
(B) 안전장치
(C) 케이블
(D) 엘리베이터

4 지문의 단어 "practical"과 의미가 가장 비슷한 것은?

(A) 우아한
(B) 중요한
(C) 유용한
(D) 필수적인

## Reading Practice 3
본문 p.34

1 (C)　　2 (C)　　3 (D)　　4 (D)

### Vocabulary Quiz

1 ⓒ　　2 ⓐ　　3 ⓐ　　4 ⓑ

### 멕시코 동굴어

멕시코 동굴어는 멕시코의 수중 석회석 동굴에 사는 종이다. 이 작은

무색 물고기의 서식지에는 빛이 없고, 산소가 거의 없으며, 먹을 것이 거의 없다. 이러한 환경에서 살아남기 위해, 그들은 몇 가지 특이한 신체적 특징들을 발달시켰다.

그들이 완전한 어둠 속에서 살기 때문에, 동굴어는 동굴에서 먹이를 찾기 위해 후각과 미각에 의존한다. 그들이 그것을 찾는 것을 돕기 위해, 멕시코 동굴에 사는 강에 사는 그들의 친척들보다 더 크고 더 많은 미뢰들을 가지고 있다. 2게다가, 그들은 압력의 변화를 감지하는 능력을 발달시켰고, 그래서 그들은 물속의 아주 작은 움직임에도 민감하다. 동굴어의 아가미 또한 다른 종류의 물고기의 것보다 더 크다. 이것은 그들이 훨씬 더 효율적으로 물에서 산소를 얻게 해준다.

아마도 동굴어의 가장 흥미로운 적응 형태는 그들이 눈을 완전히 잃어버렸다는 것이다. 수백만 년에 걸쳐, 그들의 눈은 완전히 사라질 때까지 서서히 점점 더 작아졌다. 현재 그들의 눈구멍은 비늘로 덮여 있으며 검은 점처럼 보인다. 과거에는, 사용하지 않음으로 인해 동굴어의 눈이 서서히 사라졌다고 여겨졌지만, 새로운 연구들은 그것들이 아마 다른 이유로 없어졌으리라는 것을 보여준다. 동굴어는 이미지를 처리할 필요가 없기 때문에 강에 사는 물고기보다 더 작은 뇌를 가지고 있다. 이것은 그들의 작은 뇌가 최대 30퍼센트까지 에너지를 덜 사용한다는 점에서 이점이 된다. 따라서, 동굴어는 에너지를 절약하기 위해 눈을 잃었을 가능성이 있고, 이는 그들이 혹독한 서식지에서 살아남는 것에 도움이 되었다.

species 몡종  limestone 몡석회석  habitat 몡서식지
unique 혱특이한  characteristic 몡특징  rely on ~에 의존하다
numerous 혱많은  taste bud (혀의) 미뢰  detect 동감지하다
sensitive 혱민감한  gill 몡아가미  efficiently 뫼효율적으로
adaptation 몡적응 형태  gradually 뫼서서히  eye socket 눈구멍
disuse 몡사용하지 않음  river-dwelling 혱강에 사는
advantage 몡이점  conserve 동절약하다  harsh 혱혹독한

**1** 지문의 단어 "it"이 가리키는 것은?

(A) 어둠
(B) 미각
(C) 먹이
(D) 동굴

**2** 2단락에 따르면, 다음 중 동굴어에 관해 사실인 것은?

(A) 그것의 아가미가 기능하기 위해 더 많은 산소가 필요하다.
(B) 한정된 수의 큰 미뢰들을 가지고 있다.
(C) 물속의 작은 움직임을 감지할 수 있다.
(D) 산소의 제약 때문에 작은 아가미를 가지고 있다.

**3** 지문의 단어 "they"가 가리키는 것은?

(A) 비늘
(B) 검은 점
(C) 동굴어
(D) 눈

**4** 지문의 단어 "harsh"와 의미가 가장 비슷한 것은?

(A) 불규칙적인
(B) 드문
(C) 음울한
(D) 극심한

## Reading Practice 4

본문 p. 36

**1** (D)   **2** (C)   **3** (C)   **4** (A)

**Vocabulary Quiz**

**1** ©   **2** ⓑ   **3** ⓑ   **4** ⓐ

### 명왕성은 왜 행성이 아닐까?

1930년에 명왕성이 처음 발견되었을 때, 그것은 태양계에서 아홉 번째이자 가장 작은 행성이 되었다. 하지만, 2006년에 과학자들이 명왕성이 더 이상 행성이 아니라고 공표했을 때 그것은 바뀌었다. 이 놀라운 사건은, 해왕성 너머 태양계 바깥에 위치한 지역인 카이퍼 벨트에 있는 새로운 행성의 발견 때문에 일어났다. 이 새로운 행성 에리스는 실제로 명왕성보다 질량이 더 컸을 뿐만 아니라, 그것의 성분 또한 이 아홉 번째 행성과 비슷했다.

이제, 천문학자들은 결정을 내려야 했다. 에리스가 태양계의 열 번째 행성이 되어야 할까, 만약 아니라면, 명왕성이 행성으로 간주되어야 할까? 신중한 고찰 후에, 그들은 행성의 정의를 바꾸기로 결정했다. 행성이 되기 위해서, 천체는 세 가지 필요조건을 만족해야 한다. 즉, 그것은 태양의 궤도를 돌아야 하고, 대체로 둥근 모양이어야 하며, 그것의 주변 영역에서 물체들을 제거할 만큼 강한 중력을 지녀야 한다. 명왕성은 처음 두 가지의 필요조건에는 문제가 없었지만, 세 번째 조건에 문제가 있었다. 3명왕성은 주변의 암석과 다른 잔해들을 모두 자신의 궤도로 끌어당기거나 우주로 밀어낼 수 없었다. 따라서, 그것의 분류가 바뀔 필요가 있었다.

이에 대응하여, 과학자들은 명왕성과 그것의 이웃인 에리스를 위해 왜소행성이라 불리는 완전히 새로운 범주를 만들었다. 왜소행성은, 그들의 이름이 암시하듯, 크기가 더 작고 충분한 중력이 없는 행성들을 가리킨다. 이제, 명왕성은 더 이상 태양계의 마지막 행성이 아니다. 대신, 카이퍼 벨트 내의 모든 천체 중에서는, 그것이 가장 가깝다.

solar system 태양계  declare 동공표하다
come about 일어나다  region 몡지역  mass 몡질량
composition 몡성분  astronomer 몡천문학자
consideration 몡고찰  definition 몡정의  celestial 혱천체의
requirement 몡필요조건  orbit 동궤도를 돌다; 몡궤도
round 혱둥근  debris 몡잔해  classification 몡분류
dwarf planet 왜소행성  refer to ~을 가리키다
sufficient 혱충분한  gravitational force 중력

**1** 지문의 단어 "declared"와 의미가 가장 비슷한 것은?

(A) 관찰했다
(B) 실험했다
(C) 토론했다
(D) 발표했다

**2** 지문의 단어 "its"가 가리키는 것은?

(A) 태양계
(B) 해왕성
(C) 에리스
(D) 명왕성

**3** 2단락에 따르면, 명왕성의 분류는 왜 왜소행성으로 바뀌었는가?

(A) 태양계 바깥에 위치해 있었다.
(B) 중력이 전혀 없다고 판명되었다.

(C) 그것의 주변 물체들을 제거하지 않았다.

(D) 에리스보다 작았다.

**4** 지문의 단어 "it"이 가리키는 것은?

(A) 명왕성

(B) 행성

(C) 태양계

(D) 카이퍼 벨트

## iBT Reading Test

본문 p. 38

1 (C)  2 (B)  3 (B)  4 (B)
5 (A)  6 (B)  7 (D)  8 (A)
9 (B)  10 (A), (C), (F)

### 흑사병

페스트라고도 알려진 흑사병은 지금까지 인류 역사에 기록된 가장 치명적인 전염병 중 하나였다. ²흑사병은 아시아에서 기원했다고 여겨지지만, 그것은 1347년에 곡류와 씨앗 무역선들이 시칠리아에 정박했을 때 유럽에 도달했다. 시칠리아인들은 대부분의 선원들이 죽은 것을 발견하고 겁에 질렸다. 이 "죽음의 배들"은 즉시 바다로 돌려보내졌지만, 유감스럽게도, 이미 너무 늦은 것이었다.

흑사병은 배들에서 나온 쥐들에 붙어살던 벼룩들을 통해 퍼졌다. 그것들이 사람들을 물고 난 다음 흑사병은 사람에서 사람으로 빠르게 퍼졌다. 페스트에 걸린 사람들은 열이 났고 허약해졌다. 그들은 사타구니와 겨드랑이에 사과 하나만 한 크기로 자라는 심한 종기를 경험했다. ⁵게다가, 몸이 검은 상처들로 뒤덮였는데, 여기에서 흑사병은 그 이름을 얻게 되었다. 치료받지 않고 방치되면, 사람들은 보통 72시간 내에 사망했다.

현재 우리에게는 페스트를 치료할 약이 있지만, 그 당시의 의사들은 무엇을 해야 할지 몰랐다. ⁷ᴮ일반적인 관행은 몸에서 "나쁜 피"를 빼내는 것을 포함했다. ⁷ᶜ많은 사람들이 식초를 마시거나 에메랄드 같은 으깨진 광물을 먹어보기도 했다. 물론, 이 치료법들 중 어떤 것도 도움이 되지 않았다. 흥미롭게도, 생존 가능성이 가장 큰 것은 오늘날에도 여전히 사용되는 전략인 사회적 거리 두기였다. ⁷ᴬ이것은 잠재적인 피해자들이 다른 사람들로부터 안전한 거리를 유지했다는 것을 의미한다. 그러나, 오직 부유한 사람들만이 혼잡한 도시에서 달아나 다른 이들로부터 떨어져 있었던 외딴 사유지로 갈 수 있었다.

결국, 대부분이 그 무서운 질병에 걸렸고 많은 사람들이 죽었다. 높은 사망률, 쉬운 전염, 치료법 부재의 조합은 대략 2천5백만 명의 사람들의 목숨을 빼앗았는데, 이는 유럽 인구의 거의 절반이었다. 인구 수준이 이전의 수준으로 회복되는 데 200년이 걸렸다.

plague 몡페스트, 전염병  fatal 톙치명적인  epidemic 몡전염병
originate in ~에서 기원하다  dock 툉정박하다
horrified 톙겁에 질린  flea 몡벼룩  swelling 몡종기, 부기
sore 몡상처  common 톙일반적인  withdraw 툉빼내다
victim 몡피해자  flee 툉달아나다  remote 톙외딴
estate 몡사유지  stay away from ~으로부터 떨어져 있다
fatality rate 사망률  transmission 몡전염  recover 툉회복하다

**1** 지문의 단어 "horrified"와 의미가 가장 비슷한 것은?

(A) 우울한

(B) 실망한

(C) 충격을 받은

(D) 기쁜

**2** 1단락에 따르면, 다음 중 흑사병에 관해 사실인 것은?

(A) 아시아의 의사들에 의해 처음 발견되었다.

(B) 그것의 유럽에서의 시작점은 시칠리아였다.

(C) 선원들이 다른 사람들보다 그것에 더 많이 걸렸다.

(D) 씨앗을 통해 유럽의 다른 지역으로 퍼졌다.

**3** 지문의 단어 "They"가 가리키는 것은?

(A) 선원들

(B) 벼룩들

(C) 쥐들

(D) 배들

**4** 2단락에서, 글쓴이는 왜 "an apple"을 언급하는가?

(A) 가능성 있는 치료법을 제시하기 위해

(B) 증상의 심각성을 강조하기 위해

(C) 전염의 수단을 밝히기 위해

(D) 종기의 원인을 나타내기 위해

**5** 2단락에 따르면, 흑사병이라는 이름이 붙은 것은

(A) 그것의 증상이 검은 상처들을 포함했기 때문이다

(B) 검은 쥐들에 의해 퍼졌기 때문이다

(C) 피가 검게 변하도록 했기 때문이다

(D) 그것의 피해자들의 무덤에 검은 묘비가 있었기 때문이다

**6** 지문의 어구 "stayed away from"과 의미가 가장 비슷한 것은?

(A) 조롱했다

(B) 피했다

(C) 위로했다

(D) 비판했다

**7** 3단락에 따르면, 다음 중 사람들이 흑사병을 견뎌 내기 위해 시도한 방법이 아닌 것은?

(A) 인구가 밀집된 지역을 떠나는 것

(B) 몸에서 피를 내보내는 것

(C) 으깨진 돌을 섭취하는 것

(D) 식초로 상처를 씻는 것

**8** 아래 문장 중 지문 속의 음영된 문장의 핵심 정보를 가장 잘 표현한 것은? 오답은 문장의 의미를 크게 바꾸거나 핵심 정보를 생략한다.

(A) 이 치명적이고 전염성 있는 병을 치료하는 것에 대한 무능력은 유럽 인구의 절반이 사망하는 결과를 낳았다.

(B) 이 치명적인 병의 확산을 막은 것이 유럽에서 사상자의 수를 제한했다.

(C) 효과적인 치료법이 발견되지 않았기 때문에 수백만 명의 유럽인들이 이 병으로 인해 사망했다.

(D) 유럽 인구의 큰 비율이 이 대단히 감염성 높은 질병에 감염되었다.

**9** 네 개의 네모[■]는 다음 문장이 삽입될 수 있는 곳을 나타내고 있다.

**물론, 이 치료법들 중 어떤 것도 도움이 되지 않았다.**

이 문장은 어디에 들어가는 것이 가장 적절한가?

**10 지시:** 지문 요약을 위한 도입 문장이 아래에 주어져 있다. 지문의 가장 중요한 내용을 나타내는 보기 3개를 골라 요약을 완성하라. 어떤 문장은 지문에 언급되지 않은 내용이나 사소한 정보를 나타내므로 요약에 포함되지 않는다. 이 문제는 2점이다.

> **흑사병은 14세기 내내 퍼진 끔찍한 질병이었다.**
> · (A) 흑사병은 절반에 가까운 유럽 인구를 없애 버렸다.
> · (C) 당시의 의학적 지식은 페스트를 다루기에 충분하지 않았다.
> · (F) 흑사병은 곤충들이 그것을 사람들에게 옮긴 이후 사람들 사이에서 빠르게 퍼졌다.

(B) 몸에서 피를 빼내는 것은 알려진 가장 효과적인 치료법이었다.
(D) 흑사병 중에 유럽 내 사상자의 대부분은 시칠리아에 있었다.
(E) 페스트가 끝난 후에, 질병을 치료하는 새로운 약물들이 개발되었다.

## Vocabulary Review
본문 p.42

| | | |
|---|---|---|
| 1 transmission | 2 numerous | 3 alleviate |
| 4 expectations | 5 outcome | 6 gradually |
| 7 (C) | 8 (A) | 9 (C) | 10 (B) |
| 11 (C) | 12 (A) | 13 (A) | 14 (D) |

---

# Sentence Simplification

## Example
본문 p.45

1 (C)    2 (B)

### 공룡은 온혈이었을까 냉혈이었을까?

공룡은 항상 고생물학자들에게 많은 수수께끼를 제시해왔다. 가장 이해할 수 없는 것들 중 하나는 그들의 체온이었다. 포유류와 조류 같은 온혈동물은 일정한 체온을 유지하기 위해 몸 내부에서 열을 발생시킨다. 파충류 같은 냉혈동물은 체온을 조절할 수 없고 환경으로부터 열을 얻는다. 하지만 공룡은 어떨까?

이것을 알아내기 위해, 과학자들은 신진대사를 살펴보기로 결정했다. 온혈동물은 더 빠른 성장 속도, 더 높은 지능, 더 빠른 움직임을 가능하게 하는 빠른 신진대사를 가지고 있다. 냉혈동물은 이러한 특징들은 없지만, 에너지와 먹이에 있어 더 경제적인데, 말하자면, 그들은 매우 적은 먹이로 오랜 기간 생명을 유지할 수 있다는 것이다. 흥미롭게도, 화석 연구는 공룡이 이러한 특징들을 결합해서 가지고 있었음을 보여주었다. ¹그들은 포유류처럼 체열을 조절할 수 있었지만, 그것을 계속 할 수는 없었다.

과학자들은 이 독특한 중간 단계가 공룡에게 생태학적인 이점을 주었다고 생각한다. 그들은 아마 파충류보다 더 영리하고 빨랐을 것이다. ²그러나, 공룡은 이러한 특징들을 유지하기 위해 비슷한 크기의 포유

---

류만큼 많은 먹이가 필요하지 않았을 것이다. 요컨대, 공룡은 정확히 그들만의 범주에 속했다. 우리가 이 오래전에 없어진 생물에 계속 매료되어 있는 것은 놀랄 일이 아니다.

paleontologist 몡 고생물학자    puzzling 혱 이해할 수 없는
warm-blooded 혱 온혈    mammal 몡 포유류
cold-blooded 혱 냉혈의    reptile 몡 파충류    regulate 통 조절하다
metabolism 몡 신진대사    brainpower 몡 지능    lack 통 ~이 없다
trait 몡 특징    economical 혱 경제적인    sustain 통 (생명을) 유지하다
characteristic 몡 특징    continually 뷔 계속
in-between 혱 중간의    ecological 혱 생태학적인
fascinate 통 매료시키다    long-gone 혱 오래전에 없어진

**1** 아래 문장 중 지문 속의 음영된 문장의 핵심 정보를 가장 잘 표현한 것은?
(A) 포유류와 공룡은 둘 다 열을 일정하게 유지할 수 있었다.
(B) 포유류는 공룡만큼 체열을 잘 조절할 수 없다.
(C) 공룡은 포유류처럼 체온을 항상 조절할 수는 없었다.
(D) 공룡은 포유류보다 체열을 더 잘 조절했다.

**2** 아래 문장 중 지문 속의 음영된 문장의 핵심 정보를 가장 잘 표현한 것은?
(A) 그들이 많은 특질들을 가지고 있었기 때문에, 공룡은 많은 먹이를 먹어야만 했다.
(B) 일부 특징들을 유지하기 위해, 공룡은 포유류보다 적은 먹이를 필요로 했다.
(C) 포유류와 공룡은 많이 먹었기 때문에 비슷한 크기였다.
(D) 공룡이 먹은 양은 그것이 지닌 특징들을 결정했다.

## Reading Practice 1
본문 p.46

1 (B)    2 (D)    3 (B)    4 (B)

**Vocabulary Quiz**

1 ⓐ    2 ⓒ    3 ⓐ    4 ⓑ

### 알래스카가 49번째 주가 된 방법

알래스카는 미국의 49번째이자 가장 큰 주다. 그곳은 아름다움과 풍부한 천연자원으로 가득 찬 지역이다. 그 지역의 약 5퍼센트는 빙하로 덮여 있고, 수백만 에이커의 훼손되지 않은 황야가 있다. 그러나, 알래스카가 항상 그렇게 매력적인 장소로 여겨졌던 것은 아니다.

러시아가 영토를 확장하기 시작했을 때까지 수천 년 동안, 토착 부족들이 그 지역의 유일한 주민들이었다. 17세기 동안, 러시아인들은 그 지역에 모피 무역소와 다른 정착지들을 세웠다. 그곳에서의 삶은 쉽지 않았다. 기후는 혹독했으며, 농업은 거의 불가능했다. ¹그곳에서 사는 것이 전반적으로 너무 불편했고 외딴 정착지들을 유지하는 것이 전혀 이익이 되지 않았기 때문에, 러시아는 결국 미국에 알래스카를 매각하기로 결정했다.

유감스럽게도, 한 사람을 제외하고 누구도 그 지역을 사는 것에 관심이 없었다. 미국의 국무장관인 윌리엄 슈어드는 그 거대한 땅덩어리가 미국의 크기를 20퍼센트만큼 늘릴 것이기 때문에 그것을 취득하는 것을 주장했다. 그는 알래스카가 미국에게 가치 있는 재산이 될 것이라고 믿

었다. [3]반면, 대부분의 미국인들은 그 거래가 돈 낭비라고 생각했으며 그것을 "슈어드의 어리석음"이라고 불렀다. 결국, 그 매입은 1867년 상원에서 단 한 표 차이로 승인되었다.

다행히도, 슈어드의 고집은 성과를 거두었다. 그 거래 직후에 그곳에서 금이 발견되었고, 수백 명의 시민들이 그 북쪽 영토로 향했다. 알래스카는 더 많은 부를 제공했다. 그곳은 북극곰, 흰돌고래, 카리부를 포함한 다양한 야생 동물의 서식지였다. [4]미국은 또한 모피, 구리, 생선, 목재, 석유로 수천억 달러를 얻었다. 오늘날, 알래스카는 미국에서 가장 부유한 주들 중 하나이고, 이는 슈어드의 어리석음이 사실 대단한 업적이었음을 의미한다.

abundant 형 풍부한   natural resource 천연자원
untouched 형 훼손되지 않은   wilderness 명 황야
attractive 형 매력적인   native 형 토착의   settlement 명 정착지
agriculture 명 농업   unpleasant 형 불편한   remote 형 외딴
profitable 형 이익이 되는   insist on ~을 주장하다
acquire 동 취득하다, 획득하다   landmass 명 땅덩어리
possession 명 재산   folly 명 어리석음   senate 명 상원, 의회
insistence 명 고집   pay off 성과를 거두다
petroleum 명 석유

1 아래 문장 중 지문 속의 음영된 문장의 핵심 정보를 가장 잘 표현한 것은?
 (A) 비록 그곳에서의 삶은 어려웠지만, 미국은 알래스카를 매입하려고 애썼다.
 (B) 러시아는 그 땅에 이점이 없었기 때문에 알래스카를 미국에 매각하기로 결정했다.
 (C) 미국은 쓸모없는 지역을 러시아에 팔아 이득을 얻기를 바랐다.
 (D) 알래스카에 식민지를 보유하는 것은 러시아에게 너무 어렵고 비용이 많이 드는 것이었다.

2 지문의 단어 "acquiring"과 의미가 가장 비슷한 것은?
 (A) 정복하는 것
 (B) 개발하는 것
 (C) 요구하는 것
 (D) 얻는 것

3 아래 문장 중 지문 속의 음영된 문장의 핵심 정보를 가장 잘 표현한 것은?
 (A) 슈어드는 더 나은 거래를 협상하지 않은 것에 대해 미국인들에게 비난받았다.
 (B) 미국에서는 재정적인 이유로 그 거래에 대한 강력한 반대가 있었다.
 (C) 미국 내에서는 써야 하는 돈의 액수에 대해 의견이 나뉘었다.
 (D) 미국인들은 슈어드의 계획에 대해 충분한 정보를 제공받지 못했다.

4 4단락에 따르면, 슈어드가 알래스카에 관해 옳았다고 증명된 것은
 (A) 그곳의 인구가 늘어나기 시작했기 때문이다
 (B) 그 지역이 중요한 천연자원을 포함했기 때문이다
 (C) 미국의 다른 주들이 그곳의 매입에 기여했기 때문이다
 (D) 다른 나라 국민들이 그곳으로 이주했기 때문이다

## Reading Practice 2

1 (C)   2 (D)   3 (B)   4 (C)

**Vocabulary Quiz**

1 ⓐ   2 ⓑ   3 ⓐ   4 ⓒ

### 철사 엄마 실험

철사 엄마 실험은 1960년대에 미국인 심리학자 해리 할로에 의해 고안된 유명한 실험이었다. [1]20세기 초반에, 많은 심리학자들은 단순히 엄마가 음식과 물을 제공하기 때문에 아기가 엄마에게 감정적으로 애착을 갖게 된다고 생각했다. 그러나, 할로는 이 주장이 의심스러웠다. 그는 그것이 사실인지 확인하기 위해 한 가지 실험을 고안했다.

그의 연구는 갓 태어난 붉은털원숭이를 이용하는 것을 포함했다. 그는 태어난 지 불과 몇 시간 만에 새끼들을 엄마로부터 떼어내어 두 인형 엄마에 의해 길러지게 했다. 첫 번째 것은 철사로 만들어졌고 먹이를 제공했다. 두 번째 것은 부드러운 헝겊으로 만들어졌고 먹이를 제공하지 않았다. 할로는 원숭이들이 이러한 조건에서 어떻게 행동하는지 관찰했다.

그는 새끼 원숭이들이 배가 고플 때 먹이를 위해 철사 엄마에게 갔다는 것을 발견했다. 그러나, 그들은 헝겊 엄마와 대부분의 시간을 보냈다. 그 새끼들은 부드러움에서 정서적인 위안과 안도감을 얻는 것처럼 보였다. 게다가, 새로운 방에 놓이는 것처럼 낯선 상황에 직면했을 때 그들은 다르게 행동했다. [2]새끼 원숭이들은 헝겊 엄마와 함께 방에 있을 때는 안심하고 방을 탐색했지만, 그것이 치워지면 얼어붙고, 소리를 질렀으며, 두려움에 울곤 했다.

할로의 실험은 사랑과 애정이 건강한 아동 발달에 있어 대단히 중요한 요소라는 것을 보여주었다. 그것들이 제공되었을 때는 긍정적인 영향이 있었고, 없을 때는 치명적인 결과가 있었다. [4]그의 획기적인 연구는 오늘날까지 여전히 연구되고 있고 계속해서 인간 행동 연구에 지식을 제공하고 있다.

emotionally 부 감정적으로   attached 형 애착을 가진
suspicious 형 의심스러운   claim 명 주장   devise 동 고안하다
newborn 형 갓 태어난   rhesus monkey 붉은털원숭이
be made of ~으로 만들어지다   condition 명 조건
comfort 명 위안   security 명 안도감   unfamiliar 형 낯선
freeze up 얼어붙다   affection 명 애정   critical 형 대단히 중요한
devastating 형 치명적인   consequence 명 결과   absent 형 없는
groundbreaking 형 획기적인   inform 동 지식을 제공하다

1 아래 문장 중 지문 속의 음영된 문장의 핵심 정보를 가장 잘 표현한 것은?
 (A) 심리학자들은 엄마가 오직 정서적인 이유로 아기에게 음식물을 제공한다고 생각했다.
 (B) 심리학자들에 따르면, 음식을 향한 아기의 욕구는 엄마가 있어야 할 필요성을 나타냈다.
 (C) 심리학자들은 아기가 영양분을 제공받기 때문에 엄마와 유대감을 형성한다고 주장했다.
 (D) 애정과 음식물 사이에서, 심리학자들은 아기가 후자를 고를 것이라고 주장했다.

2 아래 문장 중 지문 속의 음영된 문장의 핵심 정보를 가장 잘 표현한 것은?
 (A) 헝겊 엄마와 함께 새로운 공간에 놓였을 때, 새끼 원숭이들은 무서워했다.

CHAPTER 03 | Sentence Simplification   **11**

(B) 대부분의 새끼 원숭이들은 헝겊 엄마 없이 새로운 방에 들어가는 것을 너무 두려워했다.

(C) 헝겊 엄마가 치워졌을 때, 새끼 원숭이들은 어떻게 행동해야 할지 몰랐다.

(D) 새끼 원숭이들은 헝겊 엄마가 있으면 안정감을 느꼈지만 그것이 없으면 겁에 질렸다.

**3** 지문의 단어 "devastating"과 의미가 가장 비슷한 것은?

(A) 예상하지 못한

(B) 해로운

(C) 악의적인

(D) 혼란스러운

**4** 4단락에 따르면, 할로가 수행한 실험은

(A) 확정적이지 않은 결과를 제공했다

(B) 최근 연구들에 의해 신빙성을 잃었다

(C) 현대의 연구와 관련이 있다

(D) 인간 행동에 대한 문제를 드러낸다

## Reading Practice 3 본문 p. 50

1 (D)    2 (A)    3 (B)    4 (D)

**Vocabulary Quiz**

1 ⓑ    2 ⓐ    3 ⓑ    4 ⓒ

### 프리다 칼로

[1]1907년에 태어난 프리다 칼로는 멕시코 전통에 크게 영향을 받은 그녀의 자화상들 덕분에 화가로서 국제적인 명성을 얻었다. 그녀가 작품으로 성공을 얻기는 했지만, 칼로의 삶은 편안한 것과 거리가 멀었다.

여섯 살이라는 어린 나이에, 그녀는 소아마비를 앓았고, 이는 그녀의 오른쪽 다리를 못 쓰게 만들었다. 십 대에는, 거의 그녀의 목숨을 빼앗을 뻔한 끔찍한 버스 사고를 당했다. 그것은 그녀를 심각하게 다치게 했다. 그녀는 30번 이상의 수술을 받았고 침대에서 회복하는 데 여러 달을 보냈다. 유감스럽게도, 그녀는 평생 동안 계속해서 심한 통증을 느꼈다.

하지만 희망의 조짐이 있었다. 침대와 신체 속에 갇혀 있다고 느끼면서, 칼로는 시간을 보내며 자신의 역경을 잊기 위해 자화상을 그리기 시작했다. 화가로서 정식 교육을 한 번도 받지 않았음에도 불구하고, 칼로는 타고난 능력을 보였다. 그녀는 선명하고 밝은색과 멕시코 민속 예술에서 직접적으로 영감을 받은 표현법을 사용했다. [3]회복한 이후에도, 칼로는 계속 그림을 그렸고 결국 화가로서의 경력을 추구하기 위해 의학 공부를 포기했다.

[4]비록 많은 전문 예술 비평가들이 칼로를 초현실주의 화가로 여겼지만, 그녀는 이 꼬리표를 거부했다. 그 대신, 칼로는 그녀의 그림들이 자신의 경험에 대한 정확한 묘사라고 주장했다. 실제로, 그녀의 자화상들은 그녀가 직면했던 어려움에 대한 감정 상태를 솔직하게 묘사하고 있기 때문에, 그녀가 평생에 걸쳐 겪은 많은 개인적인 고통이 작품에 반영되어 있다. 삶과 예술을 분리하기를 거부함으로써, 칼로는 오늘날에도 여전히 중요한 예술적 유산을 창조했다.

renown 몡명성    self-portrait 몡자화상    heritage 몡전통, 유산

suffer from ~을 앓다    polio 몡소아마비    nearly 뷰거의
severely 뷰심각하게    undergo 통(수술을) 받다
silver lining (불행한 상황에서) 희망의 조짐    adversity 몡역경
innate 톙타고난    inspire 통영감을 주다    abandon 통포기하다
art critic 예술 비평가    label 몡꼬리표    accurate 톙정확한
hardship 몡어려움    separate 통분리하다    legacy 몡유산
influential 톙중요한

**1** 아래 문장 중 지문 속의 음영된 문장의 핵심 정보를 가장 잘 표현한 것은?

(A) 칼로는 전 세계의 관객들에게 멕시코 예술을 소개한 것으로 널리 존경받았다.

(B) 칼로는 초상화에 집중했는데, 이는 이 예술 형식이 그녀의 모국에서 인기 있었기 때문이다.

(C) 칼로는 새로운 초상화 기법을 개발함으로써 다른 멕시코 화가들에게 영향을 미쳤다.

(D) 칼로는 자신의 문화를 반영한 자화상을 그려서 유명해졌다.

**2** 지문의 단어 "innate"와 의미가 가장 비슷한 것은?

(A) 천부적인

(B) 의식하는

(C) 비범한

(D) 꾸준한

**3** 아래 문장 중 지문 속의 음영된 문장의 핵심 정보를 가장 잘 표현한 것은?

(A) 의학에 대한 칼로의 관심은 그녀가 화가가 되도록 이끌었다.

(B) 칼로는 회복 이후 화가가 되기 위해 의학을 포기했다.

(C) 칼로는 회복하는 동안 의학 공부를 중단해야 했다.

(D) 예술에 방해가 되었기 때문에 칼로는 의학 경력을 중단했다.

**4** 4단락에 따르면, 다음 중 프리다 칼로에 관해 사실인 것은?

(A) 그녀의 도전적인 삶 때문에 미술 작품을 창조하려고 분투했다.

(B) 그림을 개인적인 어려움으로부터의 기분 전환으로 간주했다.

(C) 자신을 초현실주의 화가라고 생각했다.

(D) 자신의 작품에 대한 전문가의 의견에 동의하지 않았다.

## Reading Practice 4 본문 p. 52

1 (D)    2 (B)    3 (A)    4 (C)

**Vocabulary Quiz**

1 ⓐ    2 ⓐ    3 ⓒ    4 ⓑ

### 손 씻기의 역사

손 씻기는 우리가 어릴 때 가장 먼저 배우는 일과 중 하나이다. 그것은 질병을 예방하는 쉽고 매우 효과적인 방법이다. 하지만, 하나의 관습으로서, 그것은 당초에는 유행하지 않았던 꽤 최근의 발전이다.

그것은 1840년대에 유럽에서 구체화되기 시작했다. [2]이는 끔찍한 시기였는데, 많은 산모들이 사회적 지위나 초기의 건강과는 무관하게 병에 걸려 죽어가고 있었기 때문이다. 출산 직후, 산모들은 빠른 심박수, 열, 심한 복통을 겪곤 했다. 결국, 그들은 병으로 죽곤 했다. 그 병은 "산욕열"로 알려져 있었다. 이그나스 제멜바이스라는 이름의 한 헝가리

의사는 비엔나 종합 병원의 산부인과 병동에서 근무하면서 이것을 반복해서 목격했다. 그는 그 원인을 찾기로 굳게 결심했다.

[4A]제멜바이스는 그 병원에 있던 두 개의 산부인과 병동을 관찰했다. 하나는 의사들에 의해 운영되었고, 다른 하나는 산파들에 의해 운영되었다. [4B]그는 산파들이 담당했던 곳에서 산욕열에 의한 사망이 훨씬 적다는 것을 알아차렸다. 두 병동을 비교하고 모든 차이를 배제한 후에, 제멜바이스는 마침내 정답을 알아냈다. 산파들이 아기를 받기만 했던 반면, 의사들은 병원에서 부검을 포함한 다수의 다른 업무들도 수행했다. 제멜바이스는 의사들에 의해 특정 "입자들"이 시신들로부터 산모들에게 옮겨지고 있다는 가설을 세웠다. 그는 의사 병동의 의료진에게 비누로 손을 씻고 염소 용액으로 의료 도구들을 씻으라고 지시했다. [4D]그 효과는 즉각적이었다. 사망률이 극적으로 감소한 것이다.

불행하게도, 그의 이론이 처음에 의학계에서 거부되었다는 점에서, 제멜바이스의 생각은 그의 시대에 앞선 것이었다. 그의 사후가 되어서야 비로소 손 씻기가 일상적으로 받아들여졌고 궁극적으로 전 세계의 위생 건강을 바꾸었다.

prevent 동 예방하다    practice 명 관습    fairly 부 꽤
catch on 유행하다    take form 구체화되다
abdominal pain 복통, 배앓이    childbed fever 산욕열
maternity ward 산부인과 병동    determined 형 굳게 결심한
midwife 명 산파    rule out ~을 배제하다    task 명 업무
autopsy 명 부검    hypothesize 동 가설을 세우다    particle 명 입자
chlorine 명 염소    solution 명 용액    immediate 형 즉각적인
mortality rate 사망률    dramatically 부 극적으로    hygiene 명 위생

1  지문의 어구 "catch on"과 의미가 가장 비슷한 것은?

   (A) 발생하다
   (B) 접근하다
   (C) 드러나다
   (D) 퍼지다

2  아래 문장 중 지문 속의 음영된 문장의 핵심 정보를 가장 잘 표현한 것은?
   (A) 임신한 여성이 죽어갈 때가 역사상 가장 절망적인 시기였다.
   (B) 모든 계층과 다양한 건강 상태의 여성들이 죽었다.
   (C) 사회적 지위와 건강함은 여성들이 죽어가는 데 작은 역할을 했다.
   (D) 이 기간 동안, 임신은 여성이 병에 걸리는 가장 큰 원인이었다.

3  아래 문장 중 지문 속의 음영된 문장의 핵심 정보를 가장 잘 표현한 것은?
   (A) 의사들은 다양한 의료 행위를 수행했지만, 산파들의 유일한 업무는 아기를 받는 것이었다.
   (B) 산파들은, 많은 다양한 책임이 있던 의사들보다 아기를 받기 위한 시간이 더 많았다.
   (C) 의사들의 주요 업무가 부검을 하는 것이었던 반면, 산파들의 주요 업무는 아기를 받는 것이었다.
   (D) 산파들은 다양한 업무를 수행했지만, 의사들은 오직 아기만 받았다.

4  3단락에 따르면, 다음 중 사실이 아닌 것은?
   (A) 제멜바이스는 두 개의 다른 산부인과 병동들을 관찰했다.
   (B) 제멜바이스는 두 환자 집단의 사망률 차이에 주목했다.
   (C) 손과 도구를 씻으라는 요구는 산파들에게 적용되었다.
   (D) 새로운 조치들이 적용된 후에 의사 병동의 사망자 수가 감소했다.

1 (C)    2 (B)    3 (B)    4 (C)
5 (D)    6 (A)    7 (D)    8 (B)
9 (A)    10 (B), (D), (E)

## 녹색 빙하

거의 모든 빙하들이 하얗거나 파랗지만, 그 대신에 어두운 에메랄드빛의 녹색을 보이는 적은 비율이 있다. 녹색 빙하라고 알려진 이 특이한 것들은 남극 대륙의 특정 지역들에서만 발견된다. 한 세기 이상 동안 녹색 빙하에 대한 기록들이 있었지만, 최근까지 누구도 그것들의 색의 이유를 설명하지 못했다.

일반적인 빙하들은 얼음으로 변하는 압축된 눈으로 구성된다. 햇빛이 얼음에 닿으면, 그것은 적색 빛을 흡수하고 청색 빛을 반사한다. 얼음의 청색 빛이 우리가 일반적으로 보는 것이다. 그러나, 녹색 빙하는 눈이 아니라, 빙붕 밑면에 해수가 얼어붙은 해빙으로 구성된다. [2]녹색 빙하를 만드는 해빙은 훨씬 어둡고 뚜렷한 녹색 빛깔을 띤다.

처음에, 과학자들은 얼음 내부의 용해된 유기 물질이 그 색의 이유라고 생각했다. [5]그것은 노르스름한 색이기 때문에, 그것을 순수한 청색 얼음과 섞으면 녹색 빛깔을 만들어낼 것이다. 그러나, 그들이 빙하를 표본 조사했을 때, 그들은 녹색과 청색 해빙에 동일한 양의 유기 물질이 있다는 것을 발견했다. 더욱이, 연구자들은 그 양이 색상의 차이를 만들기에 너무 적다는 것을 알아냈고, 이는 다른 무언가가 원인이 되어야 한다는 것을 시사했다.

그들은 그 빙하 속 철분의 수준을 측정하던 중에 단서를 우연히 발견했다. 놀랍게도, 녹색 빙하에는 일반 빙하보다 철분이 500배 더 많았다. 암석 안의 산화철이 대체로 노란색이기 때문에, 과학자들은 빙하에 있는 산화철의 존재에 기반한 새로운 이론을 세우기 시작했다. [7/8A/8C]남극 대륙의 빙하가 기반암 위로 이동함에 따라, 그것들은 암석을 갈아 "암분"이라 불리는 가루로 만들었다. 이 암분은 바다로 흘러들어가 해빙의 일부로 얼어붙었다. [8D]청색 얼음과 노란 산화철의 결합이 빙하의 가장자리에 녹색 빛깔을 만들어냈다. 이 조각들이 분리되었을 때, 그것들은 희귀한 녹색 빙하가 되었다.

iceberg 명 빙하    oddity 명 특이한 것    compressed 형 압축된
typically 부 일반적으로    ice shelf 빙붕    distinct 형 뚜렷한
hue 명 빛깔    dissolve 동 용해시키다    organic matter 유기 물질
sample 동 표본 조사하다    determine 동 알아내다    quantity 명 양
responsible 형 원인이 되는    come across ~을 우연히 발견하다
measure 동 측정하다    iron oxide 산화철    bedrock 명 기반암
grind 동 갈다    combination 명 결합

1  지문의 단어 "distinct"와 의미가 가장 비슷한 것은?

   (A) 유기의
   (B) 기이한
   (C) 뚜렷한
   (D) 처음의

2  2단락에 따르면, 다음 중 녹색 빙하에 관해 사실인 것은?

   (A) 청색 빙하보다 더 흔하다.
   (B) 일반적인 빙하만큼 밝지 않다.
   (C) 압축된 눈으로 만들어졌다.
   (D) 많은 서로 다른 지역들에서 발견된다.

**3** 지문의 단어 "It"이 가리키는 것은?

(A) 눈
(B) 유기 물질
(C) 얼음
(D) 색

**4** 아래 문장 중 지문 속의 음영된 문장의 핵심 정보를 가장 잘 표현한 것은? 오답은 문장의 의미를 크게 바꾸거나 핵심 정보를 생략한다.

(A) 그들은 녹색과 청색 해빙 표본에서 유기 물질을 발견했다.
(B) 녹색 빙하와 청색 빙하는 각각의 형태에 유기 물질이 얼마나 있는지 알아내기 위해 검사되었다.
(C) 녹색 해빙에 있는 유기 물질의 양은 청색 해빙에서 발견된 것과 동일했다.
(D) 빙하 속 유기 물질의 종류는 그것들이 청색일지 녹색일지 결정했다.

**5** 3단락에 따르면, 다음 중 사실인 것은?

(A) 청색 해빙은 유기 물질을 포함하지 않았다.
(B) 적은 양의 유기 물질은 빙하의 색을 바꿀 수 있다.
(C) 청색 얼음과 녹색 얼음은 때때로 섞일 수 있다.
(D) 얼음 속 유기 물질은 노르스름한 색이다.

**6** 지문의 어구 "came across"와 의미가 가장 비슷한 것은?

(A) 발견했다
(B) 제시했다
(C) 확인했다
(D) 접근했다

**7** 다음 중 4단락에서 산화철에 관해 추론할 수 있는 것은?

(A) 그것의 색깔은 그것이 어디에 위치해 있는지에 따라 바뀐다.
(B) 그것의 존재는 빙하의 움직임을 방해한다.
(C) 그것은 남극 대륙의 빙하에서 발견되는 가장 흔한 광물이다.
(D) 그것은 남극 대륙의 기반암에서 발견된다.

**8** 4단락에 따르면, 다음 중 암분에 관해 사실이 아닌 것은?

(A) 그것은 미세하게 갈아진 돌로 이루어진다.
(B) 그것은 얼 때 청색으로 변한다.
(C) 그것은 빙하의 움직임에 의해 형성된다.
(D) 그것은 녹색 빙하의 구성 요소이다.

**9** 네 개의 네모[■]는 다음 문장이 삽입될 수 있는 곳을 나타내고 있다.

**햇빛이 얼음에 닿으면, 그것은 적색 빛을 흡수하고 청색 빛을 반사한다.**

이 문장은 어디에 들어가는 것이 가장 적절한가?

**10** 지시: 지문 요약을 위한 도입 문장이 아래에 주어져 있다. 지문의 가장 중요한 내용을 나타내는 보기 3개를 골라 요약을 완성하라. 어떤 문장은 지문에 언급되지 않은 내용이나 사소한 정보를 나타내므로 요약에 포함되지 않는다. 이 문제는 2점이다.

> 수백 년 동안 존재해 왔음에도 불구하고, 녹색 빙하는 과학자들에게 불가사의로 남아 있었다.
>
> · (B) 남극 대륙의 해빙으로 형성되는 빙하는 때때로 뚜렷한 색을 갖는다.
> · (D) 유기 물질은 그것의 노란 색깔 때문에 처음에 녹색 빙하의 원인에 대한 주요 후보가 되었다.
> · (E) 산화철을 함유하는 암분이 빙하가 녹색이 된 이유였다.

(A) 남극 대륙은 특이한 빙하 현상 때문에 과학자들에게 특별한 장소이다.
(C) 과학자들은 광물을 연구했어야 할 때 유기 물질을 연구하느라 시간을 너무 많이 보냈다.
(F) 녹색 빙하는 고농도의 철분 때문에 훨씬 더 가치가 있다.

## Vocabulary Review
본문 p.58

| 1 possessions | 2 untouched | 3 dissolved |
| 4 sustain | 5 hypothesized | 6 hardships |

**7** (B) **8** (A) **9** (C) **10** (D)
**11** (D) **12** (A) **13** (B) **14** (B)

---

CHAPTER 04
# Fact

## Example
본문 p.61

**1** (B)  **2** (D)

### 모뉴먼트 밸리

미국 남서부에 위치한 모뉴먼트 밸리는 붉은 모래사막에 있는 한 무리의 거대한 사암 암석의 형성물들이며, 이것들 중 가장 인상적인 것들은 높이가 250미터가 넘는다. 이 자연의 불가사의는 장기간에 걸쳐 발생한 지질 작용들의 결과이다.

¹수백만 년 전, 모뉴먼트 밸리의 위치는 고지대로 둘러싸여 있었다. 그 결과, 인근의 로키산맥에서 나온 많은 양의 암석과 모래가 그 지역에 퇴적되었다. 이것은 다양한 종류의 암석이 층층이 형성되도록 했다. 비슷한 시기에, 지하 깊숙한 곳으로부터의 압력이 점진적으로 저지대를 들어 올리면서, 고원이라 불리는 높은 평지를 만들었다.

이 시점에, 바람과 물이 그 고원의 일부를 파괴하기 시작했다. ²이 침식 과정은 다양한 암석층에 다르게 작용했고, 더 부드러운 것들이 더 단단한 것들보다 더 빠르게 침식했다. 모뉴먼트 밸리에서 볼 수 있는 형성물들은 가장 튼튼한 종류의 암석으로 구성되어 있다.

locate ⑧위치시키다　sandstone rock 사암 암석
formation ⑲형성물; 형성　impressive ⑳인상적인
wonder ⑲불가사의　geological ⑳지질의　occur ⑧발생하다
site ⑲위치　surround ⑧둘러싸다　deposit ⑧퇴적하다
gradually ⑨점진적으로　elevate ⑧들어 올리다　plateau ⑲고원
erosion ⑲침식　affect ⑧작용하다　wear away 침식하다
visible ⑳볼 수 있는　compose ⑧구성하다　durable ⑳튼튼한

**1** 2단락에 따르면, 다음 중 모뉴먼트 밸리에 관해 사실인 것은?

(A) 수역으로 둘러싸여 있었다.
(B) 인접한 지역들보다 낮았다.
(C) 로키산맥에 더 가까웠다.
(D) 한 종류의 암석으로만 구성되었다.

**2** 3단락에 따르면, 침식은 어떻게 모뉴먼트 밸리의 형성으로 이어졌는가?

(A) 다양한 암석의 층들을 형성했다.
(B) 고원의 표면을 평평하게 했다.
(C) 그 지역에 다양한 암석을 퇴적했다.
(D) 다른 물질에 다른 속도로 영향을 주었다.

## Reading Practice 1
본문 p. 62

**1** (A)　　**2** (B)　　**3** (D)　　**4** (B)

### Vocabulary Quiz

**1** ⓒ　　**2** ⓐ　　**3** ⓐ　　**4** ⓑ

### 무성 영화의 이야기 전달

1800년대 후반부터 1920년대까지, 영화는 소리 없이 제작되었다. 무성 영화로 알려진 그것들은 음악이나 음향 효과, 대화를 포함하지 않았다. 따라서, 그것들은 주로 시각적인 형태의 오락이었다. 이러한 한계에도 불구하고, 초기 영화 제작자들은 관객들에게 이야기를 전달하기 위해 여러 방법들을 개발했다.

가장 중요한 것 중 하나는 배우의 과장된 표정과 신체 언어 사용이었다. 이것은 등장인물의 감정을 관객들에게 명백하게 드러냈다. 예를 들어, 만약 한 등장인물이 놀라기로 되어 있었다면, 그 배우는 허공에 손을 들어 올리면서 눈을 크게 뜨곤 했다. 이러한 유형의 장면 동안에, 감독은 보통 배우의 얼굴에 카메라의 초점을 맞추곤 했다. ²근접 화면은 등장인물이 어떻게 느끼고 있는지 관객이 알기 쉽게 해주었다.

무성 영화는 또한 타이틀 카드를 포함했는데, 이것들은 장면들 사이에 있는, 글을 포함한 영화 프레임이었다. 그것들은 보통 대화나 등장인물의 내면의 생각을 보여주었다. 타이틀 카드는 현대 영화의 내레이터와 같은 역할을 하기도 했다. ³그것들은 화면에서 일어나고 있는 일에 대한 배경 정보를 제공하곤 했다. 무성 영화가 더욱 복잡해지면서, 타이틀 카드는 점점 더 중요해졌다. 영화 제작자들은 콘텐츠를 제작하기 위해 전문직 작가들과 함께 작업했다. 그들은 또한 삽화와 다른 장식적인 특징들을 만들기 위해 예술가들도 고용했다.

또 하나의 방법은 극장에 실황 연주자들을 고용하는 것이었다. 이것은 음악의 사용이 적절한 분위기를 만들고 기분을 표현할 수 있도록 했다. 영화 제작자들은 연주자들에게 영화들이 상영되는 동안 따를 지시사항들을 제공했다. 이것들은 보통 화면상의 연기에 맞는 음향 효과를 만드는 방법에 대한 정보를 포함했다. 예를 들어, 폭풍우의 천둥소리를 표현하기 위해 큰 드럼 소리가 연주될 수 있었다.

motion picture 영화　　silent film 무성 영화　　dialogue 똉대화
limitation 똉한계　　exaggerated 똉과장된
facial expression 표정　　be supposed to ~하기로 되어 있다
close-up shot 근접 화면　　display 똉보여주다
increasingly 뙝점점 더　　professional 똉전문직의
illustration 똉삽화　　decorative 똉장식적인　　feature 똉특징
employment 똉고용　　suitable 똉적절한, 알맞은
atmosphere 똉분위기　　instructions 똉지시사항
onscreen 똉화면상의　　represent 똉표현하다

**1** 지문의 단어 "exaggerated"와 의미가 가장 비슷한 것은?

(A) 지나치게 강조된
(B) 절제된
(C) 기발한
(D) 정확한

**2** 2단락에 따르면, 배우 얼굴의 근접 화면은

(A) 서로 다른 등장인물들 사이의 대화를 보여주었다
(B) 관객들이 감정 상태를 파악하도록 했다
(C) 관객들이 줄거리를 따라가도록 장려했다
(D) 신체 언어를 이해하기 어렵게 만들었다

**3** 무성 영화의 감독들은 어떻게 영화 관람객들에게 배경 정보를 제공했는가?

(A) 영화 촬영 세트장을 만들기 위해 예술가들이 고용되었다.
(B) 연주자들이 주제와 관련된 인기곡을 연주했다.
(C) 극장에 실황 내레이터들이 고용되었다.
(D) 몇 줄의 글이 영화에 포함되었다.

**4** 지문의 단어 "These"가 가리키는 것은?

(A) 극장
(B) 지시사항들
(C) 연주자들
(D) 영화들

## Reading Practice 2
본문 p. 64

**1** (D)　　**2** (B)　　**3** (A)　　**4** (D)

### Vocabulary Quiz

**1** ⓐ　　**2** ⓐ　　**3** ⓒ　　**4** ⓑ

### 점자 체계

점자는 시각 장애인들을 위한 글자 체계이다. 각 문자는 하나 이상의 볼록한 점들로 구성된다. 점자로 쓰여진 메시지는 시각 대신 촉각으로 읽힐 수 있다. 그것이 처음 개발된 이후, 점자는 전 세계에 걸쳐 시각적으로 장애가 있는 사람들에 의해 사용되게 되었다.

점자는 프랑스 황제 나폴레옹을 위해 만들어진 군사 암호에 기원이 있다. ¹그는 병사들이 밤에 빛을 사용하지 않고 메시지를 읽을 수 있는 방법을 원했다. 이에 답하여, 발명가 샤를 바르비에가 촉각으로 읽을 수 있는, 숫자를 쓰기 위한 볼록한 점들의 간단한 체계를 개발했다. 어린 나이에 시각을 잃었던 프랑스의 교육자 루이 브라유는 그 체계를 개선했다. 1905년까지, 브라유는 시각 장애인들을 위한 완전한 글자 체계를 만들어냈고, 그것은 그의 이름을 따서 명명되었다.

점자는 세계 많은 지역에서 사용되는 라틴 알파벳에 기초했다. 점자의 가장 기본적인 구성 요소는 칸이다. 이것은 여섯 개의 점들이 세 개씩 두 개의 세로열로 배열되어 있는 패턴이다. 알파벳의 특정 문자들을 나타내기 위해, 칸에는 서로 다른 점들이 솟아나 있다. 예를 들어, 칸의 좌측 상단에 있는 볼록한 점 하나는 문자 A를 상징한다. ³이 체계는 또한 구두점과 숫자 같은 다른 종류의 문자들도 포함한다.

점자가 다른 국가들로 확산되면서, 변형들이 도입되었다. 이것들은

언어들 사이의 차이 때문에 필요했다. [4]그러나, 1951년에, 다양한 점자 문자들 사이의 일관성을 확보하기 위해 국제회의가 열렸다. 이것은 라틴 알파벳이 아닌 글자들과 라틴 알파벳을 맞추기 위한 방법을 고안하는 것을 포함했다. 결과적으로, 한 국가에서 점자를 읽고 쓰는 능력을 얻은 시각 장애인은 보통 다른 국가에서 사용되는 문자를 읽을 수 있다.

character 몡문자   visually 붜시각적으로
impaired 헹장애가 있는   origin 몡기원   sight 몡시각
improve 둉개선하다   component 몡구성 요소
arrange 둉배열하다   column 몡세로열   specific 헹특정한
stand for ~을 상징하다   punctuation mark 구두점
variation 몡변형   international 헹국제의   conference 몡회의
ensure 둉확보하다   consistency 몡일관성   script 몡문자
achieve 둉얻다   literacy 몡읽고 쓰는 능력

**1** 샤를 바르비에에 의해 만들어진 체계의 목적은 무엇이었는가?

   (A) 적들에 의해 군사 계획이 읽혀지는 것을 방지했다.
   (B) 군대가 적군의 암호를 이해할 수 있게 했다.
   (C) 나폴레옹이 동맹국들에게 메시지를 보낼 수 있게 했다.
   (D) 병사들이 어둠 속에서 메모를 읽을 수 있게 했다.

**2** 지문의 어구 "stands for"와 의미가 가장 비슷한 것은?

   (A) 예약하다
   (B) 상징하다
   (C) 모방하다
   (D) 밝히다

**3** 3단락에 따르면, 점자의 특징은 무엇인가?

   (A) 구두점이 표현될 수 있다.
   (B) 필요하면 여섯 개 이상의 점들이 사용될 수 있다.
   (C) 모든 문자가 동일한 패턴으로 쓰여질 수 있다.
   (D) 하나의 점이 한 단어 전체를 표현할 수 있다.

**4** 4단락에 따르면, 1951년에 열린 다양한 점자 문자들에 관한 회의는

   (A) 그것들의 식자율을 알아내기 위해 열렸다
   (B) 그것들을 다른 국가들에 소개하기 위해 열렸다
   (C) 그것들의 오류를 제거하기 위해 열렸다
   (D) 그것들을 더 획일적으로 만들기 위해 열렸다

## Reading Practice 3
본문 p. 66

1 (C)   2 (A)   3 (B)   4 (D)

**Vocabulary Quiz**

1 ⓐ   2 ⓑ   3 ⓐ   4 ⓒ

### ADHD

주의력 결핍 과잉 행동 장애(ADHD)는 흔한 아동기 정신 건강 장애이다. 미국에서, 전체 아이들 중 거의 10퍼센트가 이 질환을 진단받았다. 그것은 환자들에게 심각한 문제들을 일으킬 수 있다.

ADHD는 학교에서 제 역할을 하는 것을 어렵게 만드는 다양한 증상들의 원인이 된다. [2]가장 두드러지게, 이 장애를 가진 아이들은 쉽게 산만해지고, 따라서 그들의 학업에 오랫동안 집중할 수 없다. 게다가, 그들은 가만히 앉아 있는 것에 어려움을 겪고, 자주 다른 이들을 방해할 것이다. 결과적으로, ADHD를 가진 아이들은 자주 꾸지람을 듣게 되고, 이것은 자존감 문제로 이어질 수 있다.

ADHD의 정확한 원인들은 밝혀지지 않았다. [3]그러나, 연구자들은 유전이 중요한 역할을 한다고 생각한다. 실제로, 최근의 한 연구는 이 장애를 가진 아이들의 75퍼센트가 ADHD를 가진 친척이 있다는 것을 보여준다. 다른 요인들 또한 이 질환의 발병 위험을 꽤 증가시킬 수 있다는 증거가 있다. 예를 들어, 어린 나이에 납과 같은 특정 유해 물질에 노출되는 것이 하나의 원인이 될 수 있다. 머리 부상도 ADHD의 발병으로 이어질 수 있다.

원인과 무관하게, ADHD는 치료할 수 있다. 일반적으로, 행동 치료만으로도 가벼운 증상에 대처하기에 충분하다. 치료사는 긍정적인 행동들은 장려하고 부정적인 것들을 막는 계획을 세우기 위해 아이와 부모 모두와 함께 노력할 것이다. [4]심각한 경우에는, 주의력을 개선하는 뇌 안의 화학 물질 생성을 증가시키는 약물이 처방될 수 있다. 다행스럽게도, 아이가 성인기에 도달하면 치료가 덜 필요해지는데, 이는 20대에 이르면 ADHD의 증상들이 보통 상당히 호전되기 때문이다.

condition 몡질환   diagnose 둉진단하다   approximately 붜거의
challenge 몡문제   symptom 몡증상   distract 둉산만하게 하다
interrupt 둉방해하다   get in trouble 꾸지람을 듣다
self-esteem 몡자존감   genetics 몡유전   moderately 붜꽤, 제법
exposure 몡노출   hazardous 헹유해한   substance 몡물질
contributor 몡원인   treatable 헹치료할 수 있는
cope with ~에 대처하다   discourage 둉막다
medication 몡약물   prescribe 둉처방하다

**1** 지문의 단어 "diagnosed"와 의미가 가장 비슷한 것은?

   (A) 치료되었다
   (B) 방지되었다
   (C) 확인되었다
   (D) 전염되었다

**2** 2단락에 따르면, ADHD는 아이들의 학교 성적에 영향을 미치는데, 이는 그것이

   (A) 집중하는 능력을 저해하기 때문이다
   (B) 에너지의 수준을 낮추기 때문이다
   (C) 대화를 피하게 하기 때문이다
   (D) 낯을 가리게 하기 때문이다

**3** 3단락에 따르면, 다음 중 아동 ADHD의 가장 흔한 원인으로 여겨지는 것은?

   (A) 인간 관계
   (B) 선천적인 특성
   (C) 해로운 화학 물질
   (D) 신체 부상

**4** 4단락에 따르면, ADHD 약물이 처방될 가능성이 가장 높은 때는 환자가

   (A) 다른 치료에 반응할 때이다
   (B) 성인기에 접어들 때이다
   (C) 행동 치료를 시작할 때이다
   (D) 심각한 증상들을 보일 때이다

## Reading Practice 4 본문 p. 68

1 (D)   2 (D)   3 (B)   4 (C)

**Vocabulary Quiz**

1 ⓐ   2 ⓒ   3 ⓒ   4 ⓐ

### 바빌론

대략 기원전 2300년에 건립된 바빌론은 오늘날의 바그다드 바로 남쪽의 유프라테스강 강가에 있었던 고대 도시이다. 그곳은 수천 년 동안 그 지역에서 중요한 권력의 중심지였다.

비록 그곳의 초기 역사에 대해서는 알려진 바가 거의 없지만, 바빌론은 기원전 1792년에 두각을 드러냈다. 이 연도는 함무라비 왕의 통치 기간의 시작으로 특징지어진다. 통치자로서 거의 40년 동안, 함무라비는 메소포타미아 남부의 도시 국가들 중 대부분을 정복했다. 그의 왕국은 바빌로니아 제1제국으로 알려지게 되었다. 그는 바빌론을 수도로 지정했고 방어 목적으로 그곳의 성벽을 강화했다. ²그는 또한 국민들을 위해 함무라비 법전이라 불리는 복잡한 법체계도 수립했다.

함무라비의 후손들은 수백 년 동안 바빌론을 통치했다. 이 기간 동안, 그 도시는 인구가 증가하여 세계에서 가장 큰 도시 중 하나가 되었다. 그때는 많은 인상적인 건축물들이 지어진 시기이기도 했다. 이것들은 에테메난키라고 불리고 추정상 높이가 90미터 이상이었던 거대한 신전을 포함했다. ³일부 역사학자들은 이것이 성경 속 바벨탑 이야기에 영감을 준 것이었다고 생각한다. 유감스럽게도, 바빌론은 기원전 1595년에 외국에 의해 정복당했다. 이것은 그 도시의 장기적인 쇠퇴로 이어졌다.

기원전 626년, 바빌론은 반란을 일으켰고, 이는 바빌로니아 제2제국의 시작을 나타냈다. ⁴새로운 왕국은 마침내 기존 바빌로니아 제국의 국경 너머까지 확장하였고, 중동의 대부분을 지배하게 되었다. 외국의 지배 기간 동안 방치되었던 많은 건축물들이 복원되었다. 그러나, 기원전 539년에, 그 도시는 다시 독립을 잃었다. 그 도시의 중요성은 서서히 줄어들었고, 기원전 275년쯤에, 그곳은 거의 완전히 버려졌다.

establish ⑧건립하다, 수립하다   rise to prominence 두각을 드러내다
reign ⑱통치 기간   conquer ⑧정복하다   city-state ⑱도시 국가
reinforce ⑧강화하다   defensive ⑱방어의   complex ⑱복잡한
descendant ⑱후손   govern ⑧통치하다
impressive ⑱인상적인   massive ⑱거대한
supposedly ⑨추정상   inspiration ⑱영감을 주는 것
decline ⑱쇠퇴   rebel ⑧반란을 일으키다   neglect ⑧방치하다
restore ⑧복원하다   independence ⑱독립   abandon ⑧버리다

**1** 지문의 단어 "reinforced"와 의미가 가장 비슷한 것은?

(A) 결합했다
(B) 검사했다
(C) 설계했다
(D) 강화했다

**2** 2단락에 따르면, 다음 중 함무라비 왕에 관해 사실인 것은?

(A) 새 도시를 건립했다.
(B) 십 년보다 짧게 통치했다.
(C) 외국의 제국과 동맹을 맺었다.
(D) 법률 체계를 만들었다.

**3** 글쓴이의 에테메난키에 대한 논의는 다음 중 무엇을 언급하는가?

(A) 함무라비 왕에 의해 지어졌다.
(B) 경전의 이야기에 영감을 주었다.
(C) 기원전 1595년에 파괴되었다.
(D) 외국 도시의 건물과 유사했다.

**4** 4단락에 따르면, 다음 중 바빌로니아 제2제국에 관해 사실인 것은?

(A) 새로운 농법을 개발했다.
(B) 통치했던 도시들에서 여러 반란에 직면했다.
(C) 제1제국보다 더 많은 영토를 지배했다.
(D) 기원전 275년까지 독립을 유지했다.

## iBT Reading Test 본문 p. 70

1 (B)   2 (B)   3 (D)   4 (D)
5 (D)   6 (D)   7 (A)   8 (C)
9 (D)   10 (B), (D), (E)

### 식물의 방어 기제

식물은 스스로를 방어할 수단이 없는 것처럼 보일 수도 있는데, 그것들이 사람의 눈에는 꽤 수동적으로 보일 수 있기 때문이다. 그러나, 모든 식물은 사실 포식자들에 맞서는 다양한 방어 방법들을 열심히 활용한다.

일반적으로, 가장 우선하는 방어책은 물리적이다. ²이것은, 가장 완강한 곤충들을 제외한 모든 것들을 들어오지 못하게 하는 여러 겹의 나무껍질과 같이, 장벽의 형태를 취할 수 있다. 많은 다른 식물들은 장미처럼 가시가 있거나 선인장처럼 따끔따끔한 가시털이 있다. 이것들은 초식동물들을 저지함으로써 식물군에게 적절한 이점을 준다. 몇몇 물리적인 방어책들은 훨씬 더 교묘하다. 예를 들어, 한 열대 덩굴 식물종은 잎에 헬리코니우스 나비의 알과 닮은 노란색 반점들을 가지고 있다. ³이것은 그 나비들이 알을 낳는 것을 막는데, 이는 이 곤충의 유충이 덩굴 식물을 먹고 살기 때문에 이점이다.

식물들은 화학적인 방어책을 이용하기도 한다. 만약 식물의 외부가 손상되거나 훼손되면, 그것은 다른 체계에 의지해야만 한다. ⁵따라서, 수천 년에 걸쳐, 식물들은 동물들이 피해야 한다고 학습한 쓴맛이 나는 화학 물질이나 유독한 독소를 생산해내도록 진화해왔다. 이차 대사물로 알려진 이러한 화학 물질들은 식물의 성장, 발달, 또는 번식에 직접적으로 관련되어 있지 않다. 다시 말해서, 그것들은 오로지 방어의 목적으로만 생산된다.

방어의 형태에서 가장 일반적인 두 가지이기는 하지만, 물리적인 기제와 화학적인 기제가 식물들이 사용할 수 있는 유일한 것들은 아니다. 예를 들어, 개미식물들은 개미와 공생 관계를 형성한다. ⁸ᴬ/⁸ᴮ그것들은 개미들이 먹을 꿀을 생산하며, 그들이 안에 집을 짓기에 적합한 속 빈 내부 구조를 가지고 있다. ⁸ᴰ이에 대한 보답으로, 개미들은 그 식물을 훼손하려는 모든 초식동물들을 공격할 것이다. 이것은 스스로를 보호하는 것에 관해서라면 식물들이 얼마나 기발해질 수 있는지를 보여준다.

means ⑱수단   passive ⑱수동적인   utilize ⑧활용하다
barrier ⑱장벽   determined ⑱완강한   prickly ⑱따끔따끔한
cactus ⑱선인장   flora ⑱식물군   deter ⑧저지하다
herbivore ⑱초식동물   discourage ⑧막다   larva ⑱유충

exterior 몡외부    compromise 동손상시키다
resort to ~에 의지하다    toxin 몡독소    metabolite 몡대사물
symbiotic 혱공생의    hollow 혱속이 빈    ingenious 혱기발한

**1** 지문의 단어 "passive"와 의미가 가장 비슷한 것은?

(A) 공격적인

(B) 소극적인

(C) 약한

(D) 비슷한

**2** 2단락에 따르면, 다음 중 나무들에 관해 사실인 것은?

(A) 그것들의 껍질은 가시나 가시털보다 덜 효과적인 방어책이다.

(B) 그것들의 외부는 오직 몇몇 곤충들에 의해서만 관통될 수 있다.

(C) 다른 식물 종에게 방어를 제공할 수 있다.

(D) 먹을 수 없는 겉싸개를 자라게 해서 초식동물을 저지한다.

**3** 다음 중 2단락에서 헬리코니우스 나비들에 관해 추론할 수 있는 것은?

(A) 그들이 모방하는 식물은 열대 지역에서만 발견된다.

(B) 각 유충은 많은 양의 덩굴 식물 잎을 먹는다.

(C) 그들의 알에 있는 노란색 반점들은 위장으로써 기능한다.

(D) 여러 개체가 같은 위치에 알을 낳는 것을 피할 것이다.

**4** 지문의 어구 "resort to"와 의미가 가장 비슷한 것은?

(A) 방해하다

(B) 보여주다

(C) 요구하다

(D) 활용하다

**5** 3단락에 따르면, 동물들은 화학적 독소가 있는 식물에 어떻게 반응하는가?

(A) 그것들이 자라거나 발달하지 못하게 한다.

(B) 그것들에 대한 생물학적 해독제를 발달시킨다.

(C) 어느 것들이 유독한지 알아낸다.

(D) 그것들을 피해야 한다는 것을 알게 된다.

**6** 아래 문장 중 지문 속의 음영된 문장의 핵심 정보를 가장 잘 표현한 것은? 오답은 문장의 의미를 크게 바꾸거나 핵심 정보를 생략한다.

(A) 식물들은 생존하기 위해 여러 종류의 방어 체계를 동시에 이용해야 한다.

(B) 다른 방어 체계를 이용하는 대부분의 식물들은 화학적이거나 물리적인 것들을 사용하지 않는다.

(C) 물리적이고 화학적인 기제는 그것들의 효과성 때문에 가장 일반적으로 사용된다.

(D) 물리적이고 화학적인 기제 외에 식물들이 이용하는 다른 방어의 형태들이 있다.

**7** 지문의 단어 "ingenious"와 의미가 가장 비슷한 것은?

(A) 영리한

(B) 모호한

(C) 길들여지지 않은

(D) 관대한

**8** 4단락에 따르면, 다음 중 개미식물에 관해 사실이 아닌 것은?

(A) 개미 거주에 적합한 구역들을 포함한다.

(B) 곤충이 먹는 물질을 만들어낸다.

(C) 많은 초식동물 종에게 유독하다.

(D) 다른 종류의 생물에 의해 보호된다.

**9** 네 개의 네모[■]는 다음 문장이 삽입될 수 있는 곳을 나타내고 있다.

**다시 말해서, 그것들은 오로지 방어의 목적으로만 생산된다.**

이 문장은 어디에 들어가는 것이 가장 적절한가?

**10** 지시: 지문 요약을 위한 도입 문장이 아래에 주어져 있다. 지문의 가장 중요한 내용을 나타내는 보기 3개를 골라 요약을 완성하라. 어떤 문장은 지문에 언급되지 않은 내용이나 사소한 정보를 나타내므로 요약에 포함되지 않는다. 이 문제는 2점이다.

> 식물들이 스스로를 보호할 수 없는 것처럼 보일 수도 있지만, 그들은 사실 포식자들에 맞서는 강력한 방어 체계를 가지고 있다.
>
> · (B) 물리적인 방어책들은 가시나 가시털과 같은 명백한 종류들에 더하여 다른 것들을 모방하는 것과 같은 덜 명백한 것들도 포함한다.
>
> · (D) 독은 물리적인 방어책이 작동하지 않을 때 이용되는 화학적인 방어책의 한 종류이다.
>
> · (E) 거의 모든 식물이 물리적 또는 화학적 방어 형태를 가지고 있지만, 일부는 포식자들에 맞서 더 특화된 방법들을 사용한다.

(A) 나무껍질은 여러 다른 겹들로 이루어져 있기 때문에 곤충들에게 방해물로 작용한다.

(C) 발달, 성장, 번식이 제한되는 식물들은 스스로를 보호하기에 너무 약하기 때문에 이차 대사물이 필요하다.

(F) 식물들과 곤충들은 각 종이 다른 동물들에 맞서 더 보호될 수 있도록 하는 공생 관계를 맺는다.

## Vocabulary Review 본문 p.74

| 1 means | 2 durable | 3 specific |
|---------|-----------|------------|
| 4 wonders | 5 governed | 6 exterior |

| 7 (A) | 8 (D) | 9 (D) | 10 (C) |
|-------|-------|-------|--------|
| 11 (B) | 12 (B) | 13 (C) | 14 (B) |

## CHAPTER 05
# Negative Fact

## Example 본문 p.77

1 (C)    2 (D)

### 팍스 로마나

'팍스 로마나'는 라틴어로 "로마의 평화"를 의미한다. 이 용어는 기원전 27년부터 서기 180년까지 두 세기 동안의 로마 제국의 평화와 번영을 가리킨다. 이 시기에, 로마 제국은 북서쪽의 영국에서부터 남동쪽의 이집트에까지 이르렀다. 세계 인구의 4분의 1이 로마의 통치하에 살았다.

줄리어스 시저의 암살 이후, 아우구스투스는 강력하고 효과적인 지도력으로 시민 반란을 끝냈다. 그는 로마의 국고에서 병사들에게 수당을 지급함으로써 반란의 위협을 제거했다. [1A]이것은 제국의 군사력을 강화했다. 아우구스투스는 방어하기 더 쉬운 국경을 확립했다. [1B]그는 또한 예속된 왕들에게 그들 스스로 지역적, 종교적 결정을 내릴 수 있게 허용함으로써 그가 정복한 영토들을 만족시켰다.

이후의 황제들은 안정과 번영의 시대를 지속했다. [1D/2C]제국의 부는 극동 지역과의 무역을 통해 확대되었다. 인도인들과 중국인들은 비단과 보석을 로마의 유리와 양탄자로 교환했다. 로마인들은 이 부를 사회 기반 시설에 투자했다. [2A]그들은 새로운 발명품인 콘크리트를 사용해 제국 전역에 도로들을 건설했다. [2B]그들은 또한 수도에 인상적인 반구형의 건축물들도 지었다. 이것은 현명한 황제 마르쿠스 아우렐리우스가 죽을 때까지 계속되었는데, 그는 그의 무능한 아들 코모두스에게 제국을 남겼다.

refer to ~을 가리키다    prosperity 명번영    era 명시기, 시대
assassination 명암살    bring an end to ~을 끝내다
civil 형시민의    unrest 명반란    rebellion 명반란
pension 명수당    treasury 명국고    military might 군사력
establish 동확립하다    territory 명영토, 지역    conquer 동정복하다
content 형만족하는    permit 동허용하다    stability 명안정
infrastructure 명사회 기반 시설    impressive 형인상적인
domed 형반구형의    incompetent 형무능한

1 글쓴이가 팍스 로마나의 특징으로 언급하지 않은 것은?

(A) 군사력
(B) 영토 정복
(C) 종교적 일치
(D) 경제적 번영

2 3단락에 따르면, 다음 중 로마 제국에 관해 사실이 아닌 것은?

(A) 콘크리트로 도로들을 건설했다.
(B) 인상적인 건축물을 만들었다.
(C) 극동 지역과 무역했다.
(D) 비단과 보석을 수출했다.

## Reading Practice 1

본문 p. 78

1 (C)    2 (B)    3 (C)    4 (B)

**Vocabulary Quiz**

1 ⓐ    2 ⓑ    3 ⓐ    4 ⓒ

### 플로리다 에버글레이즈

플로리다 남부에 위치한 에버글레이즈는 미국에서 가장 큰 아열대 습지이다. [2]우기 동안, 오키초비 호가 범람하여 에버글레이즈를 담수로 채운다. 이것은 풍부한 식물과 야생 동물 군락을 부양하는 거대한 습지대를 형성한다. 플로리다퓨마, 아메리카악어, 맹그로브를 포함한 2,000여 종이 넘는 희귀 동식물들이 에버글레이즈에 서식한다. 그것은 필수적인 생태계의 역할을 할 뿐만 아니라, 플로리다 사람들에게 식수도 제공한다.

그러나, 그것은 인간 활동에 의해 위협받는다. [3A]플로리다 남부의 홍수

를 방지하기 위한 노력은 에버글레이즈에 큰 피해를 입혀 왔다. [3B]땅이 사탕수수와 다른 작물들을 경작하는 데 이용될 수 있도록 대부분의 습지에서 물이 빠졌다. [3D]플로리다의 몇몇 도시들은 도로와 건물들을 습지 지역 안쪽으로 확장하기도 했다. 오늘날에는, 원래 습지의 절반도 되지 않는 지역만 남아 있다. 게다가, 외래의 식물들과 곤충들 같은 침입종들이 사람들에 의해 그 지역에 들어왔고 위협을 가한다. 서식지 상실과 식량원의 상실은 토착종의 멸종 위험을 높이고 있다. 결과적으로, 많은 동물 종들이 멸종 위기에 처해 있다. 예를 들어, 공원에는 100마리가 채 되지 않는 퓨마만이 남아 있으며, 섭금류의 개체 수는 90퍼센트 감소했다.

20년 동안, 생태학자들과 정치인들은 이 국가적 보물을 복원하기 위해 협력해왔다. [4C]2000년에, 미국 의회는 100억 달러라는 막대한 금액을 포괄적인 에버글레이즈 복원 계획(CERP)을 포함하는 대의명분에 쏟아부었다. [4A]그것의 목표는 에버글레이즈의 담수자원을 복원하고, 보호하고, 보존하는 것이다. 이것은 그 생태계를 사람들이 그 지역으로 이주하기 전과 더 비슷하게 만들 것이다. [4D]지역의 식수 또한 더 깨끗해질 것이다. 이 복원 프로젝트에 비용이 많이 들지도 모르지만, 그것은 동물과 사람 모두에게 많은 혜택들을 가져다줄 것이다.

subtropical 형아열대의    wetland 명습지    overflow 동범람하다
vast 형거대한, 막대한    marshland 명습지대    vital 형필수적인
ecosystem 명생태계    threaten 동위협하다    drain 동물을 빼내다
invasive species 침입종    exotic 형외래의
pose a threat 위협을 가하다    habitat 명서식지
extinction 명멸종    native species 토착종
endangered 형멸종 위기에 처한
wading bird (두루미·백로 등의) 섭금류    restore 동복원하다
devote 동(돈·시간을) 쏟아붓다    comprehensive 형포괄적인

1 지문의 단어 "vital"과 의미가 가장 비슷한 것은?

(A) 흔한
(B) 번성하는
(C) 필수적인
(D) 균형 잡힌

2 1단락에 따르면, 다음 중 플로리다 에버글레이즈에 관해 사실인 것은?

(A) 세계에서 가장 큰 습지이다.
(B) 계절에 따라 범람하는 호수로부터 물이 들어온다.
(C) 커다란 담수지로 물이 빠진다.
(D) 여러 독특한 생태계들을 포함한다.

3 2단락에 따르면, 다음 중 플로리다 에버글레이드에 대한 위협이 아닌 것은?

(A) 홍수 방지
(B) 농업 활동
(C) 멸종 위기종들
(D) 도시 개발

4 3단락에 따르면, 다음 중 CERP에 관해 사실이 아닌 것은?

(A) 에버글레이즈에 담수를 보존하는 것을 목표로 한다.
(B) 동물보다 사람에게 더 유익할 것이다.
(C) 거액의 돈을 필요로 한다.
(D) 그것의 혜택들은 개선된 식수를 포함한다.

**1** (C)　　**2** (B)　　**3** (C)　　**4** (B)

**Vocabulary Quiz**

**1** ⓑ　　**2** ⓐ　　**3** ⓒ　　**4** ⓐ

### 타지마할

¹타지마할은 인도 아그라에 위치한 흰 대리석으로 이루어진 거대한 복합 건물이다. ¹ᴬ그것은 무덤과 사원의 역할을 한다. ¹ᴮ무굴 왕조의 황제 샤 자한은 1632년에 그것이 건설되어야 한다고 명령했다. 400년이 지난 후에도, 그것은 변함없이 굉장히 아름답다. 무굴 건축 양식의 걸작으로서, 그것은 1983년에 유네스코 세계문화유산으로 지정되었다.

타지마할은 많은 이들에게 순수한 사랑의 상징으로 여겨진다. 전설에 따르면, 샤 자한이 대단히 사랑했던 그의 아내 뭄타즈 마할은 그들의 14번째 아이를 출산하던 중 사망했다. ²슬픔에 잠긴 채, 샤 자한은 그녀를 영원히 예우할 안식처를 건설하기로 결심했다. 그는 당대 최고의 건축가 여럿을 불러모았다. 그들은 완성하는 데 20,000여 명의 노동자와 22년이 필요한 대규모의 건축물을 설계했다. 샤 자한은 세계에서 가장 훌륭한 건축물만이 고인이 된 아내에게 걸맞은 가치가 있다고 주장했다.

타지마할은 그것의 건축학적인 가치로 인해 오랫동안 인정받아왔다. 그것은 많은 요소들이 서로 다른 면에 반사되어 있는 듯한 완벽한 대칭으로 건축되었다. 예를 들어, 그것의 중앙 무덤은 사람들이 예배하러 올 수 있는 쌍둥이 사원들로 둘러싸여 있다. ⁴ᴬ네 개의 각 모서리는 첨탑이라 불리는 높고 폭이 좁은 똑같은 탑으로 장식되어 있다. ⁴ᴬ이전의 무굴 건축 양식에서는 전례가 없던 이 첨탑들은 타지마할이 서로 다른 양식들을 어떻게 결합하는지 보여준다. ⁴ᶜ사원들은 적색 사암으로 이루어졌고, 이는 이전의 무굴 건축에서 전통적인 것이었다. 하지만, 무덤은 흰 대리석으로 만들어졌고, 이는 다른 인도 전통에서 일반적인 것이었다. 게다가, 타지마할의 반구형 지붕은 페르시아 양식이다. 타지마할이 인도, 페르시아, 이슬람 양식의 결합에 있어서 가장 훌륭한 예시로 여겨지는 것은 놀랄 일이 아니다.

enormous 혱거대한　　complex 몡복합 건물　　marble 몡대리석
mosque 몡사원　　command 동명령하다
stunning 혱굉장히 아름다운　　masterpiece 몡걸작
architecture 몡건축 양식, 건축물　　designate 동지정하다
symbol 몡상징　　beloved 혱대단히 사랑하는
resting place 안식처　　insist 동주장하다　　recognize 동인정하다
symmetry 몡대칭　　worship 동예배하다　　identical 혱똑같은
narrow 혱폭이 좁은　　unprecedented 혱전례가 없는

**1**　1단락에 따르면, 다음 중 타지마할에 관해 사실이 아닌 것은?

　　(A) 무덤의 역할을 한다.
　　(B) 무굴의 통치자에 의해 지어졌다.
　　(C) 1983년에 복원되었다.
　　(D) 건축에 대리석이 사용되었다.

**2**　2단락에 따르면, 샤 자한이 타지마할을 지은 이유는 그가

　　(A) 그의 권력을 보여주고 싶었기 때문이다
　　(B) 아내를 위한 기념비를 짓고 싶었기 때문이다
　　(C) 사람들이 예배할 곳을 필요로 했기 때문이다
　　(D) 다양한 건축 양식들을 높이 평가했기 때문이다

**3**　지문의 단어 "symmetry"와 의미가 가장 비슷한 것은?

　　(A) 통합
　　(B) 다양성
　　(C) 균형
　　(D) 혁신

**4**　3단락에 따르면, 타지마할을 두드러지게 하는 이유가 아닌 것은?

　　(A) 다양한 건축 양식들을 결합한 것
　　(B) 각 측면에 다양한 디자인을 보여준 것
　　(C) 다양한 건축 재료를 사용한 것
　　(D) 같은 크기의 탑 네 개를 포함한 것

---

**1** (D)　　**2** (A)　　**3** (B)　　**4** (C)

**Vocabulary Quiz**

**1** ⓑ　　**2** ⓒ　　**3** ⓐ　　**4** ⓑ

### 동물들은 지진을 예측할 수 있을까?

수 세기 동안 지진 활동과 동물의 행동 사이의 연관성이 제기되어 왔다. ¹ᴮ기원전 373년의 강력한 지진이 일어나기 며칠 전에 그리스의 철학자 아리스토텔레스는 쥐, 뱀, 지네가 그들의 집 밖으로 기어 나오는 것을 목격했다. ¹ᶜ1989년에는, 한 지질학자가 신문 광고에 실린 다수의 반려동물 실종신고에 근거하여 지진을 예측했다. ¹ᴬ동물원 사육사들은 2011년의 지진이 일어나기 15분 전에 비정상적으로 소란스러운 여우원숭이들을 기록했다. 지진 전의 동물들의 이러한 특이 행동은 인간들에게 유용할 수 있다. 그것은 우리에게 아직 신뢰할 만한 장기적인 지진 예측 능력이 없기 때문이다.

동물들이 어떻게 지진이 온다는 것을 아는지는 아무도 모르지만, 한 가지 이론은 그들이 땅속의 진동을 감지할 수 있다고 시사한다. 제1차파와 제2차파(P파와 S파)로 알려진, 이러한 진동들은 지하의 암석들이 이동할 때 발생한다. ²ᴰP파는 초당 1에서 14킬로미터의 속도로 암석을 통과하여 이동한다. ²ᴮ2분 뒤에, 지면을 움직이게 하는 격렬한 S파가 일어난다. ²ᶜ동물들은 사람들이 알아차리지 못하는 더 약한 P파를 감지할 수 있을지도 모른다. 그러나, 그것은 겨우 2분 정도 앞선 경보만을 제공할 것이다.

또 하나의 가능성 있는 설명은, 동물들이 지진 며칠 전에 불편을 느낄지도 모른다는 것이다. 일부 과학자들은 지각이 이동할 때 지각에서 나온 분자들이 전하를 띠게 된다고 생각한다. 이 이온들은 공기 중으로 방출된다. 동물들은 아마 그들의 털로 이 이온화를 감지할 것이다. ⁴이것이 그 지역에서 벗어나고자 하는 동물들의 욕구를 설명할지도 모른다. 그것은 또한 사로잡힌 동물들이 왜 가만히 있지 못하는지를 설명할 것이다.

그럼에도 불구하고, 동물의 지진 예측에 대한 확실한 증거는 거의 없다. 그 발상은 대부분 확인되지 않은 이야기들에 근거하고 있다. 우리가 지진에 대한 조기 경보 시스템으로 동물의 특이한 행동 패턴을 활용할 수 있기까지는 더 많은 실험들이 필요하다.

association 몡연관성　　seismic activity 지진 활동
philosopher 몡철학자　　centipede 몡지네　　geologist 몡지질학자
predict 동예측하다　　behavior 몡행동　　ability 몡능력

vibration 명 진동　underground 형 지하의　violent 형 격렬한
detect 동 감지하다　advance 형 사전의　release 동 방출하다
ionization 명 이온화　desire 명 욕구; 바람　captive 형 사로잡힌
restless 형 가만히 있지 못하는　solid 형 확실한
unconfirmed 형 확인되지 않은

**1** 1단락에 따르면, 다음 중 지진 이전에 발생한 것이 아닌 것은?

(A) 동물원의 동물들이 소란을 피우는 것
(B) 뱀들이 땅 밖으로 나오는 것
(C) 반려동물들이 실종되는 것
(D) 쥐들이 한곳에 모이는 것

**2** 2단락에 따르면, 다음 중 P파에 관해 사실이 아닌 것은?

(A) 지면이 흔들리게 한다.
(B) S파보다 먼저 일어난다.
(C) 동물들에 의해 감지될 수 있다.
(D) 암석을 통과할 수 있다.

**3** 지문의 단어 "restless"와 의미가 가장 비슷한 것은?

(A) 복잡한
(B) 불안한
(C) 의욕을 가진
(D) 아픈

**4** 3단락에 따르면, 지진 전 공기의 이온화는 동물들이 왜

(A) 사람들보다 P파에 더 민감한지 설명할 것이다
(B) 지진 후에 울렁거림을 느끼는지 설명할 것이다
(C) 지진 활동 지역에서 도망치는지 설명할 것이다
(D) 지각의 이동을 느끼는지 설명할 것이다

---

## Reading Practice 4　본문 p.84

1 (C)　2 (D)　3 (A)　4 (C)

**Vocabulary Quiz**

1 ⓐ　2 ⓐ　3 ⓑ　4 ⓒ

---

### 토템폴

토템폴은 동물이나 사람의 형태로 조각된 높은 나무탑이다. ¹ᴬ/¹ᴰ그것들은 일반적으로 북미 태평양 연안의 북서부 지역 토착민들에 의해 삼나무로 만들어진다. ¹ᴮ전통적으로 이 북미 원주민들은 뾰족하게 깎은 돌, 조개껍데기, 또는 뼈를 이용해 손으로 토템폴을 조각했다. 그러나, 오늘날에는 현대의 목각 도구들이 사용된다. 토템폴이 완성되면, 그것은 포틀래치라고 불리는 의례적인 행사 동안 세워진다.

이 독특한 예술품들은 북서부 북미 원주민 문화에서 다양한 목적을 수행한다. ³ᴮ가장 흔하게는, 새로 온 사람들을 환영하기 위해 마을의 해변이나 집 입구의 통로에 환영의 기둥이 설치된다. ³ᴰ때때로 그 조각들은 해를 끼치고자 하는 낯선 사람들에게 겁을 주어 쫓아내려는 목적으로 쓰이기도 한다. 수치심 기둥은 잘못을 저지른 사람을 조롱하기 위해 전시된다. ³ᶜ특정 종류의 토템폴은 죽은 사람을 기억하기 위한 기념비로 설계된다. 그것들은 묘지 표석의 역할을 하거나 심지어는 고인의 유해를 담고 있을 수도 있다.

---

더 중요하게는, 토템폴은 한 가문의 역사를 알리기 위해 사용된다. 흔히, 별개의 가문들은 기둥 위의 중요한 위치를 차지하는 서로 다른 상징 동물들을 가진다. 토템폴에 조각되는 흔한 동물들은 곰, 독수리, 개구리, 범고래, 심지어 모기도 포함한다. ⁴각 가문의 토템은 각 동물의 능력에 기반한 힘을 지닌다고 여겨진다. 예를 들어, 곰은 신체적인 힘을 상징하고 독수리는 자유와 용기를 나타낸다. 토템폴에 조각된 각각의 형상들은 또한 그 가문의 선조들의 삶에서 중요한 사건들을 나타내기도 한다. 이와 같이, 토템폴은 일종의 교과서처럼 기능하면서, 세대에서 세대로 부족의 역사를 보존한다.

carve 동 조각하다　indigenous 형 토착의
sharpened 형 뾰족하게 깎은　ceremonial 형 의례적인
distinctive 형 독특한　purpose 명 목적　entryway 명 입구의 통로
newcomer 명 새로 온 사람　scare off ~에게 겁을 주어 쫓아내다
ridicule 동 조롱하다　memorial 명 기념비　remains 명 유해
the deceased 고인　occupy 동 차지하다　prominent 형 중요한
symbolize 동 상징하다　represent 동 나타내다　ancestor 명 선조
function 동 기능하다　preserve 동 보존하다

**1** 1단락에서 토템폴에 대한 다음 질문 중 답하지 못하는 것은?

(A) 그것들은 무엇으로 만들어졌는가?
(B) 그것들을 조각하기 위해 과거에 어떤 도구들이 사용되었는가?
(C) 그것들을 만드는 데 얼마나 오래 걸리는가?
(D) 누가 그것들을 만드는가?

**2** 지문의 단어 "ridicule"과 의미가 가장 비슷한 것은?

(A) 보호하다
(B) 허락하다
(C) 고마워하다
(D) 놀리다

**3** 2단락에 따르면, 다음 중 토템폴의 기능이 아닌 것은?

(A) 주요 축제일들을 기념하는 것
(B) 집의 손님을 환영하는 것
(C) 고인에게 예의를 표하는 것
(D) 원치 않는 방문자들을 제지하는 것

**4** 3단락에 따르면, 토템폴의 힘은

(A) 그것을 소유한 가문의 지위에서 나온다
(B) 그것의 물리적인 위치의 중요성에서 나온다
(C) 그것이 포함하는 동물들의 특징들에서 나온다
(D) 그것을 조각한 사람의 능력들에서 나온다

---

### iBT Reading Test　본문 p.86

1 (C)　2 (A)　3 (B)　4 (B)
5 (A)　6 (B)　7 (B)　8 (A)
9 (C)　10 (A), (D), (E)

---

### 우리가 하품하는 이유

우리는 하품이 무엇인지 안다. 그것은 입을 벌리고 깊은 숨을 들이마시는 행동이다. 하품하는 것만큼 보편적인 행동은 거의 없다. 모든 종류의 사람들이 하품한다. 심지어 개, 뱀, 물고기와 같은 동물들도 하품

한다. 우리는 하품하게 될 가능성이 가장 높을 때가 언제인지 안다. ³ᴰ우리가 지치거나 피로할 때, 하품이 뒤따르기 마련이다. ³ᶜ그것은 종종 사람이 일어나자마자 가장 먼저 하게 되는 것이다. ³ᴬ때때로 하품은 지루함의 징후이다.

그럼에도 불구하고, 우리는 아직 하품하는 것이 어떤 생물학적 목적을 수행하는지 모른다. 한 가지 일반적인 생각은, 사람들이 체내에 더 많은 산소를 받아들이기 위해 하품한다는 것이다. ⁷우리가 일반적인 호흡을 할 때보다 하품하는 동안 더 많은 산소를 들이마시고 더 많은 이산화탄소를 내쉬는 것은 사실이다. 그러나, 연구들은 사용 가능한 산소의 양이 우리가 하품할 가능성과 어떠한 관계도 없다는 것을 보여주었다. 보다 가능성 있는 설명은 우리가 스스로를 깨우기 위해 하품한다는 것이다. 이것은 하품이 기지개 켜는 것을 동반하고, 둘 다 졸음을 떨치는 데 도움이 되기 때문이다. 하품하는 것은 또한 각성도를 높이고 우리가 주변 환경을 관찰하는 것을 돕는 귓속 근육을 자극한다. ⁶놀랍게도, 우리가 뇌를 식히기 위해 하품한다는 것 또한 가능성이 있다. 우리가 하품할 때 들이마시는 공기는 뇌로 흐르는 혈액의 온도를 낮춘다.

하품은 또한 개인 간 유대감을 형성하며, 사회적인 목적을 수행한다. ⁸하품과 공감 사이에는 관련성이 있는데, 당신이 누군가에게 감정적으로 더 가까울수록, 당신이 전염되어 하품할 가능성이 더 높다. 더 높은 공감 수준을 가진 사람들은 다른 사람이 하품하는 것을 인지할 때 하품할 가능성이 더 높다. 과학자들은 여전히 이 현상을 연구 중이다. 매우 흔하지만 거의 이해되지 못한 또 다른 행동을 생각해내기는 어렵다.

yawn 동하품하다; 명하품   universal 형보편적인
description 명종류   fatigued 형피로한   boredom 명지루함
biological 형생물학적인   inhale 동들이마시다   exhale 동내쉬다
carbon dioxide 이산화탄소   available 형사용 가능한
likelihood 명가능성   stimulate 동자극하다   alertness 명각성도
monitor 동관찰하다   surroundings 명주변 환경   bond 명유대감
connection 명관련성   empathy 명공감
emotionally 부감정적으로   contagiously 부전염되어
phenomenon 명현상

**1** 지문의 단어 "universal"과 의미가 가장 비슷한 것은?

(A) 복잡한
(B) 비범한
(C) 널리 퍼진
(D) 유연한

**2** 글쓴이는 왜 "dogs, snakes, and fish"를 언급하는가?

(A) 하품하는 것이 사람에게만 국한되어 있지 않다는 증거를 제시하기 위해
(B) 하품하는 것이 필수적인 신체 기능이라고 주장하기 위해
(C) 인간과 동물 사이의 차이점을 언급하기 위해
(D) 더 많은 연구가 수행되어야 한다는 것을 보여주기 위해

**3** 1단락에 따르면, 사람이 하품하게 할 수 있는 것이 아닌 것은?

(A) 지루함을 느끼는 것
(B) 스트레스를 받는 것
(C) 잠에서 깨는 것
(D) 피곤한 것

**4** 아래 문장 중 지문 속의 음영된 문장의 핵심 정보를 가장 잘 표현한 것은? 오답은 문장의 의미를 크게 바꾸거나 핵심 정보를 생략한다.

(A) 산소와 하품하는 것 사이의 관계가 연구되었다.
(B) 연구들은 하품하는 것과 사용 가능한 산소의 관련성을 보여주는 것에 실패했다.
(C) 연구들에 따르면, 사람들은 불충분한 산소를 접하기 때문에 하품한다.
(D) 주변 환경의 산소는 하품할 가능성에 영향을 미친다.

**5** 지문의 단어 "monitor"와 의미가 가장 비슷한 것은?

(A) 관찰하다
(B) 장소를 알아내다
(C) 길을 찾다
(D) 확인하다

**6** 2단락에 따르면, 하품하는 것은 뇌에 어떤 영향을 미치는가?

(A) 인지 기능을 향상시킨다.
(B) 전반적인 온도를 낮춘다.
(C) 근육 활동을 자극한다.
(D) 혈액의 흐름을 증가시킨다.

**7** 2단락에 따르면, 다음 중 하품하는 것에 관해 사실인 것은?

(A) 이산화탄소의 흡수를 막는다.
(B) 신체의 산소 공급을 증가시킨다.
(C) 턱 근육에만 관련이 있다.
(D) 각성도를 높이지 않는다.

**8** 다음 중 3단락에서 전염성 있는 하품에 관해 추론할 수 있는 것은?

(A) 친구들과 가족 구성원들 사이에서 가장 흔히 일어난다.
(B) 시각보다는 청각 신호에 의해 촉발된다.
(C) 영향을 받은 사람들에게 더 큰 공감을 낳는다.
(D) 성인보다 아이들에게서 더 흔하게 관찰된다.

**9** 네 개의 네모[■]는 다음 문장이 삽입될 수 있는 곳을 나타내고 있다.

이것은 하품이 기지개 켜는 것을 동반하고, 둘 다 졸음을 떨치는 데 도움이 되기 때문이다.

이 문장은 어디에 들어가는 것이 가장 적절한가?

**10** 지시: 지문 요약을 위한 도입 문장이 아래에 주어져 있다. 지문의 가장 중요한 내용을 나타내는 보기 3개를 골라 요약을 완성하라. 어떤 문장은 지문에 언급되지 않은 내용이나 사소한 정보를 나타내므로 요약에 포함되지 않는다. 이 문제는 2점이다.

> **하품하는 것에는 가능한 여러 기능들이 있다.**
> · (A) 하품하는 것은 모든 사람들과 많은 동물들이 하는 행동이다.
> · (D) 하품하는 것의 생물학적 목적은 여전히 불확실하다.
> · (E) 하품은 사람들 사이에서 사회적인 역할을 하는 것으로 보인다.

(B) 하품은 입을 크게 벌리고 공기를 더 많이 들이쉬는 것을 수반한다.
(C) 과학자들은 하품하는 것이 기온의 변화에 의해 유발된다고 생각한다.
(F) 사람들은 다른 사람이 하품하는 것을 보면 종종 하품할 것이다.

1 violent          2 extinction       3 fatigued
4 description       5 might            6 unrest
7 (A)    8 (C)      9 (B)    10 (B)
11 (D)   12 (C)     13 (D)   14 (C)

# CHAPTER 06
# Inference

## Example
본문 p.93

1 (D)    2 (D)

### 문어의 지능

문어들은 그것들이 먹이를 사냥하고 포식동물들을 피할 수 있게 해주는 많은 특징들을 가지고 있다. 예를 들어, 어떤 것들은 주변 환경과 뒤섞이도록 모양과 색을 바꿀 수 있다. 그러나, 문어의 가장 인상적인 특성은 높은 지능이다.

동물의 지능에 대한 일반적인 척도는 그것의 몸의 크기와 비교한 뇌의 크기이다. 문어의 몸에서 뇌의 비율은 다른 모든 무척추동물과 일부 척추동물보다 크다. [1]그러나, 그것의 상대적인 뇌 크기는 포유류의 그것과 같은 수준에는 미치지 못한다.

문어의 행동 또한 그것이 지능적이라는 것을 입증한다. 어떤 것들은 도구를 사용하는 것이 관찰되어 왔다. 예를 들어, 인도네시아에서 관찰된 일부 문어들은 해저에서 부서진 코코넛 껍질들을 모으고 그것들에서 진흙을 털어낸다. 그런 다음 그 문어들은 그것들로 보호용 은신처를 지을 적당한 장소를 찾을 것이다.

문어들은 또한 문제를 해결할 수 있는 능력을 갖추고 있다. 한 실험에서, 연구자들은 문어 한 마리를 마지막에 보상이 있는 미로에 넣었다. [2]그 문어는 미로를 빠져나가는 길을 찾을 수 있었을 뿐만 아니라 실험의 매회마다 그것을 더 빠르게 할 수 있었다. 이것은 그것이 문제의 해답을 기억했다는 것을 시사한다.

characteristic 몡특징    prey 몡먹이    predator 몡포식동물
blend into ~과 뒤섞이다    impressive 휑인상적인
intelligence 몡지능    compared to ~과 비교한    ratio 몡비율
invertebrate 몡무척추동물    vertebrate 몡척추동물
comparative 휑상대적인    mammal 몡포유류
demonstrate 됭입증하다    observe 됭관찰하다
suitable 휑적당한    protective 휑보호용의    shelter 몡은신처
solve 됭해결하다    maze 몡미로    reward 몡보상

1  다음 중 2단락에서 동물의 지능에 관해 추론할 수 있는 것은?
   (A) 뇌의 전체적인 크기가 생물의 지능을 결정한다.
   (B) 문어들은 일부 포유류보다 더 높은 지능을 가지고 있다.
   (C) 몸에서 뇌의 비율은 일반적으로 지능과 관련이 없다.
   (D) 문어는 포유류보다 지능이 낮다.

2  글쓴이가 미로를 포함하는 실험에 관해 암시하는 것은?
   (A) 모든 미로에 각기 다른 문어가 사용되었다.
   (B) 매회마다 더 어려운 미로가 설치되었다.
   (C) 첫 번째 시도가 가장 빨리 완수되었다.
   (D) 동일한 경로가 여러 차례 제공되었다.

## Reading Practice 1
본문 p.94

1 (C)    2 (D)    3 (A)    4 (A)

**Vocabulary Quiz**

1 ⓒ    2 ⓑ    3 ⓒ    4 ⓒ

### 깨진 유리창 이론

깨진 유리창 이론은 눈에 보이는 어떤 범죄의 징후가 그 이상의 범죄행위를 조장한다고 주장한다. 그것은 또한 더 심각한 범죄를 예방하기 위해 경찰이 경범죄에 대해 법률을 집행해야 한다고 제안한다. 그러나 이 접근법의 유효성에는 논란의 여지가 있다.

이 이론은 1982년에 미국의 사회 과학자 제임스 윌슨과 조지 켈링에 의해 처음으로 제안되었다. [2]그들은 유리창이 깨진 건물과 같이, 사회적 무질서의 작은 징후조차 한 지역이 방치되어 있다는 신호라고 주장했다. 이것은 주민들이 더 파괴적인 행동을 하도록 부추겼다. 결국, 심각한 범죄들이 주기적으로 일어날 것이었다.

그들의 제안은 정치인들에게 많은 관심을 받았다. 특히, 루돌프 줄리아니는 1993년에 그가 뉴욕 시장으로 당선되었을 때, 그 이론을 적용하기로 결정했다. [3]그 결과, 이 도시의 경찰관들은 공공장소에서의 음주와 지하철 요금 회피 같은 경범죄를 엄중히 단속하기 위해 엄청난 노력을 기울이기 시작했다. 이 전략은 거의 20년 동안 계속 사용되었다. 연구들은 그것이 성공적이었다는 것을 시사해왔다. 이 기간 동안, 그 도시 전역에 걸쳐 경범죄와 중대 범죄 모두 50퍼센트의 감소했다.

이것에도 불구하고, 일부 전문가들은 이 치안 유지 방법의 유효성에 의문을 제기해왔다. 그들은 뉴욕시가 범죄의 감소를 경험했다는 것에는 동의한다. 그러나, 그들은 그것이 깨진 유리창 이론을 적용함으로써 야기된 것이 아니라고 주장한다. 같은 기간 동안, 미국의 거의 모든 대도시가 치안 유지 전략과 관계없이 상당한 범죄의 감소를 경험했다. [4]이것은 경제 발전 때문일 가능성이 높았다. 그것은 그 나라 전역에 걸친 실업과 빈곤의 감소로 이어졌다.

visible 휑눈에 보이는    encourage 됭조장하다
enforce a law 법률을 집행하다    minor crime 경범죄
effectiveness 몡유효성    debatable 휑논란의 여지가 있는
indication 몡징후    disorder 몡무질서    uncared for 방치된
prompt 됭부추기다    disruptive 휑파괴적인    apply 됭적용하다
devote 됭(노력 등을) 기울이다    crack down on ~을 엄중히 단속하다
evasion 몡회피    reduction 몡감소    policing 몡치안 유지
regardless of ~과 관계없이    unemployment 몡실업
poverty 몡빈곤

1  지문의 단어 "debatable"과 의미가 가장 비슷한 것은?
   (A) 적절한
   (B) 증명할 수 있는

(C) 불확실한

(D) 모욕적인

**2** 2단락에서 추론할 수 있는 것으로, 윌슨과 켈링은 중대 범죄가

(A) 주민들로 하여금 지역을 떠나게 한다고 생각했다

(B) 도시 내의 사회적 무질서의 주된 요인이라고 생각했다

(C) 다른 이들보다 건물 소유주들에게 더 영향을 미친다고 생각했다

(D) 관리가 잘 된 지역에서는 일어날 가능성이 낮다고 생각했다

**3** 글쓴이가 1993년 이전 뉴욕시의 경찰관들에 관해 암시하는 것은?

(A) 경범죄를 없애는 것에 집중하지 않았다.

(B) 범죄율을 낮추는 데 성공적이었다.

(C) 한 중요한 연구의 연구 대상이었다.

(D) 루돌프 줄리아니의 전략을 지지하지 않았다.

**4** 4단락에 따르면, 전국적인 범죄 감소의 가장 가능성이 높은 원인은?

(A) 경제 성장이 이루어졌다.

(B) 범죄에 대한 처벌이 강해졌다.

(C) 빈곤 퇴치 계획이 도입되었다.

(D) 치안 유지 방법이 더욱 발전되었다.

---

## Reading Practice 2　　　　　본문 p. 96

**1** (D)　　**2** (D)　　**3** (D)　　**4** (B)

### Vocabulary Quiz

**1** ⓑ　　**2** ⓑ　　**3** ⓐ　　**4** ⓒ

---

### 나스카 지상화

페루 남부에 위치한 나스카 지상화는 사막의 땅에 새겨진 그림들이다. 그것들 대부분이 너무 커서 공중에서만 관찰될 수 있다. 1927년에 그것들이 발견된 이후, 고고학자들은 그것들의 기원과 목적을 알아내기 위해 노력해오고 있다.

나스카 지상화는 나스카인들의 작품이며, 그들은 기원전 100년부터 서기 700년까지 그 지역에 거주했다. 그들은 그 그림들을 계획하기 위해 밧줄이 부착된 말뚝을 사용했다고 여겨진다. 그리고, 작업자들은 밧줄들을 따라가면서 땅에서 바위들을 제거했을 것이다. [1]이것은 그 선들이 눈에 잘 보이게 해주었는데, 지면의 바위들은 빨간색이고 아래의 모래는 노란색이기 때문이다.

이 기법들은 나스카인들이 다양한 종류의 그림들을 창작하는 것을 가능하게 했다. 가장 기본적인 것은 직선들로, 그것들 중 일부는 길이가 40킬로미터가 넘는다. 삼각형과 나선형 같은 기하학적인 모양들도 존재한다. [2]가장 복잡한 것은 동물 묘사이다. 예를 들어, 콘도르 묘사는 길이가 대략 130미터이며 발, 날개, 부리와 같은 많은 특징들을 포함한다.

연구자들은 오랫동안 나스카 지상화의 목적에 관해 논쟁해왔다. 인기 있는 초기 이론은 그것들이 천문학적 표지였다는 것이다. 이것은 당시의 많은 고대 유물들이 특정 날짜에 별이 어디에 위치할 것인지를 나타내기 때문이다. [4]그러나, 오늘날 대부분의 전문가들은 나스카 지상화가 종교 의식에 이용되었다는 것에 동의한다. 나스카인들은 신들이 비를 내리도록 격려하기 위해 그 선들을 따라 걸었다. 이 이론은 거미와

---

원숭이같이, 묘사된 동물들 중 많은 것들이 나스카 문화에서 물과 관련이 있었다는 사실에 의해 뒷받침된다.

carve ⑧새기다　　archaeologist ⑲고고학자
determine ⑧알아내다　　origin ⑲기원　　inhabit ⑧거주하다
stake ⑲말뚝　　visibility ⑲눈에 잘 보임, 가시성　　surface ⑲지면
geometric ⑲기하학적인　　spiral ⑲나선형　　portrayal ⑲묘사, 그림
depiction ⑲묘사　　numerous ⑲많은　　feature ⑲특징
debate ⑧논쟁하다　　indicate ⑧나타내다　　position ⑧위치시키다
religious ⑲종교적인　　ritual ⑲의식
be associated with ~과 관련이 있다

**1** 2단락에 따르면, 나스카 지상화를 더 눈에 띄게 만든 것은?

(A) 새겨진 그림들의 길이

(B) 색깔이 있는 밧줄의 활용

(C) 큰 바위들의 배치

(D) 아래에 깔린 모래의 노출

**2** 3단락에서 글쓴이가 동물 묘사에 관해 암시하는 것은?

(A) 모든 나스카 지상화 중에서 가장 크다.

(B) 당초에 생각했던 것보다 상당히 더 오래되었다.

(C) 복잡한 기하학적 모양들을 포함하는 경향이 있다.

(D) 다른 그림들보다 더 많은 세부 묘사를 포함한다.

**3** 지문의 단어 "rituals"와 의미가 가장 비슷한 것은?

(A) 가르침

(B) 희생

(C) 준비

(D) 의식

**4** 4단락에서 추론할 수 있는 것으로, 나스카 지상화가 천문학적 표지로 기능했다는 이론은

(A) 고고학자들 사이에서 결코 큰 지지를 받지 못했다

(B) 다른 설명을 위해 폐기되었다

(C) 나스카 문화에 관한 오해에 근거했다

(D) 당시의 다른 유물들에 대한 통찰력을 제공했다

---

## Reading Practice 3　　　　　본문 p. 98

**1** (C)　　**2** (C)　　**3** (A)　　**4** (D)

### Vocabulary Quiz

**1** ⓐ　　**2** ⓑ　　**3** ⓐ　　**4** ⓑ

---

### 사마귀

사마귀는 그것의 두드러진 앞다리에서 이름이 붙여진 큰 곤충이다. 이것들은 보통 그 곤충이 기도하고 있는 것처럼 보이게 하는 방식으로 위치해 있다. 사마귀는 그것을 매우 효과적인 포식자이게 하는 많은 진화적 적응 형태를 가지고 있다.

사마귀의 앞다리는 먹이를 잡기 위한 주된 도구이다. [2D]각 다리의 끝은 완전히 접힐 수 있다. 그 결과, 다리는 거의 집게와 같은 역할을 할 수 있다. [2B]게다가, 그것은 길고, 끝이 뾰족한 가시들로 덮여 있다. [2A]사마귀가 먹이를 붙잡기 위해 빠르게 다리를 뻗을 때, 그 가시들은 희생양을 꿰

뚫는다. 이것은 잡아먹는 것을 쉽게 만든다.

사냥할 때 사마귀의 목은 그것에게 또 다른 이점을 제공한다. 그 목은 유별나게 길고, 매우 유연하다. 실제로, 사마귀는 머리를 180도로 회전시킬 수 있으며, 이는 그것을 뒤를 볼 수 있는 몇 안 되는 곤충 중 하나로 만든다. ³이 특징은 사마귀가 몸을 움직일 필요 없이 잡아먹을 다른 곤충들을 찾아 식물을 계속 살펴볼 수 있게 한다. 그 결과, 그것은 종종 눈에 띄지 않고 먹이를 찾을 수 있다.

먹이를 찾아내는 사마귀의 능력은 훌륭한 시력에 의해 더욱 강화된다. ⁴사마귀는 입체 시각을 가지고 있다는 점에서 곤충들 중에서 특별한데, 그것의 양쪽 겹눈은 동시에 같은 물체에 초점을 맞출 수 있다. 따라서, 사마귀는 세상을 3차원으로 인지할 수 있으며, 이는 인간이 하는 것과 거의 같은 방식이다. 이것은 사마귀가 움직임을 감지하여 먹이의 상대적인 거리를 판단하는 것을 더 쉽게 해준다.

praying mantis 사마귀　prominent 형 두드러진
evolutionary 형 진화적인　adaptation 명 적응 형태　highly 부 매우
fold 동 접히다　function 동 역할을 하다　pincher 명 집게
spine 명 가시　pierce 동 뚫다　flexible 형 유연한
rotate 동 회전시키다　enable 동 ~을 할 수 있게 하다
vegetation 명 식물　enhance 동 강화하다
stereo vision 입체 시각　perceive 동 인지하다
detect 동 감지하다　judge 동 판단하다　relative 형 상대적인

1 지문의 단어 "prominent"와 의미가 가장 비슷한 것은?

　(A) 섬세한
　(B) 튼튼한
　(C) 뚜렷한
　(D) 곡선의

2 2단락에 따르면, 사마귀의 앞다리의 특징이 아닌 것은?

　(A) 빠르게 뻗어 나가는 능력
　(B) 날카로운 가시들의 존재
　(C) 보호용 덮개의 존재
　(D) 큰 각도로 구부러지는 능력

3 3단락에서 사마귀에 관해 추론할 수 있는 것은?

　(A) 먹이를 찾을 때 움직이지 않는다.
　(B) 먹이를 고정하기 위해 유연한 목을 사용한다.
　(C) 곤충과 식물을 둘 다 섭취한다.
　(D) 포식자가 다가오면 몸을 낮춘다.

4 4단락에서 글쓴이가 암시하는 것으로, 사마귀가 아닌 곤충들은

　(A) 두 눈으로 동시에 물체에 초점을 맞춘다
　(B) 큰 겹눈들을 가지고 있지 않다
　(C) 입체 시각으로 움직임을 감지한다
　(D) 3차원으로 보는 능력이 없다

## Reading Practice 4　　본문 p. 100

1 (D)　2 (D)　3 (A)　4 (B)

### Vocabulary Quiz

1 ⓒ　2 ⓐ　3 ⓑ　4 ⓐ

---

## 니콜라 테슬라

니콜라 테슬라는 1884년에 미국으로 이주해 온 세르비아의 발명가이자 공학자였다. 1943년에 그가 사망하기까지, 테슬라는 우리 세상을 변화시켰고 오늘날에도 여전히 사용되는 발명품들에 대한 수많은 특허를 냈다. 오늘날, 테슬라는 역사상 가장 뛰어난 발명가들 중 한 명으로 기억되며, 그의 혁신적인 생각들은 시대를 앞서 있었다.

아마도 그의 가장 중요한 업적은 전기 분야에 있는 듯하다. 1887년까지, 미국에서 사용된 전기는 토머스 에디슨에 의해 개발된 직류(DC)였다. 직류는 배터리에서처럼 전류가 오직 한 방향으로만 흐르게 했다. 하지만, 테슬라가 교류, 혹은 AC라고 알려진 전기 체계를 개발했고, 그것은 방향을 바꿀 수 있었다. ²교류 덕분에, 전기는 가정과 사업체에 훨씬 더 합리적인 가격으로 전달될 수 있었다. 오늘날에는, 교류가 거의 모든 전자 기기와 장치들에 사용된다.

테슬라는 또한 무전 기술에서 획기적인 발전을 이뤄낸 것으로 인정받는다. ³그는 전선 없이 멀리서 무전 신호를 송신하고 수신할 수 있다는 것을 발견했다. 이 생각에 근거하여, 테슬라는 최초의 원격 조종 보트를 개발했다. 그 보트의 속도와 방향은 무전 송신기와 수신기를 사용하여 제어되었다. 이것은 세계 최초의 무선 원격 조종으로 여겨진다.

테슬라가 개발하는 데 일조한 또 다른 기술은 X선이다. ⁴빠른 속도로 전자를 방출하는 어떤 장치로 실험을 하던 중에, 테슬라는 그의 카메라의 일부가 손상된 것을 알아차렸다. 이것은 그가 "복사 에너지"라고 불렀던 것을 연구하도록 이끌었다. 이 과정에서, 그는 빌헬름 뢴트겐이 X선의 발견을 발표한 1895년보다도 이전에 X선 사진을 포착했을 것이라고 생각된다. 불행하게도, X선 발견에 대한 그의 기여는 주목받지 못했는데, 이는 그의 실험실에서 불이 났을 때 그의 연구 중 많은 부분이 소실되었기 때문이다.

immigrate 동 이주해 오다　patent 명 특허　brilliant 형 뛰어난
innovative 형 혁신적인　significant 형 중요한
direct current 직류　electrical current 전류
alternating current 교류　reasonable 형 합리적인
appliance 명 전자 기기　breakthrough 명 획기적인 발전
radio 형 무전의　remotely 부 멀리서　transmit 동 송신하다
remote-controlled 형 원격 조종의　discharge 동 방출하다
radiant 형 복사의　capture 동 포착하다　contribution 명 기여
go unnoticed 주목받지 못하다

1 지문의 단어 "immigrated"와 의미가 가장 비슷한 것은?

　(A) 망명했다
　(B) 방문했다
　(C) 여행했다
　(D) 이동했다

2 2단락에서 교류에 관해 추론할 수 있는 것은?

　(A) 직류 이전에 개발되었다.
　(B) 그것의 전류는 방향을 바꿀 수 없다.
　(C) 1887년 이전에 미국에서 널리 사용되었다.
　(D) 직류에 비해 더 비용 효율이 높다.

3 3단락에서 글쓴이가 암시하는 것으로, 테슬라의 보트는

　(A) 그것에 연결된 전선이 없었다
　(B) 다른 보트들보다 속도가 더 빨랐다
　(C) 이전의 무선 기술을 발전시켰다
　(D) 교류나 직류를 사용할 수 있었다

**4** 4단락에 따르면, 테슬라가 X선의 연구를 시작하도록 이끈 것은?

(A) 한 사진이 다른 발명가에 의해 찍혔다.
(B) 한 장치가 실험 도중에 파손되었다.
(C) 화재가 그의 실험실을 태워버렸다.
(D) 과학적 발견이 간행물에 발표되었다.

---

## iBT Reading Test

본문 p. 102

| | | | |
|---|---|---|---|
| 1 (B) | 2 (A) | 3 (C) | 4 (C) |
| 5 (A) | 6 (C) | 7 (D) | 8 (A) |
| 9 (C) | 10 (A), (E), (F) | | |

---

### 하와이의 열점

미국의 다른 49개 주와 달리, 하와이는 북미 대륙의 일부가 아니다. 대신, 그것은 태평양에 위치한 일련의 섬들이며, 빅아일랜드, 마우이, 라나이, 몰로카이, 오아후, 카우아이 등을 포함한다. 지질학자들은 하와이의 섬들을 형성한 화산 활동에 오랫동안 매료되어 왔다.

하와이가 형성된 특별한 방식을 이해하기 위해서는, 일반적으로 화산이 생기는 방식을 이해하는 것이 도움이 된다. 지각은 지구의 표면 위를 천천히 움직이는 여러 개의 지각판으로 구성된다. 워싱턴 주의 세인트헬렌스산과 같은 전통적인 화산들은 지각판들의 경계에서 생겨난다. ²이 모형에서는, 근접한 두 개의 판이 충돌하여, 하나가 다른 것 아래로 밀려 들어간다. 판이 지구 안쪽으로 이동하면, 그것은 녹는다. 이것은 뜨거운 용암을 지표면으로 분출하도록 야기하여 화산을 형성한다.

그러나, 하와이의 화산들은 태평양판의 경계에서 약 2,000마일 떨어진 곳에 형성되었다. ⁶ᴮ/⁶ᴰ지각과 핵 사이에는 맨틀이 있는데, 이는 판 중간의 한 지점에서 특히 뜨거운 층이다. 3,000만 년 전을 시작으로, 태평양판은 매년 3에서 4인치의 속도로 이 열점 위를 미끄러져 지나갔다. ⁶ᴬ녹은 암석(용암)은 그것이 해저에서 분출하여 화산을 형성할 때까지 맨틀을 통과해 올라갔다. **화산에서 솟아오른 이 용암은 차가워지고 굳어져 섬을 형성했다.** 하나씩 차례로, 태평양판의 그 움직이는 컨베이어 벨트가 열점 위를 지나감에 따라 하와이의 섬들이 형성되었다.

하와이의 화산들은 점차 그 열점에서 멀어지고 있다. 그것들이 만들어진 원천에서 점점 더 멀어질수록, 그 섬들에서의 뜨거운 용암의 화산 분출은 점점 더 줄어든다. ⁸결국, 그 섬들을 형성했던 화산들은 사그라들 것이다. 그 결과, 그 섬들은 침식되어 바닷속으로 가라앉기 시작할 것이다. 수백만 년 후에는, 그 섬들을 운반하고 있는 태평양판이 북미 대륙판 아래로 이동할 것이다. 그것은 하와이의 섬들을 영원히 사라지게 할 것이다.

continent 영대륙  fascinated 형매료된
form 통형성하다; 형성되다  crust 영지각
be made up of ~으로 구성되다  tectonic plate 지각판
the planet 지구  arise 통생기다  boundary 영경계
neighboring 형근접한  collide 통충돌하다  force 통밀어 넣다
magma 영용암  erupt 통분출하다  molten 형녹은
ascend 통올라가다  seafloor 영해저  erode 통침식되다
sink 통가라앉다  carry 통운반하다  disappear 통사라지다

---

**1** 지문의 단어 "fascinated"와 의미가 가장 비슷한 것은?

(A) 즐거워하는
(B) 관심 있어 하는
(C) 충격을 받은
(D) 짜증이 난

**2** 2단락에 따르면, 전통적인 화산들은

(A) 두 지각판들이 서로 충돌하기 때문에 형성된다
(B) 뜨거운 용암이 지표면 깊은 곳에서 형성되기 때문에 형성된다
(C) 판이 맨틀의 뜨거운 부분 위를 미끄러져 지나가기 때문에 형성된다
(D) 지구의 핵이 녹기 때문에 형성된다

**3** 지문의 단어 "ascended"와 의미가 가장 비슷한 것은?

(A) 가라앉았다
(B) 파괴했다
(C) 올라갔다
(D) 갈랐다

**4** 지문의 단어 "it"이 가리키는 것은?

(A) 태평양판
(B) 열점
(C) 녹은 암석
(D) 맨틀

**5** 글쓴이는 왜 "conveyor belt"를 언급하는가?

(A) 태평양판이 어떻게 열점 위를 움직이는지 설명하기 위해
(B) 다른 판들과 비교하여 태평양판의 속도를 보여주기 위해
(C) 전통적인 화산들이 주기적인 간격으로 형성된다는 것을 시사하기 위해
(D) 하와이의 섬들이 다수의 화산을 포함한다는 것을 강조하기 위해

**6** 3단락에 따르면, 다음 중 하와이의 섬들을 형성했던 열점에 관해 사실이 아닌 것은?

(A) 해저의 화산 활동을 야기했다.
(B) 지각과 지구의 핵 사이에 위치한다.
(C) 판이 그것의 에너지를 흡수함에 따라 차가워진다.
(D) 지각판의 중앙에 놓여 있다.

**7** 아래 문장 중 지문 속의 음영된 문장의 핵심 정보를 가장 잘 표현한 것은? 오답은 문장의 의미를 크게 바꾸거나 핵심 정보를 생략한다.

(A) 화산들이 열점 위에 있을 때, 그것들은 덜 자주 분출했다.
(B) 분출이 가끔 일어나기는 하지만, 이전만큼 자주 일어나지 않는다.
(C) 열점은 화산에서 점점 더 멀어질 것이다.
(D) 열점과의 거리가 멀어지면 화산은 덜 빈번하게 분출한다.

**8** 다음 중 하와이를 형성한 화산들에 관해 추론할 수 있는 것은?

(A) 그것들이 형성한 섬들이 사라지기 전에 활동을 중단할 것이다.
(B) 일 년 주기로 여전히 활발하게 분출하고 있다.
(C) 더 이상 분출할 수 없게 된 후에 계속해서 크기가 커질 것이다.
(D) 태평양판이 움직임에 따라 열점 위에 남아 있을 것이다.

**9** 네 개의 네모[■]는 다음 문장이 삽입될 수 있는 곳을 나타내고 있다.
**화산에서 솟아오른 이 용암은 차가워지고 굳어져 섬을 형성했다.**
이 문장은 어디에 들어가는 것이 가장 적절한가?

---

**10** 지시: 지문 요약을 위한 도입 문장이 아래에 주어져 있다. 지문의 가장 중요한 내용을 나타내는 보기 3개를 골라 요약을 완성하라. 어떤 문장은 지문에 언급되지 않은 내용이나 사소한 정보를 나타내므로 요약에 포함되지 않는다. **이 문제는 2점이다.**

> 하와이의 섬들의 형성은 많은 지질학자들의 관심의 대상이다.
> · (A) 전통적인 화산들은 지각판들의 경계 위에 형성된다.
> · (E) 하와이는 지구의 맨틀 내부의 열점 위에서의 화산 활동에 의해 형성되었다.
> · (F) 하와이의 섬들은 열점에서 멀어질 것이고 바다에 가라앉을 것이다.

(B) 하와이는 미국의 다른 주들과 다르다.
(C) 세인트헬렌스산은 그것에서 용암이 분출한다는 점에서 전통적인 화산이다.
(D) 태평양판은 결국 북미 대륙판 아래로 이동할 것이다.

## Vocabulary Review
본문 p.106

1 neighboring    2 enabled    3 disorder
4 evasion    5 erupted    6 sink
7 (A)    8 (C)    9 (B)    10 (A)
11 (C)    12 (C)    13 (A)    14 (D)

## CHAPTER 07
# Rhetorical Purpose

## Example
본문 p.109

1 (B)    2 (A)

### 이집트 상형문자

상형문자는 약 5,000년 전에 고대 이집트인들에 의해 처음으로 사용된 문자 체계의 글자들이다. 2,000개가 넘는 상형문자가 존재한다. 각각은 고대 이집트에서 발견된 흔한 물체의 형상이다. 상형문자는 그 물체 자체나 그것의 이름에 기반한 소리를 나타낼 수 있다. 따라서, 만약 무언가가 그것에 상응하는 상형문자가 없다면, 그것은 여러 개의 글자들을 이용하여 쓰여질 수 있었다. 예를 들어, Rob이라는 이름은 상형문자의 세 개의 글자들로 표현될 수 있었으며, 각각은 영문자들 중 하나의 소리와 일치했다.

상형문자 체계가 너무 복잡하고 상세했기 때문에, 그 글자들은 상세한 표현을 그릴 시간이나 인내심이 없었던 사람들을 위해 단순화되었다. 이 단순화된 형태들은 신관 문자와 민중 문자로 알려져 있다. 신관 문자의 글자들은 상형문자의 필기체 형태로, 오직 행정적이고 종교적인 목적으로만 사용되었다. 민중 문자 또한 필기체였으며, 그것은 회계와 문학 창작의 일상적인 용도를 위한 문자로써 신관 문자를 대신했다.

hieroglyph 몡상형문자    character 몡글자    ancient 혱고대의
stand for ~을 나타내다    corresponding 혱상응하는

multiple 혱여러 개의    represent 통표현하다    match 통일치하다
detailed 혱상세한    simplify 통단순화하다    patience 몡인내심
representation 몡표현, 그림    hieratic 몡신관 문자
demotic 몡민중 문자    cursive 혱필기체의
administrative 혱행정적인    religious 혱종교적인
replace 통대신하다    script 몡문자    accounting 몡회계

**1** 1단락에서 글쓴이는 왜 "Rob"을 언급하는가?
   (A) 이집트어와 영어의 문자 체계를 대조하기 위해
   (B) 상형문자가 어떻게 각각의 소리들을 표현할 수 있는지 보여주기 위해
   (C) 상형문자가 영어에 끼친 영향을 설명하기 위해
   (D) 영문자와 상형문자 사이의 유사점들을 보여주기 위해

**2** 2단락에서, 글쓴이는 "writing literature"를 무엇의 예시로 언급하는가?
   (A) 민중 문자의 기능
   (B) 상형문자 체계의 복잡성
   (C) 민중 문자에 대한 신관 문자의 우월성
   (D) 시간이 지나면서 상형문자가 보다 단순해진 방식

## Reading Practice 1
본문 p.110

1 (B)    2 (B)    3 (D)    4 (C)

### Vocabulary Quiz

1 ⓑ    2 ⓐ    3 ⓑ    4 ⓒ

### 개미의 의사소통

개미들은 사회적인 곤충으로 여겨지는데, 이는 그들이 독립적으로 움직이기보다는 무리를 지어 활동하기 때문이다. 이 무리는 군집이라고 불린다. 군집에서 성공적으로 살아가고 활동하기 위해, 개미들은 서로 의사소통을 해야만 한다.

더듬이는 개미들이 정보를 주고받기 위해 사용하는 한 가지 방법이다. 한 일개미가 군집의 다른 구성원을 만나면, 그들은 흔히 더듬이를 맞댄다. 이것은 그 일개미가 탐험했던 길 도중에 무엇이 예상될 수 있는지에 대한 메시지를 보낸다. 비록 개미들은 사람이 들을 수 있는 소리를 듣지 못하지만, 그들의 더듬이는 귀와 같은 기능을 하기도 한다. 더듬이의 끝에는 1킬로헤르츠 정도의 음향 주파수를 포착할 수 있는 털과 같은 감지기가 있다.

더듬이가 탐지할 수 있는 다른 신호들은 페로몬이라고 알려진 화학 물질에 의해 만들어진다. 이 페로몬은 개미들에게 있어 핵심적인 의사소통 수단이다. 개미들이 이동할 때, 그들은 지면에 페로몬을 남긴다. 각각의 개미 군집이 서로 다른 페로몬을 사용하기 때문에, 그것의 구성원들은 서로를 인식할 수 있다. ³ᴬ/³ᴮ이 화학물질은 또한 먹이가 있는 장소나 짝짓기를 하려는 의도를 신호할 수 있다. ³ᶜ개미가 짓밟힐 때, 그것의 페로몬은 군집의 다른 구성원들에게 경고하는 역할을 한다.

개미들은 또한 마찰음이라고 불리는 짹짹거리는 소리를 낸다. 이것은 그들 복부의 단단한 두 부분을 서로 문지르는 것에 의해 생겨난다. 마찰음은 때로는 소리로 들리고 때로는 진동으로 느껴진다. 여왕개미들은 둥지를 지을 준비가 되었다는 것을 신호하기 위해 마찰음을 낸다. 각 개체들은 비상사태가 일어나고 있다는 것을 신호하기 위해 마찰음

을 낸다. 실제로, 연구자들은 이것이 마찰음의 가장 중요한 역할이라고 생각한다. 이러한 진동을 만들어내는 개미는 흔히 비상등의 역할을 하며, 포식자가 군집의 둥지에 침입하려 할 때 다른 개미들을 호출한다.

consider 图여기다　operate 图움직이다
independently 图독립적으로　colony 圆(동·식물의) 군집
communicate 图의사소통을 하다　antenna 圆더듬이　trail 圆길
explore 图탐험하다　frequency 圆주파수　chemical 圆화학 물질
pheromone 圆페로몬　recognize 图인식하다　intention 圆의도
mate 图짝짓기를 하다　chirp 图짹짹거리다　stridulation 圆마찰음
rub 图문지르다　abdomen 圆복부　emergency 圆비상사태
role 圆역할　summon 图호출하다

**1** 글쓴이는 왜 개미를 "social insects"라고 묘사하는가?

(A) 개미의 짝짓기 관습에 대한 논의를 소개하기 위해
(B) 개미들이 의사소통을 해야 하는 이유를 설명하기 위해
(C) 개미의 행동과 사람의 행동을 비교하기 위해
(D) 개미들이 개별적인 성격을 가지고 있다는 것을 보여주기 위해

**2** 지문의 단어 "independently"와 의미가 가장 비슷한 것은?

(A) 본래
(B) 개별적으로
(C) 사실상
(D) 즉시

**3** 3단락에 따르면, 페로몬은

(A) 먹이가 있는 곳으로 가는 길을 알려주기 위해 사용되지 않는다
(B) 짝짓기 상대를 매혹하기 위해 사용되지 않는다
(C) 군집에 위협을 신호하기 위해 사용되지 않는다
(D) 다른 개미들을 새로운 둥지로 이끌기 위해 사용되지 않는다

**4** 4단락에서 글쓴이는 왜 "an emergency beacon"을 언급하는가?

(A) 여왕개미들이 다른 개미들에 대해 갖는 통제력을 강조하기 위해
(B) 군집의 서식지에 대한 일반적인 위협을 식별하기 위해
(C) 상호작용 수단의 중요한 기능을 명시하기 위해
(D) 잘 조직된 둥지 방어의 중요성을 나타내기 위해

## Reading Practice 2　본문 p. 112

1 (A)　　2 (C)　　3 (B)　　4 (B)

**Vocabulary Quiz**

1 ⓒ　　2 ⓑ　　3 ⓐ　　4 ⓒ

### 국경 없는 의사회

국경 없는 의사회는 국제적인 인도주의 단체이다. 그것은 1971년에 한 무리의 의사들과 기자들에 의해 설립되었다. 그들은 의료서비스 이용을 필요로 하는 사람들에게 의료를 제공하기를 원했다. 오늘날, 이 단체의 직원은 전 세계 60개국에서 대략 30,000명까지 늘어났다.

³이 용감한 국제 구호원들은 자연재해, 전쟁, 기근, 전염병의 피해자들을 돕는다. 이 단체의 첫 번째 프로젝트는 1972년의 니카라과 지진 이후에 보급품과 의료서비스를 제공하는 것이었다. 그 유산은 오늘날에도 이어지고 있다. 국경 없는 의사회는 2010년의 아이티 지진 직후에

환자들을 치료했다. 그것은 또한 세계 전역의 교전 지역에서 위험에 처한 사람들을 위해 일한다. 국제 구호원들은 레바논, 체첸, 예멘과 같은 국가들에서 부상자들을 돕기 위해 그들의 목숨을 위태롭게 해왔다. 직접적인 치료를 제공하는 것에 더해, 그 단체는 음식, 깨끗한 물, 피난처와 같은 기본적인 필수품들도 제공한다.

이러한 봉사와 함께, 국경 없는 의사회는 도움을 요청하는 사람들을 대신하여 부당함에 공개적으로 맞서고 있다. 예를 들어, 이 단체는 약품에 대한 공정한 접근이 허락되지 않을 때 이의를 제기한다. 그들은 미국 제약 회사들에게 코로나바이러스 감염증-19의 백신을 세계 전역에서 저렴하게 이용할 수 있도록 만들라고 요구했다. 때때로 이러한 행동들은 국제 구호원들을 정치 폭력의 표적이 될 위험에 처하게 한다. 심지어 국경 없는 의사회의 직원들은 아프가니스탄과 소말리아에서 살해당하기까지 했다. 그럼에도 불구하고, 국경 없는 의사회는 도움이 필요한 이들을 위해 도움의 손길을 제공하고 목소리를 내는 임무를 계속해서 수행하고 있다. 노고를 인정받아, 그것은 1999년에 노벨 평화상을 수상했다.

humanitarian 图인도주의의　victim 圆피해자　disaster 圆재해
famine 圆기근　epidemic 圆전염병　legacy 圆유산
endangered 图위험에 처한　jeopardize 图위태롭게 하다
assist 图돕다　the wounded 부상자들　necessity 圆필수품
shelter 圆피난처　injustice 圆부당함　on behalf of ~을 대신하여
protest 图이의를 제기하다　fair 图공정한　challenge 图요구하다
available 图이용할 수 있는　fulfill 图수행하다　recognition 圆인정

**1** 1단락에서 글쓴이는 왜 "60 countries around the world"를 언급하는가?

(A) 수년간 이 단체가 어떻게 성장했는지를 보여주기 위해
(B) 이 단체가 더 많은 봉사자들을 필요로 한다는 것을 시사하기 위해
(C) 이 단체를 지역적인 인도주의 단체와 대조하기 위해
(D) 이 단체의 직원들의 용기를 강조하기 위해

**2** 지문의 단어 "jeopardized"와 의미가 가장 비슷한 것은?

(A) 지연했다
(B) 복잡하게 만들었다
(C) 위태롭게 했다
(D) 제한했다

**3** 2단락에 따르면, 다음 중 국경 없는 의사회에 관해 사실인 것은?

(A) 질병의 피해자들을 돕기 위해 약을 개발한다.
(B) 전쟁에 영향을 받은 사람들에게 의료 지원을 제공한다.
(C) 주로 의약용품 수송에 집중한다.
(D) 몇몇 국가에서만 국제 구호원들을 모집한다.

**4** 3단락에서, 글쓴이는 왜 "Afghanistan and Somalia"에 관해 논하는가?

(A) 분쟁 지역에서 직원들을 고용하는 것에 찬성하기 위해
(B) 그곳의 직원들이 임무 중에 직면하는 위험을 보여주기 위해
(C) 국경 없는 의사회의 평화 교섭 능력을 설명하기 위해
(D) 국경 없는 의사회가 최근에 활동했던 국가들을 열거하기 위해

1 (D)　　2 (A)　　3 (A)　　4 (C)

**Vocabulary Quiz**

1 ⓐ　　2 ⓑ　　3 ⓒ　　4 ⓐ

---

### 찰스 다윈과 갈라파고스 제도

갈라파고스 제도는 생물학자의 보물 상자이다. 남아메리카 연안에서 약 1,000킬로미터 떨어진 19개의 섬으로 구성된 갈라파고스와 그 주변 해역에는 대략 9,000여 개의 종이 서식한다. 그곳의 이구아나, 도마뱀, 코끼리거북의 일부를 포함해서, 그 종들 중 다수는 그 제도에서만 볼 수 있다.

이 놀라운 생물학적 다양성은 1835년에 영국의 유명한 생물학자인 찰스 다윈에 의해 연구되었다. 당시 그는 22살이었으며, '비글호'의 5년짜리 항해에서 동식물 연구가로 일하고 있었다. ²그의 업무는 갈라파고스에서 식물과 동물의 표본을 수집하는 것이었다. 그의 발견 중에는 서로 다른 모양의 부리를 가진 14종의 되새류가 있었다. 그는 이 새들의 부리가 서로 다른 것에 이유가 있다는 것을 깨달았다. 뾰족한 부리는 일부 되새류들이 다치지 않고 선인장 열매의 씨앗을 갉아먹는 데 도움이 되었다. 날카로운 부리는 또 다른 되새류들이 벌레를 잡는 것을 도왔다. 그는 유럽으로 돌아와 그의 관찰이 정확했는지를 확인하기 위해 조류 전문가와 상의했다.

다윈은 이전에도 동물 종들이 시간이 지나며 진화했다고 믿었지만, 갈라파고스에서의 발견은 그에게 자연선택이라는 새로운 발상을 하게 해주었다. 그는 그가 접했던 종들이 그 제도에서 살아남는 데 도움을 주는 특성들을 발달시켰음이 틀림없다고 결론지었다. 가장 유리한 자질을 가진 동물들이 살아남았다. 그들의 서식지에 적합하지 않았던 것들은 멸종했다. 1859년에, 그는 '종의 기원'이라는 그의 획기적인 저서에 이러한 관찰 결과들을 기록했다. 오늘날, 진화론과 자연선택론은 현대 생물학의 근간이다. 과학자들은 그곳의 놀라운 생물들이 어떻게 진화해왔는지를 연구하기 위해 여전히 갈라파고스를 방문한다.

treasure chest 보물 상자　　inhabit 图서식하다
remarkable 혱놀라운　　diversity 몡다양성
naturalist 몡동식물 연구가　　specimen 몡표본
finch 몡되새류　　beak 몡부리　　nibble 图갉아먹다
consult 图상의하다　　observation 몡관찰　　evolve 图진화하다
encounter 图접하다, 마주치다　　advantageous 혱유리한
be suited to ~에 적합하다　　record 图기록하다
groundbreaking 혱획기적인　　foundation 몡근간
modern 혱현대의　　creature 몡생물

**1** 글쓴이는 왜 "treasure chest"를 언급하는가?

(A) 그 제도에서 귀중한 천연자원들이 발견될 수 있다는 것을 시사하기 위해

(B) 그 제도가 그곳에 거주하는 종들에게 중요하다는 것을 암시하기 위해

(C) 그 제도가 생물학자들에게 인기 있다는 것을 강조하기 위해

(D) 그 제도의 풍부한 생물학적 다양성을 강조하기 위해

**2** 다음 중 다윈이 갈라파고스로 항해를 했을 때, 그에 관해 사실인 것은?

(A) 식물과 동물을 연구하기 위해 고용되었다.

(B) 그 제도를 방문한 최초의 사람이었다.

(C) 그의 선원들 또한 훈련된 생물학자들이었다.

(D) 그의 목적은 새로운 되새류 종을 찾는 것이었다.

**3** 지문의 단어 "advantageous"와 의미가 가장 비슷한 것은?

(A) 이로운

(B) 인상적인

(C) 영향력 있는

(D) 독특한

**4** 3단락에서 글쓴이는 왜 "The Origin of Species"를 언급하는가?

(A) 다윈이 연구했던 책의 예시를 제공하기 위해

(B) 다윈의 연구에 중요한 영향을 끼친 것을 소개하기 위해

(C) 현대 생물학 이론의 기원을 확인하기 위해

(D) 다윈이 매우 성공한 작가였음을 밝히기 위해

---

1 (C)　　2 (C)　　3 (C)　　4 (A)

**Vocabulary Quiz**

1 ⓑ　　2 ⓐ　　3 ⓐ　　4 ⓐ

---

### 캘리포니아 골드러시

1848년, 서터즈밀의 제재소 직원이 아메리칸강의 흙속에서 귀한 금속의 작은 조각들을 발견했다. 캘리포니아의 강들에서 금이 반짝거린다는 말이 퍼져 나갔다. 인생을 바꿀만한 재물에 대한 기대가 골드러시를 일으켰고, 이는 전 세계로부터 사람들을 끌어들였다.

이 대규모 이주는 캘리포니아의 미국 연방 가입의 속도를 높였다. 금이 처음 발견되었을 때, 캘리포니아는 멕시코의 영토였는데, 그곳은 미국과 전쟁 중이었다. 한 달 안에, 평화 조약이 체결되었다. 멕시코는 캘리포니아의 지배권을 미국인들에게 넘겼다. 1849년에 이 지역으로 넘어온, 금을 찾는 "포티나이너스"의 쇄도는 강력한 정부를 필요로 했다. 그것이 주의 지위를 긴급한 우선순위로 만들었다. 1850년까지, 캘리포니아는 31번째 주로 승인되었다.

이 시기에, 그 지역의 인구 통계는 급격하게 변했다. 골드러시가 시작되었을 때, 캘리포니아에는 (미국 원주민을 제외하고) 700명의 사람들이 있었다. 1859년까지, 그 숫자는 380,000으로 급증했다. 탐광자들은 미국뿐만 아니라 유럽, 호주, 아시아, 라틴 아메리카에서도 왔다. 비록 수백 명은 노예로서 그 일을 하도록 강요당했지만, 그 지역의 미국 원주민들 또한 금을 찾았다. ³ᴬ이 탐광자들은 돌과 흙, 얼어붙은 듯한 물에서 금을 찾는 것이 어렵고 위험한 작업이라는 것을 곧 알게 되었다. ³ᴮ/³ᴰ많은 이들이 질병이나 사고로 죽었다. 몇몇 이들은 많은 돈을 벌었지만, 대부분은 그렇게 운이 좋지 않았다.

골드러시는 또한 캘리포니아의 풍경을 영구적으로 변화시켰다. 얼마 지나지 않아, 개인에 의해 발견될 수 있는 금의 대부분은 사라졌지만, 산업체들은 수력 채광 기술로 더 깊이 파고들었다. 이 산업적인 채광은 댐을 침전물로 채웠고, 강을 그것을 필요로 하는 농부들로부터 다른 곳으로 향하게 했다. 이 프로젝트에 나무가 필요했기 때문에, 벌목이 그 땅에서 많은 천연자원들을 제거했다. 캘리포니아는 골드러시에 의해 영구히 변화되었고, 이는 그 주에 골든스테이트라는 별칭을 붙여주었다.

precious ⑱귀한　glitter ⑧반짝거리다　attract ⑧끌어들이다
migration ⑲이주　admission ⑲가입　territory ⑲영토
treaty ⑲조약　statehood ⑲주의 지위　urgent ⑱긴급한
demographic ⑲인구 통계　dramatically ㉰급격하게
soar ⑧급증하다　prospector ⑲(금 등을 찾는) 탐광자
permanently ㉰영구적으로　alter ⑧변화시키다　mining ⑲채광
sediment ⑲침전물　redirect ⑧다른 곳으로 향하게 하다
logging ⑲벌목　strip ⑧제거하다

**1** 글쓴이는 왜 "forty-niners"에 관해 논하는가?

(A) 외국의 영토가 획득된 방법을 묘사하기 위해
(B) 평화 조약의 필요성을 강조하기 위해
(C) 주의 지위가 빠르게 획득된 이유를 설명하기 위해
(D) 서로 다른 주 정부의 유형들을 비교하기 위해

**2** 지문의 단어 "soared"와 의미가 가장 비슷한 것은?

(A) 등록했다
(B) 계산했다
(C) 증가했다
(D) 관련됐다

**3** 3단락에 따르면, 다음 중 이주한 탐광자들이 견뎌낸 것이 아닌 것은?

(A) 차가운 물
(B) 사고
(C) 노예 제도
(D) 질병

**4** 4단락에서 글쓴이는 왜 "The Golden State"를 언급하는가?

(A) 골드러시가 캘리포니아에 영속적인 영향을 끼쳤다는 것을 강조하기 위해
(B) 환경 파괴에도 불구하고 캘리포니아가 아름다운 주라는 것을 암시하기 위해
(C) 골드러시가 캘리포니아의 주의 지위라는 결과로 이어졌다는 생각을 강화하기 위해
(D) 금이 캘리포니아를 부유한 주로 만들었다는 증거를 제공하기 위해

## iBT Reading Test

본문 p. 118

1 (A)　2 (A)　3 (C)　4 (A)
5 (B)　6 (A)　7 (C)　8 (B)
9 (C)　10 (D), (E), (F)

### 역사 속의 무대 조명 기법들

연극 예술의 2,000년 역사에 걸쳐, 극장들은 무대를 밝히는 최선의 방법을 찾기 위해 노력해왔다. ¹고대 그리스인들은 오직 태양만이 빛을 제공하는 야외극장에서 연극을 상연했다. 태양은 관객의 뒤에서 무대를 비췄다. 이것은 또한 햇빛이 관객의 눈으로 향하지 않게 했다. 게다가, 그리스인들은 변화하는 태양의 위치를 이용하기 위해 공연을 잠시 멈추곤 했다. 그들은 또한 큰 거울들을 이용하여 햇빛을 그들이 원하는 곳으로 향하게 했다.

그다음의 주요한 무대 조명의 혁신은 이탈리아 르네상스 시기에 일어났다. 1500년대 후반에는, 양초가 상들리에로 천장에 매달리거나 무

대 가장자리에 각광으로 놓이곤 했다. 충분한 조명을 제공하기 위해 수천 개의 양초가 필요했다. ⁴ᴮ물론, 당시에는 양초가 상당히 비쌌기 때문에, 이것은 연극을 상연하는 것을 더 비싸게 만들었다. ⁴ᴰ또 다른 문제는 극장에 불이 날 위험이 컸다는 것이다. ⁴ᶜ또한, 양초들이 너무 많은 산소를 소모해서, 출연자와 관객들의 숨이 차게 될 수도 있었다. 때때로 사람들이 기절하기도 했다.

⁶1783년에, 프랑스가 석유등을 도입했는데, 그것은 불꽃을 더 높거나 낮아지게 하도록 조절할 수 있었기 때문에 양초보다 우수했다. 100년 동안, 석유는 무대를 밝히는 데 선호되는 방식이었다. 그러나, 석유등은 비쌌다. 1800년대 초반에 도입된 가스등은 보다 저렴했다. 그것 또한 조절 기능을 제공했다. 배관 장치 안으로 가스를 방출하는 밸브를 이용하여, 빛은 각기 다른 각도와 밝기로 무대 위로 향해질 수 있었다.

전등은 1873년에 도입되었다. 그것들이 발명되고 1년이 지났을 때, 파리 오페라 극장은 그것들을 사용하기 시작했다. 20세기 초반에는, 전등 앞에 젤라틴을 바르는 것을 통해 전기 조명에 색이 입혀지기 시작했다. 이것은 플라스틱으로 만들어졌으며, 디자이너들에게 장면의 분위기를 조성하는 복잡한 조명 구성을 만드는 능력을 주었다. 효과를 위해 서로 다른 색깔들이 섞일 수 있었다. 조명은 연극의 감정적 효과에 있어 배우의 연기만큼 중요해졌다.

dramatic ⑱연극의　struggle ⑧노력하다
stage ⑧상연하다; ⑲무대　illuminate ⑧비추다
performance ⑲공연; 연기　take advantage of ~을 이용하다
direct ⑧향하게 하다　innovation ⑲혁신　edge ⑲가장자리
footlight ⑲(무대 앞쪽의) 각광　adequate ⑱충분한
consume ⑧소모하다　gasp ⑧숨이 차다　faint ⑧기절하다
kerosene oil 석유　superior ⑱우수한　adjust ⑧조절하다
release ⑧방출하다　plot ⑲구성　blend ⑧섞다

**1** 다음 중 1단락에서 그리스의 연극에 관해 추론할 수 있는 것은?

(A) 밤에는 공연되지 않았다.
(B) 관객들이 있는 채로 상연되지 않았다.
(C) 옥외의 불꽃을 이용해 밝혀졌다.
(D) 쉬는 시간 없이 공연되었다.

**2** 지문의 단어 "adequate"와 의미가 가장 비슷한 것은?

(A) 충분한
(B) 효과적인
(C) 무해한
(D) 감당할 수 있는

**3** 지문의 단어 "consume"과 의미가 가장 비슷한 것은?

(A) 변형하다
(B) 발산하다
(C) 다 써버리다
(D) 결합하다

**4** 2단락에 따르면, 다음 중 양초를 사용하는 것의 단점으로 제시된 것이 아닌 것은?

(A) 더 긴 준비 시간
(B) 더 높은 제작비
(C) 공기 질의 저하
(D) 화재 위험

5 아래 문장 중 지문 속의 음영된 문장의 핵심 정보를 가장 잘 표현한 것은? 오답은 문장의 의미를 크게 바꾸거나 핵심 정보를 생략한다.

(A) 가스등은 다양한 각도로 무대를 밝게 비추는 능력을 제공했다.

(B) 무대 조명의 각도와 밝기는 가스 방출에 의해 조절될 수 있었다.

(C) 가스를 사용하려면, 큰 배관 장치가 설치되어 밸브로 조절되어야 했다.

(D) 석유등이 더 밝기는 했지만, 가스는 배관망을 이용하여 제어하기가 더 쉬웠다.

6 3단락에 따르면, 석유등이 양초에 비해 개선된 것으로 여겨진 것은

(A) 그것들의 불꽃이 조절될 수 있었기 때문이다

(B) 설치하기 쉬웠기 때문이다

(C) 그것들의 연료를 쉽게 구할 수 있었기 때문이다

(D) 손상시키기 어려웠기 때문이다

7 지문의 단어 "This"가 가리키는 것은?

(A) 파리 오페라 극장

(B) 전기 조명

(C) 젤라틴

(D) 등

8 글쓴이는 왜 "the actors' performances"를 언급하는가?

(A) 연극에 색이 입혀진 조명이 필요했다는 생각을 반박하기 위해

(B) 연출에 있어서 조명의 증대된 중요성을 강조하기 위해

(C) 조명 디자이너가 배우보다 돈을 더 많이 받아야 한다고 주장하기 위해

(D) 감정이 관객에게 전달되는 방식을 확인하기 위해

9 네 개의 네모[■]는 다음 문장이 삽입될 수 있는 곳을 나타내고 있다.

**이것은 또한 햇빛이 관객의 눈으로 향하지 않게 했다.**

이 문장은 어디에 들어가는 것이 가장 적절한가?

10 **지시**: 지문 요약을 위한 도입 문장이 아래에 주어져 있다. 지문의 가장 중요한 내용을 나타내는 보기 3개를 골라 요약을 완성하라. 어떤 문장은 지문에 언급되지 않은 내용이나 사소한 정보를 나타내므로 요약에 포함되지 않는다. **이 문제는 2점이다.**

> **수 세기 동안, 극장들은 공연 중에 무대를 밝힐 좋은 방법을 찾았다.**
> · (D) 전등은 조명 디자이너에게 연극의 분위기에 대한 더 큰 통제권을 준다.
> · (E) 양초는 무대를 밝히기에 위험한 방식이라는 것이 드러났다.
> · (F) 조명 방식으로서 가스는 석유보다 개량된 것이었다.

(A) 사람들은 때때로 양초로 빛을 밝힌 연극을 보는 도중에 기절했다.

(B) 석유등의 불꽃은 크기가 커지거나 줄어질 수 있었다.

(C) 젤라틴은 조명의 색을 바꾸는 플라스틱 여과 장치이다.

## Vocabulary Review
본문 p. 122

1 superior　　　2 colony　　　3 Admission
4 illuminated　　5 corresponding　6 disaster
7 (A)　8 (C)　9 (A)　10 (B)
11 (B)　12 (A)　13 (D)　14 (D)

---

## Example
본문 p. 125

1 (B)　　2 (D)

### 마시멜로 실험

1960년대에, 심리학자 월터 미쉘은 당시 유아였던 그의 아이들이 어떻게 자제력을 발휘하는 법을 배우는지 알고 싶어 했다. 그는 한 무리의 4세 아이들이 마시멜로를 받게 되는 실험을 고안했다. **그들에게는 다음의 두 가지 선택권이 주어졌다.** 그들은 곧장 한 개의 마시멜로를 먹거나, 15분을 기다린 다음 두 개의 마시멜로를 먹을 수 있었다. 약 3분의 1의 아이들은 즉시 첫 번째 간식을 먹었다. 다른 3분의 1의 아이들은 두 배의 보상을 위해 인내심 있게 기다렸다. 나머지 아이들은 유혹에 굴복하기까지 몇 분 정도 기다렸다. 미쉘은 무엇이 이 유아들에게 만족감을 뒤로 미룰 수 있게 했는지를 알아내기 위해 오늘날 마시멜로 실험이라고 알려진 그 실험을 다양한 조건하에서 시도해보았다.

하지만, 실제로 마시멜로 실험을 유명하게 만든 것은 1980년대 후반에 있었던 미쉘의 후속 연구였다. 미쉘은 당시 30대가 된 동일한 사람들을 다시 찾아가, 그들의 삶에서 자제력의 중요성을 조사했다. 유아였을 때 더 오래 기다릴 수 있었던 아이들은 더 높은 SAT 점수를 받았으며 직장에서 성과가 더 좋았다. 그들은 또한 더 높은 자존감과 더 나은 인간관계를 갖고 있었다. 그들은 심지어 만성질환을 앓고 있을 가능성도 더 낮았다. 그러나, **충동 조절을 잘하지 못했던 아이들은 성인이 되었을 때 덜 성공적이었고, 덜 행복했으며, 덜 건강했다.** 이것은 어린 시절 유혹을 견딜 수 있는 사람들이 인생에서 성공할 가능성이 더 높다는 것을 보여준다.

psychologist 명 심리학자　　wonder 통 알고 싶어 하다
toddler 명 유아　　exercise 통 발휘하다　　self-control 명 자제력
devise 통 고안하다　　treat 명 간식　　right away 즉시
patiently 부 인내심 있게　　reward 명 보상　　give in to ~에 굴복하다
temptation 명 유혹　　condition 명 조건　　delay 통 뒤로 미루다
gratification 명 만족감　　follow-up 형 후속의
investigate 통 조사하다　　chronic 형 만성의
demonstrate 통 보여주다　　resist 통 견디다

1 1단락에서 네 개의 네모[■]는 다음 문장이 삽입될 수 있는 곳을 나타내고 있다.

**그들에게는 다음의 두 가지 선택권이 주어졌다.**

이 문장은 어디에 들어가는 것이 가장 적절한가?

2 2단락에서 네 개의 네모[■]는 다음 문장이 삽입될 수 있는 곳을 나타내고 있다.

**그러나, 충동 조절을 잘하지 못했던 아이들은 성인이 되었을 때 덜 성공적이었고, 덜 행복했으며, 덜 건강했다.**

이 문장은 어디에 들어가는 것이 가장 적절한가?

1 (A)    2 (C)    3 (D)    4 (A)

**Vocabulary Quiz**

1 ⓑ    2 ⓐ    3 ⓒ    4 ⓐ

### 맹그로브 나무

맹그로브는 해안선을 따라 자라는 나무의 한 종류이다. 대략 50에서 100개의 서로 다른 종이 있다. 미국에서, 그것들은 주로 플로리다에서 자란다. 그것들은 중앙아메리카와 동남아시아 같은 많은 다른 열대 지역에서 발견되기도 한다. 맹그로브가 일반적인 식물처럼 보일지도 모르지만, 그것들은 매우 특별한 특징을 가지고 있다. 그것들은 소금물을 견디는 유일한 나무 종이다.

그것들이 소금기 있는 환경에서 살 수 있는 두 가지 서로 다른 방법이 있다. 일부 맹그로브 종들은 소금이 그들의 몸에 들어오는 것을 거의 완전히 차단하는 여과 장치를 가지고 있다. 이 여과 장치로, 그것들은 바닷물에서 90퍼센트 이상의 소금을 차단할 수 있는데, 이것이 삼투 현상이라고 불리는 과정을 막는다. 이 과정에서, 물은 소금 농도가 낮은 곳에서 소금 농도가 높은 곳으로 이동한다. 만약 이것이 발생하게 된다면, 소금물은 나무의 수분을 완전히 빼앗아 죽게 할 것이다.

또 다른 방법은 소금이 그 식물에 들어온 이후에 그것을 관리하는 것이다. 이러한 접근법을 이용하는 맹그로브 종은 분비자라고 불린다. 그것들은 특수한 기공과 분비선을 통해 소금을 바깥으로 내보낼 수 있다. ³소금에서 수분이 증발함에 따라, 작은 소금 결정들이 잎 표면에 남겨진다.

그것들의 특별한 능력에 더하여, 맹그로브는 생태계에서 매우 중요한 역할을 수행한다. 그것들은 해안선을 안정시키고, 폭풍 해일, 파도, 조수에 의한 침식을 줄인다. ⁴ᴮ게다가, 물 바깥으로 튀어나온 뒤엉킨 굵은 뿌리들이 조수의 움직임을 늦춰, 진흙 바닥에 퇴적물이 가라앉게 만든다. ⁴ᶜ이것은 유기물과 중요한 영양분들을 가둔 서식지를 형성한다. ⁴ᴰ그것은 먹이나 포식자로부터의 은신처를 찾는 많은 물고기들과 다른 동물들에게 이상적인 환경이다.

coastline 몡해안선    tolerate 동견디다    filter 몡여과 장치
exclude 동차단하다    osmosis 몡삼투 현상
dehydrate 동수분을 빼앗다    approach 몡접근법
secretor 몡분비자    pore 몡(식물의) 기공    gland 몡분비선
moisture 몡수분    evaporate 동증발하다    ecosystem 몡생태계
stabilize 동안정시키다    erosion 몡침식    storm surge 폭풍 해일
tide 몡조수    ideal 혱이상적인    seek 동찾다

1 지문의 단어 "tolerates"와 의미가 가장 비슷한 것은?

(A) 견디다
(B) 받다
(C) 재활용하다
(D) 제거하다

2 네 개의 네모[■]는 다음 문장이 삽입될 수 있는 곳을 나타내고 있다.

이 과정에서, 물은 소금 농도가 낮은 곳에서 소금 농도가 높은 곳으로 이동한다.

이 문장은 어디에 들어가는 것이 가장 적절한가?

3 3단락에 따르면, 다음 중 분비자에 관해 사실인 것은?

(A) 소금의 침투를 막음으로써 소금을 처리한다.

(B) 그것들의 특수한 기공이 소금을 흡수한다.
(C) 소금물은 그것들 위에서 더 빠르게 증발한다.
(D) 소금 결정들이 그것들의 잎에 남는다.

4 4단락에 따르면, 다음 중 맹그로브 나무들이 중요한 이유가 아닌 것은?

(A) 폭풍 해일과 해안가의 파도를 줄인다.
(B) 그것들의 뿌리는 조수의 물이 느려지게 한다.
(C) 영양분의 공급원을 가두는 환경을 만든다.
(D) 보호가 필요한 동물들을 위한 좋은 거주지를 만든다.

1 (B)    2 (D)    3 (C)    4 (B)

**Vocabulary Quiz**

1 ⓒ    2 ⓐ    3 ⓑ    4 ⓒ

### 스텔스 기술

제2차 세계대전 중에 발명된 레이더는 항공기와 같은 움직이는 물체를 탐지하기 위해 사용된다. 그것의 광범위한 활용은 스텔스 기술에 대한 연구로 이어졌다. 이 기술의 목적은 군용기를 적에게 탐지되지 않게 만드는 것이다.

항공기를 레이더에 보이지 않게 만드는 한 가지 비결은 그것의 형태이다. 레이더는 전파를 주고받는 것을 통해 물체들을 식별한다. 무선 안테나가 전파를 내보내면, 항공기와 같은 물체들은 그것들을 다시 반사한다. 그런 다음 그 전파는 무선 안테나로 되돌아가, 그 물체에 대한 정보를 제공한다. 하지만 만약 비행기에 전파를 쉽게 튕겨 나가도록 하는 넓거나 둥근 표면이 없다면, 그것은 레이더로부터 숨을 수 있다. ³ᴬ이것이 스텔스 비행기가 대개 뾰족한 가장자리를 가지며 평평한 이유이다. 전파들은 그것들이 근원지로 되돌아가지 않게 하는 각도로 굴절된다.

³ᴮ레이더를 물리치는 또 다른 방법은 그것을 비행기의 기체 내부로 흡수하는 것이다. 금속으로 된 표면은 레이더 전파를 쉽게 반사한다. F-117 나이트호크는 1980년대에 개발된 스텔스 항공기로, 흡수력이 있는 유리 섬유와 플라스틱으로 만들어졌다. 또 다른 비행기들은 아이언 볼 페인트라고 불리는 흡수력이 있는 검은 물질로 칠해진다. ³ᴮ이 페인트는 전파를 근원지로 튕겨 되돌아갈 수 없는 열로 전환한다.

스텔스 기술에 단점이 없는 것은 아니다. 우선 첫째로, 스텔스 기술을 사용하는 비행기는 생산하기에 매우 값비싸다. 필요한 특수 물질들 때문에, F-117은 4,500만 달러의 비용이 든다. 스텔스 B-2 폭격기는 한 대에 22억 달러로 심지어 더 비싸다. 또한, 이 특이한 디자인들은 비행에 그리 효율적이지 않다. ⁴예를 들어, F-117은 특이하게 배치된 꼬리가 있으며, 이는 그것을 불안정하게 만든다. 하지만 위험한 군사 작전에서, 눈에 보이지 않는 능력은 아주 중요하다.

detect 동탐지하다    widespread 혱광범위한    utilization 몡활용
undetectable 혱탐지되지 않는    invisible 혱보이지 않는
identify 동식별하다    radio wave 전파    reflect 동반사하다
bounce off 튕기다    deflect 동굴절시키다    defeat 동물리치다
metallic 혱금속으로 된    absorbent 혱흡수력이 있는
coat 동칠하다    substance 몡물질    disadvantage 몡단점
bomber 몡폭격기    unusual 혱특이한    unstable 혱불안정한
priceless 혱아주 중요한

1 지문의 단어 "Its"가 가리키는 것은?

(A) 제2차 세계대전
(B) 레이더
(C) 물체
(D) 항공기

2 네 개의 네모[■]는 다음 문장이 삽입될 수 있는 곳을 나타내고 있다.
**그런 다음 그 전파는 무선 안테나로 되돌아가, 그 물체에 대한 정보를 제공한다.**
이 문장은 어디에 들어가는 것이 가장 적절한가?

3 지문에 따르면, 다음 중 레이더 전파가 근원지로 되돌아가는 것을 막는 방법이 아닌 것은?

(A) 뾰족한 끝을 가진 비행기를 만드는 것
(B) 레이더 전파를 열로 전환하는 것
(C) 금속으로 비행기를 만드는 것
(D) 레이더 전파를 비행기 내부로 흡수하는 것

4 지문에 따르면, F-117의 단점은?

(A) B-2 폭격기보다 많은 비용이 든다.
(B) 그것을 불안정하게 만드는 꼬리가 있다.
(C) 레이더 전파에 의해 탐지될 수 있다.
(D) 최근의 검증되지 않은 발명품이다.

## Reading Practice 3
본문 p.130

1 (C)  2 (D)  3 (B)  4 (B)

### Vocabulary Quiz

1 ⓐ  2 ⓑ  3 ⓒ  4 ⓐ

### 해마의 번식

매일 동이 트기 전, 수컷 해마와 암컷 해마가 모여 아름다운 구애 의식을 행한다. 그 암수의 쌍들은 춤을 추기 시작한다. ¹ᴬ그들의 원숭이 같은 꼬리는 서로를 고리 모양으로 감는다. ¹ᴮ그들은 하나의 선명한 색에서 다른 하나의 색으로 여러 차례 색을 바꾼다. ¹ᴰ때때로 그것들은 몇 시간, 심지어 며칠 동안 서로의 주위를 유영한다. 이 놀라운 발레는 어떤 진화적인 목적에 도움이 될까? 과학자들은 확실히 알지 못한다. 그러나, 그들은 이 짝짓기 춤이 수컷 해마가 임신하기 전까지 암수의 움직임을 일치시키기 위한 것이라고 짐작한다.

수컷이 임신하고 출산한다는 점에서 해마는 동물 세계에서 특이하다. ³암컷은 알을 만든 후에 그것들을 수컷의 복부에 있는 주머니에 집어넣는다. 수컷은 이 주머니 안에서 알들을 수정시키고 수정란들을 품는다. 수컷은 그것들에게 산소와 영양분을 제공하고, 이산화탄소와 노폐물은 제거한다. 대략 2주가 지나면, 이 알들은 아비의 주머니에서 부화한다. 그런 다음, 수컷은 주위 바다에 무려 1,000마리나 되는 작은 해마들을 배출한다.

일단 야생에 나오게 되면, 새끼 해마들은 혼자의 힘으로 살아간다. 어미와 아비는 갓 태어난 새끼들에게 보살핌이나 가르침을 제공하지 않는다. 그들은 심지어 자식들에게 **어떤 보호를 제공하는 것을 시도조차 하지 않는다.** 이 작은 해마들은 해류에 휩쓸릴 수 있고, 포식자들에게 먹힐 수 있으며, 심지어는 (만약 그것들이 태어난 장소에서 너무

오래 기다린다면) 자신들의 아비에게 먹힐 수도 있다. 결과적으로, 1,000마리의 해마 중 5마리 미만이 살아남고 자라서 그들 자신의 아름다운 짝짓기 춤을 추게 된다.

seahorse 몡해마   courtship 몡구애   ritual 몡의식
loop 동고리 모양으로 감다   vivid 톙선명한   hue 몡색
evolutionary 톙진화적인   remarkable 톙놀라운
suspect 동짐작하다   synchronize 동일치시키다
pregnant 톙임신한   deposit 동집어넣다   pouch 몡주머니
fertilize 동수정시키다   embryo 몡수정란   hatch 동부화하다
expel 동배출하다   instruction 몡가르침, 지시   consume 동먹다
consequently 톞결과적으로

1 1단락에 따르면, 다음 중 짝짓기 춤 동안의 해마에 관해 사실이 아닌 것은?

(A) 꼬리로 서로를 감싼다.
(B) 춤을 추면서 색을 바꾼다.
(C) 밤늦게 춤을 추기 시작한다.
(D) 몇 시간 혹은 며칠 동안 춤을 춘다.

2 지문의 단어 "expels"와 의미가 가장 비슷한 것은?

(A) 당기다
(B) 보호하다
(C) 통제하다
(D) 방출하다

3 2단락에 따르면, 암컷 해마들이 담당하는 행동은?

(A) 알을 수정시키는 것
(B) 알을 만드는 것
(C) 알에 영양분을 공급하는 것
(D) 알을 부화시키는 것

4 네 개의 네모[■]는 다음 문장이 삽입될 수 있는 곳을 나타내고 있다.
**그들은 심지어 자식들에게 어떤 보호를 제공하는 것을 시도조차 하지 않는다.**
이 문장은 어디에 들어가는 것이 가장 적절한가?

## Reading Practice 4
본문 p.132

1 (D)  2 (B)  3 (C)  4 (A)

### Vocabulary Quiz

1 ⓒ  2 ⓐ  3 ⓐ  4 ⓒ

### 마사 그레이엄

마사 그레이엄 세대의 대다수의 어린 여성들은 전통적인 발레를 통해 무용에 입문했다. 분홍색의 레이스 치마와 우아한 회전은 많은 어린 숙녀들에게 너무 매력적이었다. 그러나, 어렸을 때조차, 그레이엄은 달랐다. 1911년에 그녀가 힌두교 여신의 옷차림을 한 루스 세인트 데니스의 공연을 보게 되었을 때, 보다 현대적인 발레 스타일에 의해 무용에 대한 그녀의 어린 시절의 열정이 촉발되었다. 그녀는 그 **이국적인 무용에서 영감을 받았다.** 그녀의 부유한 펜실베이니아 부모에게는 실망스럽게도, 16살의 그레이엄은 그 무렵에 그녀가 인생에서 무엇을

하고 싶은지를 알고 있었다. 그들은 그녀가 대학에 가서 실용적인 일을 하기를 원했다. 그 대신, 그녀는 새로운 무용 형식을 창조했다.

그레이엄의 독특한 현대 무용 스타일은 무용계에 발레의 대안을 제공했다. 발레는 다섯 가지 고전적인 동작들을 중심으로 만들어진 우아함과 기술을 강조했다. 그것은 형식적이고 정확했다. [3B]그에 반해서, 그레이엄의 스타일은 깊은 감정 표현에 가치를 두었다. [3D]때로는 난폭하고 때로는 관능적인 그녀의 무용은 항상 열정적이었다. [3A]그것은 "수축과 이완"의 원칙에 기반을 두었다. 이것은 리듬감 있게 호흡하고 몸의 중심을 활용하면서, 그녀의 근육을 교대로 긴장시키고 이완하는 것을 의미했다. 이러한 방식으로, 그녀는 인간의 감정을 직접적이고도 강력하게 표현하는 동작들을 창조했다. 전통은 그녀에게 거의 의미가 없었다. 그녀는 그녀의 무용이 충격적이며 새롭기를 바랐다.

오늘날, 그레이엄은 20세기의 가장 위대한 무용수로 인정받는다. 1920년대에서부터 1990년대 초반까지, 그녀는 피카소가 현대 미술에서 그러했듯, 현대 무용 예술에서 중요했다. 그녀는 1926년에 마사 그레이엄 무용단을 설립했다. 비록 그녀가 1969년에 무용계에서 은퇴했고 1991년에 사망했지만, 그녀의 무용단은 계속해서 획기적인 무용을 보여주고 있다. 이 무용단은 우리 시대의 많은 훌륭한 무용수들과 안무가들을 훈련해왔다.

twirling 몡회전    irresistible 혱너무 매력적인    enthusiasm 몡열정
spark 통촉발하다    goddess 몡여신    dismay 몡실망
affluent 혱부유한    practical 혱실용적인    distinctive 혱독특한
alternative 몡대안    emphasize 통강조하다    precise 혱정확한
in contrast 그에 반해서    sensual 혱관능적인
passionate 혱열정적인    contraction 몡수축
alternately 뷔교대로    tense 통긴장시키다
retire 통은퇴하다    choreographer 몡안무가

1 네 개의 네모[■]는 다음 문장이 삽입될 수 있는 곳을 나타내고 있다.
   **그녀는 그 이국적인 무용에서 영감을 받았다.**
   이 문장은 어디에 들어가는 것이 가장 적절한가?

2 지문의 단어 "It"이 가리키는 것은?
   (A) 현대 무용 스타일
   (B) 발레
   (C) 우아함
   (D) 기술

3 2단락에 따르면, 다음 중 그레이엄의 무용 스타일에 관해 사실이 아닌 것은?
   (A) 근육의 수축과 이완을 기반으로 했다.
   (B) 감정 표현에 가치를 두었다.
   (C) 정확하고 형식적이었다.
   (D) 열정적이고 관능적이었다.

4 아래 문장 중 지문 속의 음영된 문장의 핵심 정보를 가장 잘 표현한 것은?
   (A) 현대 무용에 끼친 그녀의 영향력은 현대 미술에 끼친 피카소의 영향력에 견줄 만했다.
   (B) 그녀는 1920년대에서 1990년대 초반까지 그녀의 무용을 창조하기 위해 피카소와 협업했다.
   (C) 그녀는 피카소의 예술에서 중요한 요소들을 그녀의 무용에 포함시켰다.
   (D) 그녀의 무용은 피카소와 같은 현대 예술가들이 독특한 그림들을 창조하도록 영감을 주었다.

## iBT Reading Test

1 (A)    2 (B)    3 (D)    4 (A)
5 (D)    6 (C)    7 (B)    8 (D)
9 (C)    10 (B), (D), (E)

### 빙하기의 네안데르탈인

[3]지구의 가장 최근의 빙하기 동안, 빙하는 유라시아 본토 북부의 대부분을 덮었다. 현생 인류는 비교적 따뜻한 아프리카에서 등장하기 시작하고 있었다. 잉글랜드에서 시베리아까지의 북쪽 지역은 네안데르탈인에 의해 차지되어 있었다. 이 튼튼한 종은 우리 종과 유전적으로 가장 가까웠다. 하지만 네안데르탈인은 훨씬 더 가혹한 환경을 견뎌야 했다. 그들은 어떻게 350,000년 동안 생존했을까?

네안데르탈인은 그들이 추위 속에서 살도록 돕는 신체적인 이점들을 가지고 있었다. 그들의 짧고 덩치가 큰 신체는 열을 보존하는 데 효율적이었다. 그들은 짧은 팔과 다리를 가지고 있었는데, 이는 그들이 아주 적게 노출된 피부를 갖게 해주었다. 그들은 또한 매우 넓은 코를 가지고 있었다. [4]이 특징은 그들이 널찍한 비강 안의 차갑고 건조한 공기를 따뜻하고 축축하게 하는 것을 가능하게 해주었다.

네안데르탈인의 큰 뇌 또한 그들이 생존하도록 돕는 지능과 기술을 제공했다. [5C]예를 들어, 혁신적인 석기 제작 기술은 그들에게 효과적인 무기를 만드는 능력을 주었다. 이것은 그들이 매머드, 순록, 들소와 같은 큰 동물들을 사냥할 수 있게 했다. [5A/5B]그들은 또한 불에 능통한 사람들이었고, 은신처에 살았으며, 옷을 입은 최초의 초기 인류였다.

그러나, 결국에는 아마 유난히 춥고 건조한 빙하기가 이 종을 절멸시켰을 것이다. [8B]대략 44,000년 전, 유럽의 평균 기온은 섭씨 0도 아래로 떨어졌고, 네안데르탈인은 사라지기 시작했다. [8A]일부 과학자들은 당시에 거대한 포유류들이 멸종하면서 네안데르탈인의 식량이 부족해졌을 것이라고 생각한다. [8C]다른 과학자들은 의견이 다른데, 그들은 네안데르탈인이 그저 우리 종과 경쟁할 수 없었던 것이라고 믿는다. 여하튼, 네안데르탈인의 놀라운 생존 이야기는 끝이 났고, 한때 그들이 거주했던 지역들은 곧 호모 사피엔스의 거주지가 되었다.

glacier 몡빙하    territory 몡지역    occupy 통차지하다
hardy 혱튼튼한    genetically 뷔유전적으로    endure 통견디다
harsh 혱가혹한    bulky 혱덩치가 큰    conserve 통보존하다
minimally 뷔아주 적게    extremely 뷔매우
humidify 통축축하게 하다    nasal cavity 비강
innovative 혱혁신적인    shelter 몡은신처
extinguish 통절멸시키다    temperature 몡기온, 온도
mammal 몡포유류    compete 통경쟁하다    remarkable 혱놀라운
dwell 통거주하다

1 글쓴이는 왜 "Africa"를 언급하는가?
   (A) 현생 인류와 네안데르탈인의 상대적인 위치를 밝히기 위해
   (B) 네안데르탈인이 어떻게 추위를 피했는지 설명하기 위해
   (C) 네안데르탈인이 어디에서 가장 가혹한 환경을 경험했는지 설명하기 위해
   (D) 빙하기 동안의 남반구의 기후에 대해 논하기 위해

2 지문의 단어 "hardy"와 의미가 가장 비슷한 것은?
   (A) 이국적인
   (B) 강한
   (C) 침입하는
   (D) 고대의

**34** 영어 실력을 높여주는 다양한 학습 자료 제공 HackersBook.com

**3** 다음 중 1단락에서 지구의 기후에 관해 추론할 수 있는 것은?

(A) 과거에는 전 세계의 기후가 덜 안정적이었다.
(B) 시베리아는 한때 유라시아의 다른 지역들보다 따뜻했다.
(C) 잉글랜드는 이전에 빙하로 덮여 있었다.
(D) 이전에 여러 차례의 빙하기가 있었다.

**4** 2단락에 따르면, 네안데르탈인의 큰 코는 그들이

(A) 숨 쉬는 공기를 따뜻하게 하는 것을 도왔다
(B) 먼 거리에서 사냥감의 냄새를 맡는 것을 도왔다
(C) 신체의 작은 크기를 보완하는 것을 도왔다
(D) 입김으로 그들의 몸을 덥히는 것을 도왔다

**5** 3단락에서, 글쓴이가 네안데르탈인에 관해 언급하지 않은 것은?

(A) 불을 통제하는 능력
(B) 그들이 옷을 입었다는 사실
(C) 도구를 만드는 능력
(D) 혁신적인 사냥 기술

**6** 지문의 단어 "extinguished"와 의미가 가장 비슷한 것은?

(A) 구별했다
(B) 얼렸다
(C) 끝냈다
(D) 나타냈다

**7** 아래 문장 중 지문 속의 음영된 문장의 핵심 정보를 가장 잘 표현한 것은? 오답은 문장의 의미를 크게 바꾸거나 핵심 정보를 생략한다.

(A) 네안데르탈인의 오랜 생존은 호모 사피엔스의 확산을 늦추었다.
(B) 네안데르탈인이 멸종하자, 호모 사피엔스가 그들의 이전 땅들을 차지했다.
(C) 네안데르탈인과 호모 사피엔스의 영역은 종종 겹쳤다.
(D) 호모 사피엔스가 한 지역으로 이주하면, 네안데르탈인은 그곳을 떠났다.

**8** 4단락에 따르면, 다음 중 네안데르탈인의 멸종에 대한 가능성 있는 설명이 아닌 것은?

(A) 불충분한 영양분
(B) 혹독한 기후
(C) 서로 다른 종들 간의 경쟁
(D) 전염병

**9** 네 개의 네모[■]는 다음 문장이 삽입될 수 있는 곳을 나타내고 있다.

**이것은 그들이 매머드, 순록, 들소와 같은 큰 동물들을 사냥할 수 있게 했다.**

이 문장은 어디에 들어가는 것이 가장 적절한가?

**10** 지시: 지문 요약을 위한 도입 문장이 아래에 주어져 있다. 지문의 가장 중요한 내용을 나타내는 보기 3개를 골라 요약을 완성하라. 어떤 문장은 지문에 언급되지 않은 내용이나 사소한 정보를 나타내므로 요약에 포함되지 않는다. 이 문제는 2점이다.

> **네안데르탈인은 극도로 추운 기후에 살았음에도 불구하고 오랫동안 생존했다.**
> · (B) 네안데르탈인은 그들을 추운 기후에 적합하도록 만드는 적응 형태들을 가지고 있었다.
> · (D) 네안데르탈인은 영리했으며, 이는 그들이 추운 환경에서 살아남도록 도왔다.
> · (E) 네안데르탈인은 대략 44,000년 전에 소멸하기 시작했다.

(A) 네안데르탈인은 대단히 큰 뇌를 가지고 있었다.
(C) 네안데르탈인은 빙하와 아프리카 사이의 유라시아에 거주했다.
(F) 네안데르탈인은 현생 인류와 이종 교배를 했다.

## Vocabulary Review

| 1 enthusiasm | 2 evaporated | 3 temptation |
|---|---|---|
| 4 seek | 5 endured | 6 alternatives |
| 7 (C) | 8 (B) | 9 (A) | 10 (B) |
| 11 (C) | 12 (A) | 13 (D) | 14 (B) |

---

# CHAPTER 09
# Summary

## Example
본문 p.141

**1** (A), (C), (F)

### 악기의 왕

피아노는 악기의 왕으로 알려져 있다. 그것은 모든 관현악단의 악기들 중에서 가장 크며, 300에서 1,000파운드의 무게가 나간다. 그것은 7옥타브에 걸친 비할 데 없는 음역대를 가지고 있다. 그것은 저음을 내는 더블 바순의 가장 낮은 음과 고음을 내는 피콜로의 가장 높은 음을 낼 수 있다. 그리고 그것은 대단히 표현력이 풍부해서, 같은 음을 부드러운 속삭임같이 내거나 천둥 같은 굉음으로 낼 수 있다. 이 특별한 악기는 어떻게 생겨났을까?

피아노는 수 세기에 걸친 음악적 혁신의 정점이다. 건반 악기들은 기원전 220년에 그리스인들이 히드라울리스를 만들었을 때부터 존재해 왔다. 물 오르간이라고도 알려진 그것은 물통에서 현대 오르간의 것과 다르지 않은 일련의 파이프로 공기를 밀어 넣음으로써 소리를 냈다. 11세기에는, 중동에서 해머드 덜시머가 발명되었다. 덜시머는 작은 해머로 현들을 쳐서 작동한다. 르네상스 동안에는, 클라비코드와 하프시코드가 등장했다. 둘 중 어느 것도 풍부한 감정을 담아 연주될 수 없었다. 건반들이 아무리 세게 눌러도, 소리는 같았다.

1700년에, 바르톨로메오 디 프란체스코는 더 다양한 음조로 현들을 연주하는 해머를 사용함으로써 그 초기의 모델들을 개선했다. 이탈리아의 하프시코드 장인 크리스토포리는 그의 발명품에 이 다양성을 표현하는 능력을 강조하는 긴 이름을 붙였다. 그 이름은 "크고 부드러운 소리를 연주할 수 있는 하프시코드"로 번역되었다. 이 본래의 이름은 이후 "피아노"로 줄여졌다. 악기의 왕이 탄생한 것이다.

instrument 몡악기    orchestral 톙관현악단의
weigh 통무게가 나가다    unmatched 톙비할 데 없는
span 통~에 걸치다    expressive 톙표현력이 풍부한
thunderous 톙천둥 같은    culmination 몡정점
innovation 몡혁신    invent 통발명하다    string 몡(악기의) 현
emerge 통등장하다    emotion 몡감정    improve 통개선하다
intonation 몡음조    craftsman 몡장인    emphasize 통강조하다
capacity 몡능력    translate 통번역되다    shorten 통줄이다

**CHAPTER 09** | Summary **35**

1 **지시:** 지문 요약을 위한 도입 문장이 아래에 주어져 있다. 지문의 가장 중요한 내용을 나타내는 보기 3개를 골라 요약을 완성하라.

**피아노는 18세기가 시작될 무렵에 발명되었다.**

(A) 피아노는 마찬가지로 건반을 가지고 있었던 여러 초기 악기들의 영향을 받았다.

(B) 해머드 덜시머는 그것이 중동에서 발명되었다는 점에서 피아노와 같다.

(C) 피아노는 음악가들이 더 많은 감정을 담아 연주할 수 있게 해줌으로써 이전에 쓰이던 것들보다 개선되었다.

(D) 클라비코드와 하프시코드는 피아노의 중요한 전신이었다.

(E) 최초의 피아노는 기원전 220년에 그리스에서 발명되었다.

(F) 음악가들은 피아노를 이용하여 광범위한 소리를 낼 수 있다.

## Reading Practice 1

1 (A)   2 (C)   3 (C)   4 (A), (C), (F)

**Vocabulary Quiz**

1 ⓐ   2 ⓒ   3 ⓐ   4 ⓐ

### 탄소 발자국

탄소 발자국은 배출된 온실가스의 양을 측정하는 방법이다. 이 가스들은 열이 지구의 대기에서 빠져나가는 것을 막는다. 그 결과, 지구의 평균 기온이 상승한다. 빙하는 녹고, 해수면은 상승하며, 악천후가 더 만연해진다. 탄소 발자국은 때때로 어떠한 활동에 의해 배출되는 탄소의 양을 생산하기 위해 필요한 토지의 양으로 표현된다. 예를 들어, 만약 모든 사람이 전형적인 미국식 생활 방식으로 산다면, 세계 인구를 지탱하기 위해 지구 네 개와 맞먹는 것이 필요할 것이다.

세계 각국은 고유한 탄소 발자국을 갖는다. 중국과 미국은 가장 큰 탄소 발자국을 가지고 있다. 이 국가들은 둘이 합쳐 전 세계 탄소 배출의 43퍼센트를 차지한다. 그러나, 그 나라들은 그것의 인구의 24퍼센트만을 가지고 있다. 이 가스들의 대부분은 화석 연료를 태우는 것에 의해 발생한다. 이것들은 석탄과 석유를 둘 다 포함한다. 따라서, 환경운동가들은 풍력과 태양열같이 온실가스를 배출하지 않는 에너지 원천으로 전환하는 것을 지지한다. 그들은 또한 전 세계의 삼림들이 보존되어야 한다고 요구한다. 나무는 1에이커당 1.4톤의 이산화탄소를 흡수한다. 2015년에, 약 200개의 국가들이 파리 협정에 서명함으로써 이 목표를 약속했다.

개인의 탄소 발자국이 줄어질 수 있는 많은 방법이 있다. ³ᴬ예를 들어, 이것은 자동차 대신 기차와 자전거를 이용함으로써 이뤄질 수 있다. 소가 메탄가스를 배출하기 때문에, 1인분의 소고기는 대기에 6파운드의 온실가스를 더한다. ³ᴮ따라서, 고기를 채소로 대체하는 것은 탄소 발자국을 줄이기 위한 효과적인 전략이다. ³ᴰ식품을 운송하는 것이 대기에 이산화탄소를 내뿜기 때문에 현지에서 생산된 식품 또한 더 좋다.

greenhouse gas 온실가스   escape 图빠져나가다
atmosphere 圀대기   average 圀평균의
prevalent 圀만연한, 널리 퍼진   emit 图배출하다
equivalent 圀~과 맞먹는 것   sustain 图지탱하다
account for (부분·비율을) 차지하다   emission 圀배출
fossil fuel 화석 연료   environmentalist 圀환경운동가
advocate 图지지하다   transition 图전환하다

demand 图요구하다   preserve 图보존하다   commit 图약속하다
accomplish 图이루다   serving 圀1인분   transport 图운송하다

1 지문의 단어 "prevalent"와 의미가 가장 비슷한 것은?

(A) 일반적인
(B) 중요한
(C) 해로운
(D) 예측할 수 있는

2 지문의 단어 "its"가 가리키는 것은?

(A) 중국
(B) 미국
(C) 전 세계
(D) 탄소

3 3단락에 따르면, 다음 중 개인의 탄소 발자국을 줄이도록 돕는 것이 아닌 것은?

(A) 대중교통을 이용하는 것
(B) 채소를 더 많이 포함한 식단을 먹는 것
(C) 고기의 더 좋은 공급원을 찾아내는 것
(D) 현지에서 생산된 제품을 사는 것

4 **지시:** 지문 요약을 위한 도입 문장이 아래에 주어져 있다. 지문의 가장 중요한 내용을 나타내는 보기 3개를 골라 요약을 완성하라.

**탄소 발자국은 얼마나 많은 온실가스가 배출되는지를 측정하는 방법을 제공한다.**

(A) 각 개인은 기후 변화의 위험을 방지하는 것에 일조할 수 있다.

(B) 소는 강력한 온실가스인 메탄가스를 자연적으로 배출함으로써 온실가스를 생성한다.

(C) 사람들은 화석 연료의 사용을 줄임으로써 국가적 차원에서 기후 변화를 예방할 수 있다.

(D) 중국과 미국은 두 곳의 세계 최대 온실가스 배출국이다.

(E) 1에이커의 삼림마다, 1톤 이상의 이산화탄소가 대기에서 제거된다.

(F) 온실가스는 지구를 더욱 더워지게 하며, 이는 그것의 생존을 위태롭게 한다.

## Reading Practice 2
본문 p.144

1 (B)   2 (B)   3 (A)   4 (C), (E), (F)

**Vocabulary Quiz**

1 ⓑ   2 ⓒ   3 ⓐ   4 ⓒ

### 가뭄은 어떻게 마야 제국을 멸망시켰는가

열두 세기 동안, 마야 제국은 아메리카에서 가장 진보한 문명이었다. 마야인들은 찬란한 석조 도시를 건설했고, 고유의 문자 체계를 개발했다. 그들은 또한 수학과 천문학에서 중요한 발견들을 했다. 그러나, 서기 900년경, 그들의 사회는 붕괴했다. 한때 수백만 명의 사람들의 안식처였던 그들의 도시는 텅 비었다. 그들의 석회암 궁전과 사원들은 버려졌다. 역사가들은 이 급작스러운 쇠퇴의 원인을 알아내기 위해 오랫동안 애써왔다. 현대 과학의 도구들로 무장한 연구자들은 마침내 그 퍼즐의 조각들을 맞추기 시작하고 있다.

²많은 연구가 마야 문명이 심각한 가뭄에 의해 완전히 파괴되었다는 것을 보여준다. 과학자들은 한 호수 바닥의 광물의 퇴적물을 조사했다. 그들은 서기 750년과 1000년 사이에 강수량이 급격하게 줄어들었다는 증거를 발견했다. 그들은 또한 동굴들 내부의 종유석과 석순의 형성 연대를 추정했다. 이것들은 동일한 시기에 환경이 건조했다는 것을 보여주었다. 마야인들은 건기에 빗물을 저장하는 거대한 석조 저수지들을 갖추고 있었다. 그러나, 이 가뭄이 아마도 너무 오래 지속되어 그 저수지들이 비게 되었을 것이다. 식수를 찾는 것은 어려웠다.

마야인들은 나무를 태우고 베어 버림으로써 가뭄을 명백하게 악화시켰다. 그들은 그들 자신의 성공의 희생양이었다. 그들이 많은 인구를 먹여 살려야 했기 때문에, 삼림은 옥수수밭으로 대체되었다. 게다가, 그들의 인상적인 건축 양식은 삼림 파괴를 부채질했다. 1제곱미터의 석회암마다, 마야인들은 20그루의 나무를 태워야 했다. 태양열을 흡수할 나무들이 점점 더 적어지면서, 점점 더 적은 비구름이 마야의 영토 위에 형성되었다. 컴퓨터 시뮬레이션에 따르면, 삼림 파괴는 그 가뭄에 60퍼센트 정도의 책임이 있었다. 그들의 영리함에도 불구하고, 마야인들은 그들의 활동이 생존에 미칠 파괴적인 영향을 아직 이해하지 못했다.

advanced 형 진보한    glorious 형 찬란한    collapse 통 붕괴하다
limestone 명 석회암    abandon 통 버리다    struggle 통 애쓰다
devastate 통 완전히 파괴하다    drought 명 가뭄    deposit 명 퇴적물
steeply 부 급격하게    date 통 연대를 추정하다    reservoir 명 저수지
store 통 저장하다    prolonged 형 오래 지속되는
apparently 부 명백하게    chop down 베다
impressive 형 인상적인    fuel 통 부채질하다
deforestation 명 삼림 파괴    solar radiation 태양열

**1** 글쓴이는 왜 "pieces of the puzzle"을 언급하는가?

(A) 연구원이 마야의 역사를 연구하는 것에서 즐거움을 얻는다는 것을 보여주기 위해

(B) 마야의 쇠퇴 이유가 명백하지 않다는 것을 강조하기 위해

(C) 마야의 건축물의 건축에 많은 구성요소가 있었다는 것을 설명하기 위해

(D) 마야 제국의 붕괴가 이해하기 쉽다는 생각을 반박하기 위해

**2** 2단락에 따르면, 마야의 인구가 줄어든 것은

(A) 저수지들이 인구를 지탱할 수 있을 정도로 충분한 물을 저장할 수 없었기 때문이다

(B) 오랜 기간 동안 충분하지 않은 양의 비가 내렸기 때문이다

(C) 농경지에서 석조 건물의 건축이 일어났기 때문이다

(D) 유해한 광물이 여러 수역에 축적되었기 때문이다

**3** 지문의 단어 "fueled"와 의미가 가장 비슷한 것은?

(A) 부추겼다

(B) 시작했다

(C) 할당했다

(D) 지연했다

**4** 지시: 지문 요약을 위한 도입 문장이 아래에 주어져 있다. 지문의 가장 중요한 내용을 나타내는 보기 3개를 골라 요약을 완성하라.

**과학은 마야 문명의 급작스러운 쇠퇴에 대한 이유를 밝혀내고 있다.**

(A) 마야인들은 중요한 수학적 발견들을 했다.

(B) 종유석과 석순은 물과 광물의 기둥이다.

(C) 마야 문명은 시대에 비해 진보되어 있었고, 많은 중요한 기여

를 했다.

(D) 마야인들은 강수량이 적은 기간에 빗물을 저장하기 위한 저수지들을 지었다.

(E) 삼림 파괴는 건조한 환경을 더욱 악화시켰다.

(F) 끔찍한 가뭄이 마야 제국의 마지막 200년 동안 물을 구하기 어렵게 만들었다.

## Reading Practice 3    본문 p. 146

1 (A)    2 (A)    3 (D)    4 (A), (C), (E)

### Vocabulary Quiz

1 ⓑ    2 ⓑ    3 ⓐ    4 ⓒ

### 의학의 역사

역사의 대부분 동안, 많은 질병들이 마법과 신들의 탓으로 여겨졌다. 일반적인 감기 같은 사소한 문제들은 약초로 치료될 수 있는 자연스러운 일로 여겨졌다. 더욱 심각한 질병들은 초자연적인 존재들에 의해 야기된다고 생각되었다. 마법, 물약, 주문이 치료를 위한 일반적인 접근법들이었다.

신체에 대한 인류의 이해는 몇 세기에 걸쳐 크게 변화해왔다. 고대 이집트인들은 해부학에 거의 관심이 없었다. 그럼에도 불구하고, 그들의 영적인 믿음은 그들이 미라화의 과정을 통해 시신을 보존하도록 이끌었다. 그 결과, 우리는 그들이 직면했던 질병들이 오늘날 우리가 직면하는 것들과 유사하다는 것을 알고 있다. 그리스인들은 고유의 의료 체계를 발전시켰다. 치료는 체액의 균형을 회복시키는 것을 목표로 삼았다. 인도에서, 힌두교 신자들은 건강이 영혼, 가래, 담즙의 균형에 근거한다고 믿었다. 중국인들 또한 음과 양이라는 개념의 균형에 초점을 맞췄다.

1800년대에 이르러서, 실험에 입각한 연구가 유럽에 뿌리를 내렸다. 화학과 실험 장비의 발전은 약의 제조를 도왔다. 그러나, 아편과 퀴닌 이상의 효과적인 약물은 거의 없었다. 따라서, 유독한 금속성 화합물과 같은 쓸모없는 민간요법이 인기 있는 치료법이었다. ³로베르트 코흐, 에드워드 제너, 루이스 파스퇴르의 세균학 연구가 특정 전염성 질병들의 실제 치료로 이어졌다. 그러나, 치명적인 질병들의 감소는 공중 보건과 영양의 개선에 더 크게 기인했다. 20세기가 되어서야, 의학에서 진정한 비약적 발전이 일어났다. 이때가 약학과 수술에서의 큰 발전이 일어났던 때이다.

be attributed to ~의 탓으로 여겨지다    supernatural 형 초자연적인
being 명 존재    incantation 명 (마법의) 주문    significantly 부 크게
anatomy 명 해부학    spiritual 형 영적인    mummification 명 미라화
take root 뿌리를 내리다, 널리 받아들여지다    aid 통 돕다
opium 명 아편    quinine 명 퀴닌    folklore 명 민간, 민속
poisonous 형 유독한    compound 명 화합물
bacteriology 명 세균학    infectious 형 전염성의    lethal 형 치명적인
breakthrough 명 비약적 발전    pharmacology 명 약학

**1** 지문의 어구 "attributed to"와 의미가 가장 비슷한 것은?

(A) ~의 탓으로 돌리다

(B) ~을 언급하다

(C) ~을 감안하다

(D) ~에 의해 지연되다

**2** 글쓴이는 왜 "metal-based compounds"를 언급하는가?

(A) 쓸모없는 민간요법의 예시를 제공하기 위해
(B) 새로운 의학과 오래된 의학 사이의 차이를 설명하기 위해
(C) 과학적인 발전이 어떻게 의학을 개선하였는지 보여주기 위해
(D) 현대 의학에서의 금속의 이용을 설명하기 위해

**3** 3단락에 따르면, 세균학 실험은 어떤 영향을 끼쳤는가?

(A) 체액의 균형을 회복시켰다.
(B) 아편과 같은 약물의 이용을 늘렸다.
(C) 전통적인 치료법을 더 효과적으로 만들었다.
(D) 과학자들에게 질병을 치료하는 방법을 제공했다.

**4** **지시**: 지문 요약을 위한 도입 문장이 아래에 주어져 있다. 지문의 가장 중요한 내용을 나타내는 보기 3개를 골라 요약을 완성하라.

**질병은 한때 초자연적인 힘에 의해 야기된다고 생각되었다.**

(A) 인체에 대한 우리의 이해는 몇 세기에 걸쳐 크게 발전해왔다.
(B) 고대에는 일반적인 감기가 약초로 치료되었다.
(C) 실험은 19세기의 의학에서 중요한 요소였다.
(D) 힌두교 신자들은 가래가 건강을 유지하는 데 중요한 요인이라고 믿었다.
(E) 의학의 비약적 발전은 20세기에 이르러서야 시작됐다.
(F) 아편과 퀴닌은 의사들에 의해 사용된 가장 초기의 약물에 속했다.

## Reading Practice 4 본문 p. 148

**1** (D)  **2** (C)  **3** (D)  **4** (A), (B), (C)

**Vocabulary Quiz**

**1** ⓒ  **2** ⓐ  **3** ⓑ  **4** ⓑ

### 태평양 제도 원주민들의 기원

태평양 제도의 최초 정착민들의 기원이 과학자들에 의해 점차 짜 맞추어 지고 있다. DNA 기술은 그들에게 현재와 이전의 섬 주민들에 대한 더 나은 지식을 제공해오고 있다. 태평양 제도의 두 지역인 멜라네시아와 폴리네시아의 역사는 유전자 연구들의 결과로써 이제 막 논의되기 시작했다.

증거는 멜라네시아가 사람들에 의해 거주된 첫 번째 지역이라는 것을 보여준다. ¹ᴬ대략 70,000년 전에, 오늘날의 인도네시아에서 온 사람들이 파푸아 뉴기니에 도착했다. ¹ᴮ이 파푸아인들 중 많은 이들이 대략 4,000년 전부터 뉴기니 동쪽의 섬들 안쪽으로 퍼져 나갔다. 그들은 대체로 검은 피부를 가지고 있었다. ¹ᶜ그 결과, 유럽의 탐험가들은 그 지역에 멜라네시아, 즉 "검은 제도"라는 이름을 붙였다.

학자들은 오랫동안 최초의 폴리네시아인들이 멜라네시아에서 왔는지에 대해 논쟁해왔다. 언어학자들은 폴리네시아의 언어들이 파푸아인들의 그것들보다 동아시아인들의 그것들과 더 많이 유사하다는 것에 주목했다. 초기의 DNA 연구들은 폴리네시아인들이 멜라네시아인들과 섞였다는 것을 시사했다. 이 두 가지 사실들은 서로 모순되는 것으로 보였다. 그러나, 이 모순은 최근에 해결되었다. 과학자들은 네 명의 고대 폴리네시아 여성들의 DNA를 분석했다. 그것은 그 여성들이 멜라네시아가 아니라 대만과 필리핀에서 온 조상들을 가지고 있었을 가능성이 높다는 것을 밝혀냈다. 게다가, 그 분석은 폴리네시아인들이 동아

시아인들의 유전자보다 파푸아인들의 유전자를 훨씬 더 최근에 얻었다는 것을 보여주었다.

DNA 분석으로부터 흥미로운 새로운 그림이 드러났다. 대략 3,000년 전에, 동아시아 출신의 사람들은 태평양에서 아주 위험한 통나무배 여행을 하기 시작했다. 그들은 멜라네시아의 섬들을 지나 폴리네시아로 나아갔다. 수천 년 후에, 멜라네시아인들이 폴리네시아에 도착했다. 그들은 이미 그곳에 있었던 사람들과 결혼했다. 유전 과학이 없었다면, 이 역사는 수수께끼로 남았을 것이다.

settler 명 정착민  current 형 현재의  previous 형 이전의
inhabitant 명 주민  genetic 형 유전자의  indicate 동 보여주다
spread out 퍼져 나가다  linguist 명 언어학자  note 동 주목하다
mingle 동 섞이다  conflict 동 모순되다; 명 모순
resolve 동 해결하다  analyze 동 분석하다  reveal 동 밝혀내다
ancestor 명 조상  acquire 동 얻다  fascinating 형 흥미로운
perilous 형 아주 위험한  proceed 동 나아가다

**1** 2단락에 따르면, 파푸아인에 관한 다음 주장들 중 증거가 있는 것이 아닌 것은?

(A) 오늘날 인도네시아의 일부인 지역에서 왔다
(B) 다른 섬들에 정착하기 위해 뉴기니에서 동쪽으로 이동했다
(C) 유럽에서 온 탐험가들과 접촉했다
(D) 대략 7만 년 전에 멜라네시아를 떠났다

**2** 지문의 단어 "those"가 가리키는 것은?

(A) 폴리네시아인들
(B) 언어학자들
(C) 언어들
(D) 동아시아인들

**3** 지문의 단어 "perilous"와 의미가 가장 비슷한 것은?

(A) 비싼
(B) 해상의
(C) 피곤하게 하는
(D) 위험한

**4** **지시**: 지문 요약을 위한 도입 문장이 아래에 주어져 있다. 지문의 가장 중요한 내용을 나타내는 보기 3개를 골라 요약을 완성하라.

**태평양 제도 원주민들의 역사는 이제 막 이해되기 시작했다.**

(A) 최초의 멜라네시아인들은 인도네시아에서 뉴기니로 왔다.
(B) 과학자들은 폴리네시아인들의 기원에 관해 의견이 달랐다.
(C) 폴리네시아의 최초 정착민들은 동아시아에서 왔다.
(D) 멜라네시아라는 용어는 멜라네시아인들의 피부색을 지칭한다.
(E) 최초의 파푸아인들은 통나무배를 타고 멜라네시아로 왔다.
(F) DNA 기술은 과학자들에게 초기의 태평양 제도 원주민들이 어떻게 여행했는지를 보여준다.

## iBT Reading Test 본문 p. 150

**1** (C)  **2** (D)  **3** (B)  **4** (D)
**5** (A)  **6** (B)  **7** (B)  **8** (D)
**9** (D)  **10** (A), (D), (F)

## 우주 방사선

²ᴬ우주 방사선은 빛의 속도보다 약간 느리게 우주를 여행하는 원자보다 작은 입자들이다. ²ᶜ일부는 태양 표면의 폭발에서 방출되고, 일부는 은하계의 더 깊은 곳이나 심지어는 은하의 바깥에서 기원한다. ⁷ᴰ매초마다, 지구는 1제곱미터당 대략 10,000개의 우주 방사선에 의해 충격을 받는다. ²ᴮ이 우주 방사선의 대부분이 지구의 자기장 보호막에 의해 굴절되지만, 일부는 대기 상층부와 지표면에 도달한다.

우주 방사선을 연구하는 것이 항상 쉽지는 않다. 그것들이 우주에서 자기장 보호막에 의해 굴절될 수 있기 때문에, 우주 방사선은 그것들의 근원까지 직접적으로 추적될 수 없다. 대신, 과학자들은 그것들의 양과 구성을 조사함으로써 우주 방사선의 기원을 추정한다. ⁷ᶜ오스트리아의 물리학자 빅터 헤스는 열기구를 타고 대기 상층부에 올라가 방사선을 측정함으로써 1912년에 처음으로 우주 방사선을 발견했다. ⁶그는 방사선이 지구의 핵에서 생겨난다는 가설을 실험하는 중이었지만, 우주 방사선의 존재로 인해 그가 더 높이 올라갈수록 방사선의 양이 증가한다는 것이 밝혀졌다. 그 이후로, 과학자들은 우주 방사선의 약 89퍼센트는 가벼운 수소 양성자이고, 10퍼센트는 헬륨이며, 1퍼센트는 우라늄과 같은 더 무거운 핵이라는 것을 알아냈다.

⁷ᴬ과학자들은 이 작은 입자들이 별의 생성이나 소멸과 같은 우주 깊은 곳 거대한 별의 사건들의 비밀을 밝혀줄 것이라는 희망을 가지고, 지구에 도달하는 우주 방사선을 연구하기 위해 노력한다. 그들은 초신성의 잔해가 우주에서 폭발할 때 더 높은 에너지의 우주 방사선이 방출된다고 오랫동안 추측해 왔다. ⁸2017년에, 연구자들은 그들이 두 중성자별의 융합에서 나온 파동들을 감지했을 때 이것이 사실임을 확인했다. 중성자별들은 상대적으로 작지만, 밀도가 높은 초거성의 잔해이다. 이것은 과학자들로 하여금 그것들이 생성하는 우주 방사선을 확인함으로써, 그들이 미래에 유사한 현상들을 연구할 수 있을 것이라고 믿게 해주었다.

cosmic rays 우주 방사선　　subatomic 형 원자보다 작은
solar flare 태양 표면의 폭발　　bombard 동 충격을 가하다, 공격하다
radiation 명 방사선　　deflect 동 굴절시키다　　trace 동 추적하다
deduce 동 추정하다　　abundance 명 (많은) 양
hypothesis 명 가설　　presence 명 존재　　lightweight 형 가벼운
proton 명 양성자　　nucleus 명 핵　　stellar 형 별의
supernova 명 초신성　　remnant 명 잔해　　explode 동 폭발하다
merger 명 융합　　neutron star 중성자별　　phenomenon 명 현상

**1** 지문의 단어 "bombarded"와 의미가 가장 비슷한 것은?

(A) 개최되다
(B) 반사되다
(C) 충격을 받다
(D) 빼앗기다

**2** 다음 중 글쓴이가 우주 방사선에 관해 묘사하지 않는 것은?

(A) 우주를 지나가는 동안의 속도
(B) 자기장 보호막과 충돌했을 때의 반응
(C) 태양 표면의 폭발에서 기원한다는 것
(D) 지구의 핵을 관통하는 능력

**3** 아래 문장 중 지문 속의 음영된 문장의 핵심 정보를 가장 잘 표현한 것은? 오답은 문장의 의미를 크게 바꾸거나 핵심 정보를 생략한다.

(A) 그것들이 상호작용하는 다양한 자기장을 연구함으로써 우주 방사선을 탐지하는 것이 가능하다.
(B) 자기장과의 상호작용으로 인해 그것들의 경로가 바뀌기 때문에

우주 방사선을 추적하는 것은 불가능하다.
(C) 우주 방사선은 자기장에서 자기장으로 튕겨 나가기 때문에 그것들을 찾는 것은 어렵다.
(D) 우주 방사선이 종종 자기장을 우회하기 때문에, 그것들이 따라서 나아가는 경로를 추적하는 것은 어렵다.

**4** 지문의 단어 "their"가 가리키는 것은?

(A) 자기장 보호막
(B) 과학자들
(C) 기원
(D) 우주 방사선

**5** 지문의 단어 "composition"과 의미가 가장 비슷한 것은?

(A) 구성
(B) 기록
(C) 창조성
(D) 부패

**6** 다음 중 빅터 헤스에 관해 추론할 수 있는 것은?

(A) 그는 방사선이 별에 관한 사건들에서 생겨난다는 것을 확인하고 싶어 했다.
(B) 그는 열기구가 하늘 위로 올라갈수록 방사선이 감소할 것이라고 예상했다.
(C) 그는 여행에서 우주 방사선의 화학 성분을 실험했다.
(D) 그의 가설은 열기구 실험에 의해 뒷받침되었다.

**7** 지문에 따르면, 다음 중 우주 방사선을 연구하는 과학자들에 관해 사실이 아닌 것은?

(A) 먼 우주의 사건들을 알아내기 위해 지구에 도달한 입자들을 이용한다.
(B) 지구에 도달하는 우주 방사선의 기원을 확인하지 못한다.
(C) 백 년 이상 우주 방사선을 연구해오고 있다.
(D) 지구에 도달하는 우주 방사선의 수를 추정할 수 있다.

**8** 3단락에 따르면, 초신성에 의해 방출되는 우주 방사선은

(A) 인간에게 위협이 된다
(B) 격렬한 우주 충돌을 야기한다
(C) 직선으로 이동한다
(D) 특히 강력하다

**9** 네 개의 네모[■]는 다음 문장이 삽입될 수 있는 곳을 나타내고 있다.

**중성자별들은 상대적으로 작지만, 밀도가 높은 초거성의 잔해이다.**

이 문장은 어디에 들어가는 것이 가장 적절한가?

**10** 지시: 지문 요약을 위한 도입 문장이 아래에 주어져 있다. 지문의 가장 중요한 내용을 나타내는 보기 3개를 골라 요약을 완성하라. 어떤 문장은 지문에 언급되지 않은 내용이나 사소한 정보를 나타내므로 요약에 포함되지 않는다. **이 문제는 2점이다.**

> **우주 방사선은 우주 공간에서 오는 입자들이다.**
> · (A) 우주 방사선에 관한 자료를 수집하는 것은 어려울 수 있다.
> · (D) 과학자들은 거대한 천체의 사건들에 대해 알아내기 위해 원자보다 작은 입자들을 연구한다.
> · (F) 우리 행성은 많은 양의 우주 방사선에 계속 노출된다.

(B) 지구에 도달하는 대부분의 우주 방사선은 다른 은하계에서 생겨난다.

(C) 우주 방사선은 열기구 여행에서 발견되었다.
(E) 중성자별들의 융합이 우주 방사선을 방출했다.

## Vocabulary Review

본문 p. 154

| | | |
|---|---|---|
| 1 unmatched | 2 remnants | 3 previous |
| 4 store | 5 presence | 6 explodes |
| 7 (A) | 8 (D) | 9 (A)    10 (A) |
| 11 (A) | 12 (C) | 13 (B)    14 (B) |

CHAPTER 10
# Category Chart

## Example

본문 p. 157

1 DNA: (B), (E), (F)  RNA: (C), (D)

### DNA와 RNA

유기체의 모든 세포에는 유전 정보를 포함하는 두 가지 핵산이 존재하는데, 이것들은 데옥시리보핵산(DNA)과 리보핵산(RNA)이다. 그것들은 많은 공통점을 가지고 있지만, 둘 사이에는 중대한 기능적이고 구조적인 차이가 있다.

DNA가 본질적으로 생물의 청사진인 반면, RNA는 더 활동적인 역할을 한다. DNA는 단백질 생산을 위한 지시사항들을 포함하는데, 단백질은 모든 생물을 구성하는 세포의 기본 단위이다. 따라서, 한 유기체의 DNA는 그것의 특성들을 결정한다. RNA의 주된 역할은 이 정보들을 DNA에서 리보솜으로 운반하는 것인데, 리보솜은 세포에서 단백질이 생산되는 부분이다.

구조적으로, RNA는 불완전한 DNA처럼 보인다. DNA는 나선형의 계단처럼 서로 감겨 있는 두 가닥의 당인산으로 구성된다. 이 계단을 가로지르는 것은 짝을 이룬 계단의 (염기라고 불리는) "단"인데, 이것은 아데닌, 티민, 사이토신, 구아닌으로 이루어져 있다. 그에 반해서, RNA는 한 가닥의 구불구불한 당인산만을 가지고 있으며, 그것의 염기는 짝을 이루지 않는다. 이 염기의 화학적 구성은 티민이 우라실로 대체된다는 점을 제외하면 DNA와 동일하다.

이 두 가지 핵산은 세포의 서로 다른 위치에서 발견된다. DNA는 세포의 핵 내부나 중앙에 있다. 또한 세포의 미토콘드리아에 적은 양의 DNA가 있으며, 이것이 에너지를 음식에서 세포로 전달한다. RNA는 주로 세포질에서 발견되는데, 세포질은 외부의 세포막과 핵 사이의 끈적끈적한 용액이다.

nucleic acid 핵산   organism 몡유기체, 생물
functional 혱기능적인   essentially 뿐본질적으로
instruction 몡지시사항   protein 몡단백질   determine 동결정하다
strand 몡가닥   sugar phosphate 당인산   wind 동감다
spiral 혱나선형의   staircase 몡계단   base 몡염기
twisty 혱구불구불한   composition 몡구성   transfer 동전달하다
cytoplasm 몡세포질   solution 몡용액   membrane 몡세포막

---

1 지시: 주어진 선택지에서 적절한 어구를 선택하여 관계있는 핵산의 종류에 연결하라.

| 선택지 | DNA |
|---|---|
| (A) 리보솜이라 불리는 특별한 세포를 생산한다<br>(G) 티민과 우라실의 짝을 포함한다 | · (B) 나선형의 계단처럼 보인다<br>· (E) 유기체의 특징들을 결정한다<br>· (F) 세포의 핵 내부에 위치한다 |
| | RNA |
| | · (C) 정보를 세포의 다른 부분으로 운반한다<br>· (D) 한 가닥의 당인산을 가지고 있다 |

## Reading Practice 1

본문 p. 158

1 (C)   2 (A)   3 (D)
4 Comic strips: (A), (G)  Comic books: (B), (D), (E)

**Vocabulary Quiz**

1 ⓒ   2 ⓒ   3 ⓐ   4 ⓐ

### 미국의 만화

만화는 그림과 글을 둘 다 가지고 있는 칸들을 특징으로 하는 매체 형태이다. 이 칸들은 순차적인 서술을 하기 위해 보통 시간 순서대로 배열된다. 미국에서, 만화의 두 가지 주요 형태는 연재만화와 만화책이다.

연재만화는 일반적으로 신문에 매일 게재되며, 최대 8개의 칸을 갖는다. 그것들은 두 가지 만화 형식 중 더 오래된 것인데, 최초의 연재만화는 '옐로우 키드'로, 1895년부터 1898년까지 연재되었다. 연재만화는 대개 유머에 집중하며, 각각의 개별적인 연재만화는 하나의 농담이나 재미있는 상황을 전개시킨다. 이것의 이유는 제한된 칸의 수가 복잡한 줄거리를 표현하는 것을 어렵게 하기 때문이다. 게다가, 신문에 연재만화가 포함되는 것은 그것들이 논쟁의 여지가 있는 내용을 담을 수 없다는 것을 의미한다.

만화책은 훨씬 더 많은 자유를 제공한다. 칸들로 이루어진 20여 페이지가 넘는 개별적인 간행물들이 한 달에 한 번씩 출간되기 때문에, 작가들은 더 다양한 범위의 주제를 가진 더욱 정교한 이야기들을 전개시킬 수 있다. 최초의 만화책은 1933년에 출간되었고, 이 형식은 슈퍼맨과 캡틴 아메리카 같은 인기 있는 슈퍼 영웅의 등장으로 이후 20년 이상 엄청난 인기를 경험했다. 제2차 세계대전 동안, 독일과 일본의 군인들과 싸우는 등장인물들에 관한 이야기들은 미국 군인들의 사기를 북돋우기 위해 미국 정부에 의해 적극적으로 장려되었다. 그러나, 1950년대에, 만화책이 아이들에게 미치는 부정적인 영향에 대한 우려가 커졌다. ³정부의 규제를 피하기 위해, 주요 만화책 출판사들은 만화 출판 규약(CCA)을 만들고 따르는 것에 동의했다. 이 규약 모음은 과도한 폭력의 묘사와 사회적으로 부적절한 주제에 대한 언급을 제한한다.

feature 동특징으로 하다   arrange 동배열하다
in chronological order 시간 순서대로   linear 혱순차적인

narrative 몡 서술    typically 閅 일반적으로    inclusion 몡 포함
controversial 혬 논쟁의 여지가 있는    issue 몡 간행물
elaborate 혬 정교한    boom 몡 엄청난 인기    actively 閅 적극적으로
encourage 통 장려하다    boost 통 북돋다    morale 몡 사기, 의욕
military personnel 군인    regulation 몡 규제    excessive 혬 과도한
reference 몡 언급    inappropriate 혬 부적절한

**1** 글쓴이는 왜 "*The Yellow Kid*"를 언급하는가?

(A) 연재만화가 책보다 더 사랑받았다는 것을 시사하기 위해

(B) 만화가 왜 신문에 포함되었는지를 설명하기 위해

(C) 한 만화 유형에서 최초로 알려진 예시를 밝히기 위해

(D) 논쟁의 여지가 있는 연재만화에 대한 설명을 제공하기 위해

**2** 지문의 단어 "boost"와 의미가 가장 비슷한 것은?

(A) 증진하다

(B) 분배하다

(C) 영향을 주다

(D) 회복하다

**3** 3단락에 따르면, 다음 중 CCA에 관해 사실인 것은?

(A) 폭력적인 그림들을 금지하는 것에 국한되어 있다.

(B) 전쟁 시기의 문제에 대한 반응이었다.

(C) 정부에 의해 강요되었다.

(D) 일련의 자발적인 지침들이었다.

**4** **지시:** 주어진 선택지에서 적절한 어구를 선택하여 관계있는 만화의 종류에 연결하라.

| 선택지 | 연재만화 |
|---|---|
| (C) 시간순의 서술을 포함하는 것을 피했다<br>(F) 신문에 등장한 이야기들을 기반으로 했다 | · (A) 19세기에 처음 등장했다<br>· (G) 희극적인 내용에 집중하는 경향이 있다 |
| | 만화책 |
| | · (B) 초능력을 가진 유명한 등장인물들을 도입했다<br>· (D) 한 달 주기로 출간되었다<br>· (E) 처음에는 정부에 의해 장려되었다 |

## Reading Practice 2    본문 p.160

1 (C)    2 (D)    3 (B)

4 Chimpanzees: (A), (D), (G)    Bonobos: (B), (F)

**Vocabulary Quiz**

1 ⓑ    2 ⓐ    3 ⓐ    4 ⓒ

---

### 침팬지와 보노보

동물의 왕국에서 침팬지와 보노보보다 인간과 유전적으로 가까운 종은 없다. 이 세 개의 종은 DNA의 98.8퍼센트 정도를 공유한다. 그들은 또한 하나의 공통된 조상 종을 가지고 있을 가능성이 크다. 그러나, 침

팬지와 보노보는 훨씬 더 밀접하게 연관되어 있다. 그것들은 불과 약 200만 년 전에 유전적으로 갈라졌는데, 이는 인간이 별개의 종이 되고 난 지 대략 500만 년이 지난 이후였다.

이 두 유인원 종은 여전히 신체적으로 매우 유사하지만, 몇 가지 중요한 차이점들이 있다. 예를 들어, 침팬지가 더 힘이 세지만, 보노보는 더 얌전하다. 또한, 침팬지는 다리가 더 짧은 반면에, 보노보는 머리가 더 크다. 게다가, 침팬지는 나이가 들수록 어두워지는 밝은 색의 얼굴을 가지고 태어난다. 보노보는 평생 피부가 검다.

그럼에도 불구하고, 신체적인 차이는 행동의 차이에 비해 거의 두드러지지 않는다. 두 종 모두 대단히 사회적이기는 하지만, 침팬지는 보노보에 비해 훨씬 더 많은 폭력과 다른 집단 구성원과의 갈등을 경험한다. 침팬지의 에너지의 대부분은 먹이와 짝을 위한 경쟁으로 향해진다. 수컷들은 지배적이며 종종 암컷들에게 공격적이다. 그에 반해서, 보노보 사회는 암컷들에 의해 지배된다. 따라서 그것은 아마 더 평화로울 것이다. 침팬지 사회에서 종종 발생하는 영아살해는 보노보 사회에서는 전례가 없는 일이다.

이러한 행동의 차이는 지리에 의해 설명될지도 모른다. 보노보는 콩고강 남부의 작은 영역에서만 발견된다. 약 2백만 년 전의 가뭄이 한때 그 지역에서 살았던 고릴라들을 멸종시켰다. ³그 결과, 보노보는 자원을 위한 큰 경쟁이 없는 환경에서 진화했다. 이것이 그것들을 상대적으로 온화하게 만들었다. 그에 반해, 침팬지는 고릴라와 공유하는 강 북부의 더 넓은 지역에서 산다. 먹이와 영역을 위해 지속적으로 경쟁해야 할 필요성이 그것들을 그렇게 공격적으로 만들었을 가능성이 크다.

genetically 閅 유전적으로    ancestor 몡 조상    related 혬 연관된
diverge 통 갈라지다    approximately 閅 대략, 거의
distinct 혬 별개의    remarkably 閅 매우    graceful 혬 얌전한, 우아한
striking 혬 두드러진    behavioral 혬 행동의    conflict 몡 갈등
direct 통 향하다    dominant 혬 지배적인    aggressive 혬 공격적인
perhaps 閅 아마    infanticide 몡 영아살해    geography 몡 지리
relatively 閅 상대적으로    compete 통 경쟁하다

**1** 지문의 단어 "diverged"와 의미가 가장 비슷한 것은?

(A) 진화했다

(B) 증가했다

(C) 분리되었다

(D) 결합되었다

**2** 아래 문장 중 지문 속의 음영된 문장의 핵심 정보를 가장 잘 표현한 것은?

(A) 침팬지는 서로 자주 싸우며, 때때로 그 갈등은 부상을 야기한다.

(B) 보노보는 좀처럼 다른 보노보와 몸싸움을 하지 않는 우호적인 동물이다.

(C) 침팬지가 보노보보다 폭력적이기는 하지만, 보노보는 더 많은 비신체적 갈등을 겪는다.

(D) 침팬지가 보노보보다 서로 더 많이 충돌하기는 하지만, 두 종 모두 사회적이다.

**3** 4단락에 따르면, 보노보가 침팬지에 비해 더 온화한 것은 보노보가

(A) 수컷들에 의해 지배되기 때문이다

(B) 먹이를 위한 경쟁이 더 적었기 때문이다

(C) 신체적으로 더 얌전하기 때문이다

(D) 콩고강의 북쪽에 살기 때문이다

**4** **지시:** 주어진 선택지에서 적절한 어구를 선택하여 관계있는 종에 연결하라.

| 선택지 | 침팬지 |
|---|---|
| (C) 200만 년 전에 인간과 갈라졌다<br>(E) 인간에게 공격적이다 | · (A) 고릴라와 영역을 공유한다<br>· (D) 다리가 더 짧다<br>· (G) 종종 그들의 자식을 죽인다 |
| | 보노보 |
| | · (B) 암컷에 의해 지배되는 집단에서 산다<br>· (F) 더 얌전하다 |

## Reading Practice 3

본문 p. 162

1 (A)  2 (D)  3 (B)
4 The United Kingdom: (A), (F), (G)
  The United States: (B), (E)

**Vocabulary Quiz**

1 ⓑ  2 ⓐ  3 ⓒ  4 ⓑ

### 산업혁명

산업혁명은 대서양의 양 측면에 전례 없는 속도로 거대한 변화를 가져왔다. 그러나, 그것은 미국보다 영국에서 훨씬 먼저 시작했다. [2C]제스로 툴이 파종기를 발명하여 씨앗을 심는 과정을 완전히 바꿔 놓았던 1701년에 이미 기술의 변화가 영국 전역을 휩쓸었다. 영국인 이민자 새뮤얼 슬레이터가 로드아일랜드에 방직 공장을 열었던 1793년이 되어서야 비로소, 이러한 변화가 진정으로 미국에 혁신을 일으키기 시작했다.

방직 산업은 산업혁명에 의해 변화된 최초의 산업에 속한다. 1700년대 중반에, 개인 방직공들과 방적공들로 구성된 영국의 가내공업은 방직 공장들로 대체되고 있었다. [2B]8개의 물레 가락을 하나의 바퀴에 연결했던 다축 방적기는 실의 생산 속도를 높였다. [2A]동력 직조기는 방직 과정을 자동화함으로써, 의류가 매우 저렴하게 만들어질 수 있게 했다. 이러한 혁신들은 18세기 말에 이르러서 미국으로 나아가기 시작했다. 미국의 발명가 엘리 휘트니는 조면기를 개발했는데, 그것은 노예를 이용하는 면직물 산업을 강화했다.

이와 유사한 기술의 향상이 산업 전반을 휩쓸고 지나감에 따라, 상품과 원자재를 장거리로 실어 나르기 위한 운송수단이 필요했다. 영국은 구식 도로망을 개선했고 배들이 전국을 횡단할 수 있도록 운하를 건설했다. 산업혁명을 특징짓는 동력원인 증기기관은 18세기 후반까지 석탄과 물을 이용하여 증기선과 열차에 동력을 제공했다. 미국에서는, 이러한 혁신들이 서부의 정착을 촉진했다.

이 빠른 발전에는 대가가 있었다. 영국의 경우, 도시화가 인구 과밀, 오염, 질병을 가져왔다. 중류층과 상류층은 번성했지만, 하류층은 끔찍한 근로 환경을 겪었다. 미국의 경우에는, 백만장자인 공장 소유주들은 이윤을 얻었지만, 가난한 사람들, 특히 이민자들은 고통받았다. 산업혁명의 어두운 측면을 완화하기 위해 아동 노동법과 환경 규제 같은 개혁들이 요구되었다.

unprecedented 휑전례 없는  pace 몡속도  sweep 통휩쓸다

---

seed drill 파종기  transform 통완전히 바꿔 놓다
textile mill 방직 공장  truly 뷘진정으로
revolutionize 통혁신을 일으키다  weaver 몡방직공
spinner 몡방적공  power loom 동력 직조기
automate 통자동화하다  shuttle 통실어 나르다
primitive 휑구식의  canal 몡운하  traverse 통횡단하다
facilitate 통촉진하다  thrive 통번성하다  profit 통이윤을 얻다
mitigate 통완화하다

1 글쓴이는 왜 "Eli Whitney"를 언급하는가?
(A) 미국에서 기술의 변화가 일어났다는 것을 입증하기 위해
(B) 미국의 산업에서 노예들이 흔하게 이용되었다는 것을 보여주기 위해
(C) 영국의 방직 산업과 미국의 방직 산업을 대조하기 위해
(D) 미국의 발명가들이 영국의 발명가들보다 뛰어났다는 것을 시사하기 위해

2 지문에 따르면, 다음 중 산업혁명에서 기술에 의해 변화된 것이 아닌 것은?
(A) 저렴한 의류를 생산하는 것
(B) 원자재에서 실을 제조하는 것
(C) 농장에 씨앗을 심는 것
(D) 공기와 물을 깨끗하게 하는 것

3 지문의 단어 "mitigate"와 의미가 가장 가까운 것은?
(A) 어둡게 하다
(B) 줄이다
(C) 유지하다
(D) 끝내다

4 지시: 주어진 선택지에서 적절한 어구를 선택하여 관계있는 국가에 연결하라.

| 선택지 | 영국 |
|---|---|
| (C) 증기기관으로 동부에서의 정착을 촉진했다<br>(D) 운하를 통해 유럽 대륙에 원자재를 운송했다 | · (A) 파종기의 발명과 함께 산업화 과정을 시작했다<br>· (F) 새로운 도로 체계를 만들었다<br>· (G) 방직공들로 구성된 가내공업을 대체했다 |
| | 미국 |
| | · (B) 방직 산업을 강화하기 위해 조면기를 사용했다<br>· (E) 백만장자인 공장 소유주들을 부유하게 만들었다 |

## Reading Practice 4

본문 p. 164

1 (B)  2 (D)  3 (D)
4 Gothic: (B), (C), (F)  Renaissance: (A), (E)

**Vocabulary Quiz**

1 ⓑ  2 ⓐ  3 ⓒ  4 ⓒ

## 고딕 양식과 르네상스 양식의 스테인드글라스

스테인드글라스 창문들은 중세의 지배적인 미술 형식이었다. 이 다채로운 창문들의 유리는 금속 가루가 섞인 모래와 나무의 재로 만들어졌다. 그런 다음 그것에 색이 칠해졌고, 그것의 조각들이 납으로 된 선으로 결합되었다. "스테인드글라스"라는 용어는 창문의 한쪽 면에 발린 은색 염료에서 비롯되었다. 10세기에서 16세기까지, 스테인드글라스의 역사는 두 가지 양식의 시대로 나뉠 수 있는데, 바로 고딕 양식과 르네상스 양식이다.

1400년대 초반까지, 성경의 이야기들을 묘사하는 다채로운 창문들에 대한 큰 수요가 있었다. 이것은 장인과 화가들에게 그 시기의 가장 야심 찬 건축 양식의 특징이 되는 표현 수단을 제공했다. 고딕 양식의 교회들과 대성당들의 아찔한 수직 높이는 높은 스테인드글라스의 전시를 가능하게 했다. 일반적으로 종교학자들이 도안을 전담했다. 이것은 그들에게 글을 모르는 대중에게 신학적인 메시지를 전달할 지속적인 기회를 주었다. 유럽 전역에서 국가적 정체성이 형성됨에 따라, 스테인드글라스의 뚜렷한 국가적 양식이 발전했다. 독일의 양식은 어둡고 심각했다. 영국인들은 그로테스크 풍의 매우 상세한 그림들을 선호했다. 프랑스인들은 화가들의 빠른 스케치 능력을 돋보이게 했다.

1430년대에 이르러서, 고딕 양식의 스테인드글라스는 위대한 르네상스 화가들의 더욱 현실적인 접근법으로 대체되기 시작했다. 비록 건축물에서 스테인드글라스가 덜 두드러지기는 했지만, 그것은 또한 더 화려해졌다. 예술 작품의 현실성을 높이기 위해 납으로 된 선이 덜 강조되었다. 유머가 도안에 스며들었다. 세속적인 주제들이 더 흔해졌다. 이 시기 동안에는 유리도 덜 비쌌다. 그 결과, 스테인드글라스는 주택에서 점점 더 인기가 많아졌다. 그러나, 이 표현 수단은 많은 예술가들에게 매력을 상실했다. [3]그 이유는, 사용되는 물감의 양이 많아져 빛이 유리를 통해 비치는 것을 막았기 때문이었다.

dominant 형지배적인, 우세한　apply 동바르다
medium 명표현 수단　ambitious 형야심 찬
architecture 명건축 양식; 건축물　dizzying 형아찔한
vertical 형수직의　cathedral 명대성당　lasting 형지속적인
deliver 동전달하다　theological 형신학적인
illiterate 형글을 모르는, 문맹의　showcase 동돋보이게 하다
prominent 형두드러진　ornate 형화려한
deemphasize 동덜 강조하다　enhance 동높이다
secular 형세속적인　appeal 명매력

**1** 네 개의 네모[■]는 다음 문장이 삽입될 수 있는 곳을 나타내고 있다.

그런 다음 그것에 색이 칠해졌고, 그것의 조각들이 납으로 된 선으로 결합되었다.

이 문장은 어디에 들어가는 것이 가장 적절한가?

**2** 지문의 단어 "ornate"와 의미가 가장 비슷한 것은?

(A) 악명 높은
(B) 중요한
(C) 낙관적인
(D) 정교한

**3** 3단락에 따르면, 스테인드글라스가 예술가들 사이에서 인기를 잃은 것은

(A) 종교적인 논쟁이 종교 예술에 대한 반감을 초래했기 때문이다
(B) 대중이 종교적인 배경 속에서의 유머 사용에 대해 부정적으로 반응했기 때문이다
(C) 유리가 엄청나게 비싼 물질이 되었기 때문이다
(D) 사용된 물감의 양이 자연광을 차단하기 시작했기 때문이다

**4** 지시: 주어진 선택지에서 적절한 문장을 선택하여 관계있는 양식에 연결하라.

| 선택지 | 고딕 양식 |
| --- | --- |
| (D) 스테인드글라스의 제작 과정은 많은 장인들에게 위험했다.<br>(G) 빠른 스케치 양식이 이 시기의 특징이 되었다. | · (B) 여러 국가들이 그들만의 독특한 양식을 발전시켰다.<br>· (C) 종교학자들은 신학적인 목적을 위해 도안을 만들어 냈다.<br>· (F) 지배적인 건축 양식이 스테인드글라스의 전시 장소를 제공했다. |
| | 르네상스 양식 |
| | · (A) 종교적인 주제가 스테인드글라스의 유일한 주제는 아니었다.<br>· (E) 현실적인 삽화 양식이 더 일반적이 되었다. |

## iBT Reading Test

본문 p.166

1 (A)　2 (D)　3 (C)　4 (C)
5 (C)　6 (C)　7 (B)　8 (B)
9 (C)　10 Orientation: (B), (C), (G)　Navigation: (A), (E)

## 철새들이 경로를 찾는 방법

매년 봄에, 수백만 마리의 새들은 견딜 수 없을 정도로 덥지 않은 지역을 향해 북쪽으로 이동한다. [2]이 온화한 지역들은 먹이를 찾을 기회를 더 많이 제공한다. 그러고 나서, 가을이 되면, 새들은 가혹한 겨울을 피하기 위해 남쪽의 따뜻한 지역들로 돌아간다. 이 놀라운 여정은 16,000마일까지 길어질 수 있다. 과학자들은 그들이 어떻게 그것을 하는지 알아내기 위해 여전히 실험을 하고 있으며, 그 해답은 새들의 방향을 설정하는 능력과 길을 찾는 능력에 있다.

방향을 설정하는 것은 자기 나침반의 방향을 결정하는 것이다. [6]과학자들은 그들이 "클러스터 N"이라 부르는, 일부 새들의 뇌 앞부분을 발견했다. 뇌의 이 부분은 야간에 비행할 때 새의 눈과 상호작용하는 것처럼 보이며, 그것들을 북쪽으로 향하게 한다. 하지만, 클러스터 N이 활성화되지 않을 때도, 새들은 여전히 북쪽을 찾기 위해 인간이 하는 것처럼 석양이나 별들의 위치를 이용할 수 있다. 연구자들은 밤하늘의 시각적 표현을 나타내는 큰 돔형 극장인, 천체 투영실에서 실험을 시행함으로써 이것을 확인했다. 새들은 일반적으로 올바른 방향으로 향하기 위해 북극성을 이용한다. 그러나, 천체 투영실의 별들이 북극성 대신 베텔게우스를 중심으로 회전했을 때, 새들은 방향을 설정하기 위해 베텔게우스를 이용했다.

새들이 가지고 있는 것이 틀림없는 두 번째 능력은 길을 찾는 것인데, 이는 비행 중에 그것의 위치를 가늠하는 것을 의미한다. 새들이 이 재주를 해내는 방법 중 하나는 후각에 의존하는 것이다. 그것들의 부리는 경로를 따라 냄새의 후각 지도를 만들어 낸다. 예를 들어, 그들은 한 지역에서는 바다 냄새로 지도를 만들고, 또 다른 한 지역에서는 늪의 냄새로 지도를 만들 수 있다. [8]새의 또 다른 비결은 아마 특정 위치에서

지구의 자기장이 얼마나 강한지를 알아내기 위해 부리에 있는 삼차 신경을 이용하는 것일 것이다. 이 방식으로, 그들은 자신들이 지구의 극이나 적도에 얼마나 가까이 있는지를 판단할 수 있다. 새들은 어떤 상황에서도 길을 찾을 수 있도록 방향을 설정하고 길을 찾는 다양한 방법들을 가지고 있는 것처럼 보인다.

migrate ⑧ (철새가) 이동하다    oppressively ⑨ 견딜 수 없을 정도로
temperate ⑲ 온화한    harsh ⑲ 가혹한    orient ⑧ 방향을 설정하다
navigate ⑧ 길을 찾다    magnetic compass 자기 나침반
interact ⑧ 상호작용하다    setting sun 석양    confirm ⑧ 확인하다
conduct ⑧ 시행하다    planetarium ⑲ 천체 투영실
representation ⑲ 표현    revolve ⑧ 회전하다    assess ⑧ 가늠하다
feat ⑲ 재주, 업적    odor ⑲ 냄새    avian ⑲ 새의    equator ⑲ 적도
circumstance ⑲ 상황

1  지문의 단어 "oppressively"와 의미가 가장 비슷한 것은?
   (A) 견딜 수 없게
   (B) 가볍게
   (C) 특이하게
   (D) 확실히

2  1단락에 따르면, 새들이 북쪽으로 이동하는 것은
   (A) 그들의 몸이 극도로 가혹한 기후에 대처할 수 없기 때문이다
   (B) 선천적으로 봄에 따뜻한 기후를 추구하기 때문이다
   (C) 그 여정이 남쪽으로 향하는 여정만큼 길지 않기 때문이다
   (D) 온화한 기후인 지역에 더 많은 먹이가 있기 때문이다

3  지문의 단어 "them"이 가리키는 것은?
   (A) 과학자들
   (B) 뇌
   (C) 새들
   (D) 눈

4  아래 문장 중 지문 속의 음영된 문장의 핵심 정보를 가장 잘 표현한 것은? 오답은 문장의 의미를 크게 바꾸거나 핵심 정보를 생략한다.
   (A) 만약 새가 클러스터 N을 이용할 수 없다면, 그것은 태양의 위치를 확인해서 사람처럼 행동할 것이다.
   (B) 클러스터 N과 석양 외에도, 새들은 인간들이 북쪽을 찾기 위해 무엇을 할지 알아내기 위해 밤하늘을 올려다본다.
   (C) 새들은 그것들의 뇌가 클러스터 N을 사용할 수 없을 때, 인간처럼 태양과 별을 통해 길을 찾는다.
   (D) 별의 위치는 새들이 클러스터 N을 활성화시키는 데 도움을 주고, 인간처럼 어디가 북쪽인지를 알아내도록 돕는다.

5  글쓴이는 왜 "the star Betelgeuse"를 언급하는가?
   (A) 북극성이 새들이 방향을 설정하기 위해 이용하는 유일한 별이 아니라고 주장하기 위해
   (B) 새들이 방향을 설정하기 위해 별을 볼 수 있어야 한다는 것을 설명하기 위해
   (C) 새들이 방향을 설정하기 위해 별에 의존한다는 것의 증거를 제공하기 위해
   (D) 방향을 설정하는 새들에게 과학자들이 별들을 잘못 보여주었다고 비판하기 위해

6  2단락에 따르면, 클러스터 N은
   (A) 새들이 사용하는 비행 기법이다
   (B) 밤하늘을 기억하는 방법이다

(C) 새 뇌의 부분이다
(D) 눈과 부리 사이의 접속부이다

7  지문의 단어 "assess"와 의미가 가장 비슷한 것은?
   (A) 관찰하다
   (B) 평가하다
   (C) 바꾸다
   (D) 낮추다

8  3단락에 따르면, 새의 삼차 신경은
   (A) 자기 나침반의 북쪽 방향을 찾는 역할을 한다
   (B) 지구 자기장의 강도를 확인하는 역할을 한다
   (C) 새의 여정에서 서로 다른 주요 지형지물의 냄새를 맡는 역할을 한다
   (D) 새가 자신의 위치를 판단하는 것을 돕기 위해 눈과 상호작용하는 역할을 한다

9  네 개의 네모[■]는 다음 문장이 삽입될 수 있는 곳을 나타내고 있다.
   **예를 들어, 그들은 한 지역에서는 바다 냄새로 지도를 만들고, 또 다른 한 지역에서는 늪의 냄새로 지도를 만들 수 있다.**
   이 문장은 어디에 들어가는 것이 가장 적절한가?

10 지시: 주어진 선택지에서 적절한 문장을 선택하여 관계있는 능력의 종류에 연결하라. **이 문제는 3점이다.**

| 선택지 | 방향 설정 |
|---|---|
| (D) 새들은 이동 방향을 결정하기 위해 새소리로 의사소통한다. <br> (F) 새의 날개는 펄럭일 때 자기장에 반응한다. | · (B) 새들은 여정의 방향을 결정하기 위해 북극성을 이용한다. <br> · (C) 새들은 석양의 위치를 관찰한다. <br> · (G) 새의 뇌는 그것을 북쪽으로 향하게 하는 기제를 갖고 있다. |
| | 길 찾기 |
| | · (A) 새들은 지구의 자기장을 이용하여 자신의 위치를 감지할 수 있다. <br> · (E) 새의 후각은 그것이 정확한 위치를 찾는 것을 돕는다. |

## Vocabulary Review

본문 p. 170

| | | |
|---|---|---|
| 1 related | 2 unprecedented | 3 conducting |
| 4 typically | 5 transformed | 6 feat |
| 7 (B) | 8 (C) | 9 (A) | 10 (B) |
| 11 (B) | 12 (D) | 13 (D) | 14 (A) |

# Actual Test 1

## Passage 1

본문 p. 172

1 (B)　　2 (B)　　3 (C)　　4 (B)
5 (D)　　6 (C)　　7 (A)　　8 (C)
9 (D)　　10 (A), (D), (F)

### 광물

그들이 음식에 소금을 뿌리든, 다이아몬드 반지를 끼든, 불로 이를 닦든, 대부분의 사람들은 그것들이 무엇인지 이해하지 못한 채 그들의 일상에서 매일 광물과 상호작용한다. 모든 광물이 공유하는 네 가지 본질적인 특성이 있다.

우선, 광물은 자연적으로 형성된다. 4A/4C광물의 특성을 모방하는, 실험실에서 만들어지는 많은 물질들이 있지만, 엄밀히 말하면 이것들은 광물이 아니다. 4D예를 들어, 인조 에메랄드는 진짜인 것과 비슷한 녹색 광채를 가질 수 있고, 심지어 동일한 화학 물질들로 만들어질 수 있다. 하지만, 만약 에메랄드가 지각 깊은 곳의 용암에서 빠져나온 베릴륨으로부터 자연적으로 형성된 것이 아니라면, 그것은 진짜 광물이 아니며, 따라서, 동일한 가치를 갖지 않는다. 많은 광물이 냉각된 용암에서 형성되며, 그 밖의 다른 것들은 물속에서 결정체를 이룬다.

일부 광물이 물속에서 형성되기는 하지만, 어떤 물질이 광물로 분류되기 위해서는 반드시 고체여야 한다. 실제로, 광물은 지구상에서 가장 단단한 고체에 속할 수 있다. 지질학자들은 모스 척도를 사용하여 광물의 굳기를 측정하는데, 그것은 광물을 긁어 상처를 내기가 얼마나 쉬운지를 측정한다. 다이아몬드는 긁어 상처를 내는 것이 사실상 불가능하기 때문에 모스 척도에서 10점 만점에 10점이 매겨진다. 반면에, 활석은 (화장품이나 베이비파우더에서 발견되는) 활석 분으로 쉽게 으깨질 수 있기 때문에, 그것은 모스 척도에서 1점이 매겨진다. 그 점수는 모든 광물 중에서 활석이 가장 무른 것임을 나타낸다.

6광물의 세 번째 특징은 그것들이 원자 수준까지 일관된 화학 구조를 지닌다는 것이다. 다시 말해서, 광물을 구성하는 원자들은 특정한 화학적 비율을 유지해야 한다. 예를 들어, 지구의 가장 흔한 광물인 석영은 한 부분이 규소이고 두 부분은 산소이다. 금과 같은 일부 광물들은 하나의 원소로 구성된다.

마지막으로, 모든 광물은 결정 구조를 가지고 있으며, 이것은 원자들이 기하학적 형태로 조직되어 있다는 것을 의미한다. 이러한 이유로, 광물은 지구에서 가장 아름다운 물질에 속한다. 8로마인들은 오팔이 신비로운 힘을 가지고 있다고 믿었는데, 이는 그것의 결정체가 빛의 스펙트럼에 있는 모든 색을 비출 수 있기 때문이다.

sprinkle 동뿌리다　　fluoride 명불소
interact with ~과 상호작용하다　　essential 형본질적인, 필수적인
laboratory 명실험실　　property 명특성, 성질
technically 부엄밀히 말하면　　synthetic 형인조의
crystallize 동결정체를 이루다　　classify 동분류하다　　talc 명활석
talcum powder 활석분　　consistent 형일관된
composition 명구조　　atomic 형원자의　　constitute 동구성하다
quartz 명석영　　silicon 명규소　　geometric 형기하학적인
mystical 형신비로운

1 글쓴이는 왜 사람들이 "sprinkling salt on their food"하는 것을 언급하는가?

(A) 광물을 먹을 수 있다는 증거를 제공하기 위해
(B) 사람들이 매일 광물을 사용한다는 것을 예를 들어 설명하기 위해
(C) 음식에 너무 많은 소금을 사용하는 사람들을 비판하기 위해
(D) 광물들이 작은 입자로 갈릴 수 있다는 것을 보여주기 위해

2 지문의 단어 "these"가 가리키는 것은?

(A) 광물
(B) 물질들
(C) 실험실
(D) 특성

3 아래 문장 중 지문 속의 음영된 문장의 핵심 정보를 가장 잘 표현한 것은? 오답은 문장의 의미를 크게 바꾸거나 핵심 정보를 생략한다.

(A) 지구의 핵에서 녹은 액체로부터 형성된 에메랄드만큼 가치 있는 것은 없다.
(B) 지구의 핵에서 형성된 에메랄드는 광물이 아니며, 가치도 없다.
(C) 자연적인 과정에 의해 형성되지 않은 에메랄드는 실제 광물이 아니기 때문에 가치가 낮다.
(D) 에메랄드가 베릴륨을 포함할 때, 그것은 항상 광물로 간주된다.

4 2단락에 따르면, 다음 중 인조 에메랄드에 관해 사실이 아닌 것은?

(A) 실험실에서 제조된다.
(B) 자연산과 쉽게 구분된다.
(C) 광물의 특성을 보인다.
(D) 화학적인 베릴륨을 포함할지도 모른다.

5 지문의 단어 "classified"와 의미가 가장 비슷한 것은?

(A) 감춰지다
(B) 상상되다
(C) 특징이 되다
(D) 분류되다

6 4단락에 따르면, 광물을 구성하는 화학 물질들은

(A) 지구에서 가장 가치 있는 원소들에 속한다
(B) 동일한 광물 유형의 각 표본에서 서로 다른 비율로 존재한다
(C) 특정 광물의 모든 표본에서 동일한 비율을 유지한다
(D) 실험실에서 사용되는 화학 물질보다 더 흔하다

7 지문의 단어 "substances"와 의미가 가장 비슷한 것은?

(A) 물질
(B) 예시
(C) 구조
(D) 종류

8 5단락에 따르면, 로마인들은 오팔이 특별한 힘을 가지고 있다고 믿었는데, 이는 그것의

(A) 화학적 균일성 때문이다
(B) 파괴할 수 없는 굳기 때문이다
(C) 색을 굴절시키는 능력 때문이다
(D) 지하로부터의 원천 때문이다

9 네 개의 네모[■]는 다음 문장이 삽입될 수 있는 곳을 나타내고 있다.
**그 점수는 모든 광물 중에서 활석이 가장 무른 것임을 나타낸다.**
이 문장은 어디에 들어가는 것이 가장 적절한가?

**10** 지시: 지문 요약을 위한 도입 문장이 아래에 주어져 있다. 지문의 가장 중요한 내용을 나타내는 보기 3개를 골라 요약을 완성하라. 어떤 문장은 지문에 언급되지 않은 내용이나 사소한 정보를 나타내므로 요약에 포함되지 않는다. **이 문제는 2점이다.**

> 광물은 명확한 기준으로 정의된다.
> - (A) 광물은 결정 구조를 가지고 있다.
> - (D) 광물은 자연적으로 발생한다.
> - (F) 광물은 일정한 화학적 구성을 갖는다.

(B) 광물은 실험실에서 만들어질 수 있다.
(C) 광물은 때때로 가루로 갈릴 수 있다.
(E) 광물은 신비로운 힘을 가지고 있다고 여겨진다.

## Passage 2
본문 p. 176

| | | | |
|---|---|---|---|
| 11 (D) | 12 (B) | 13 (C) | 14 (B) |
| 15 (C) | 16 (B) | 17 (A) | 18 (D) |
| 19 (C) | 20 (A), (C), (E) | | |

### 아나사지 절벽 주거지

아나사지라고 알려진 고대 북미 원주민의 절벽 주거지는 전 세계의 관광객들을 끌어들여 왔다. 그 건축물들은 크기, 디자인, 내구성에 있어서 매우 뛰어나다. ¹³ᴰ그것들은 돌로 만들어졌으며, 콜로라도 주의 메사 베르데 절벽 위에 건설되었다. 언뜻 보기에, 그 주거지들은 사각형의 창문들은 있지만 문은 없는 다층의 대형 아파트 단지로 보인다. ¹³ᴮ아나사지인들은 사다리를 타고 올라가 지붕에 있는 구멍을 통해 그 건물들에 들어갔다. ¹³ᴬ역사가들은 아나사지인들이 이 주거지를 건축하는 데 80년이 걸렸을 것이고, 그것들이 완성된 지 불과 100년만에, 아나사지인들이 이 아름답고 견고한 집들을 버렸다고 추측한다.

이 절벽 주거지는 그곳에 살았던 사람들에 관해 많은 것들을 밝혀주는 고고학적인 금광이다. 고대의 콜로라도 사막의 기후 조건은 혹독할 수 있었는데, 이는 장기간의 가뭄을 포함했다. 하지만, 그 주거지는 그것들이 꽤 안정적이었던 역사의 한 시점(서기 1190년경)에 건축되었다. ¹⁷아나사지의 인구는 최고조에 달했다. 이것이 일부가 땅속에 있는 단순한 움집에서 절벽 안의 더 정교한 주거지로의 이주를 촉진했다. 그들은 사슴과 큰뿔야생양을 사냥했고 가축화된 칠면조를 먹었다. 그들은 키가 5피트 1인치에서 5피트 5인치 정도인 작은 민족이었기 때문에, 좁은 사다리들을 쉽게 오르내릴 수 있었다.

아나사지인들은 왜 그렇게 갑자기 이 놀라운 건축물들을 떠났을까? 여러 가지 이유가 있는 것으로 보인다. ¹⁸ᴮ그들이 식량으로 큰 사냥감을 더 많이 사냥할수록, 그 동물들은 점점 덜 풍부해졌다. 삼림 벌채 또한 이용 가능한 자원의 부족에 기여했다. 나무는 콜로라도의 혹독한 겨울 동안 땔감의 주요 원천이었다. ¹⁸ᴬ1276년에는, 23년 동안 지속된 가뭄이 발생했다. ¹⁸ᶜ이러한 불리한 환경 조건에 더해, 아나사지인들은 그들의 주거지 안에서 공격을 받았을지도 모른다. 고고학자들은 전혀 격식을 갖춰 매장되지 못한 어느 34명의 유해를 발굴했다. 적어도 그 유해 중 8구는 폭력에 의한 사망 원인의 증거를 지녔다. 이유가 무엇이었건 간에, 살아남은 아나사지인들은 애리조나와 뉴멕시코 지역을 향해 남쪽으로 이주했다. 이 절벽 주거지들의 잔해는 1880년대에 카우보이들에 의해 발견되기 전까지 수 세기 동안 비어 있었다. 오늘날, 그것들은 국립공원에 보존되어 있다.

---

dwelling 명 주거지　　exceptional 형 매우 뛰어난, 특출난
durability 명 내구성　　speculate 동 추측하다　　abandon 동 버리다
sturdy 형 견고한　　archaeological 형 고고학적인　　brutal 형 혹독한
drought 명 가뭄　　pit house 움집　　elaborate 형 정교한
feast on ~을 먹다　　domesticated 형 가축화된
abruptly 부 갑자기　　game 명 사냥감　　abundant 형 풍부한
deforestation 명 삼림 벌채　　contribute to ~에 기여하다
unfavorable 형 불리한　　uncover 동 발굴하다

**11** 지문의 단어 "durability"와 의미가 가장 비슷한 것은?
(A) 복잡성
(B) 건축
(C) 매력
(D) 견고함

**12** 지문의 단어 "speculate"와 의미가 가장 비슷한 것은?
(A) 결론을 내리다
(B) 짐작하다
(C) 올리다
(D) 재촉하다

**13** 다음 중 1단락에서 절벽 주거지에 관해 언급되지 않은 것은?
(A) 그것들을 지은 사람들의 정체
(B) 거주민들이 그것들에 들어가기 위해 사용한 방법
(C) 그것들에 거주했던 사람들의 수
(D) 그것들을 건축하는 데 사용된 재료들

**14** 글쓴이는 왜 "archaeological goldmine"을 언급하는가?
(A) 아나사지인들의 생존 방식을 묘사하기 위해
(B) 아나사지인들에 관한 정보가 어떻게 얻어졌는지를 설명하기 위해
(C) 아나사지인들의 가난에 대한 오해를 반박하기 위해
(D) 아나사지인들을 이해하기 위해 더 많은 연구가 필요하다고 주장하기 위해

**15** 지문의 단어 "they"가 가리키는 것은?
(A) 절벽 주거지
(B) 사람들
(C) 기후 조건
(D) 기간

**16** 아래 문장 중 지문 속의 음영된 문장의 핵심 정보를 가장 잘 표현한 것은? 오답은 문장의 의미를 크게 바꾸거나 핵심 정보를 생략한다.
(A) 아나사지인들의 키는 그들이 많은 숫자로 절벽 주거지에 들락날락할 수 있게 했다.
(B) 아나사지인들은 작아서, 그들이 주거지에서 작은 사다리를 사용하는 데 어려움이 없었다.
(C) 아나사지인들은 위아래로 움직이며 절벽에 있는 그들의 집을 들락날락했다.
(D) 일부 아나사지인들은 5피트 1인치만큼 작았으며, 이것은 집을 나가는 것을 쉽게 했다.

**17** 2단락에 따르면, 아나사지인들이 움집을 떠난 것은 그들이
(A) 수용해야 할 인구가 더 많았기 때문이다
(B) 산에서 큰 사냥감을 발견했기 때문이다
(C) 작은 집에 살기에는 너무 컸기 때문이다
(D) 절벽에서 더 따뜻한 환경을 경험했기 때문이다

**18** 다음 중 아나사지인들이 절벽에서 떠난 것에 대한 글쓴이의 설명이 언급하지 않은 것은?

(A) 대단히 긴 가뭄

(B) 그 기간 동안의 고기의 부족

(C) 절벽 내 전투의 증거

(D) 건축물의 상태 저하

**19** 네 개의 네모[■]는 다음 문장이 삽입될 수 있는 곳을 나타내고 있다.

**나무는 콜로라도의 혹독한 겨울 동안 땔감의 주요 원천이었다.**

이 문장은 어디에 들어가는 것이 가장 적절한가?

**20 지시:** 지문 요약을 위한 도입 문장이 아래에 주어져 있다. 지문의 가장 중요한 내용을 나타내는 보기 3개를 골라 요약을 완성하라. 어떤 문장은 지문에 언급되지 않은 내용이나 사소한 정보를 나타내므로 요약에 포함되지 않는다. **이 문제는 2점이다.**

> 아나사지인들은 산 절벽 위에 놀라운 주거 망을 건설했다.
> · (A) 이상하게도 절벽 주거지는 건설된 지 얼마 되지 않아 버려졌다.
> · (C) 고고학자들은 그들의 주거지를 연구함으로써 아나사지인들에 관해 많은 것을 알아냈다.
> · (E) 여러 요인들이 아나사지인들의 절벽 주거지로부터의 이른 이탈에 기여했다.

(B) 아나사지인들은 대가족에게는 너무 작았던 아파트 같은 주거지에서 살았다.

(D) 절벽 주거지에 살았던 사람들은 읽고 쓸 수 없었다.

(F) 절벽 주거지에서 대규모 전투가 일어났고, 이는 대부분의 아나사지인들을 죽였다.

---

## Passage 3 본문 p.180

21 (B)    22 (B)    23 (D)    24 (A)
25 (B)    26 (B)    27 (C)    28 (B)
29 (B)    30 (A), (B), (D)

### 에디슨의 축음기

녹음의 역사는 토머스 에디슨이 축음기를 발명했을 때 시작되었다. 에디슨은 그의 "말하는 기계"가 결국 미국의 모든 가정에 있게 될 것이라고 상상했다. 그의 시대에, 가정에서 듣는 음악은 주로 부자들에 의해 누려진 사치였다. 축음기의 대량 생산을 통해, 그는 모든 이들에게 가정에서 음악을 듣는 것이 적당한 가격이 되기를 바랐다. ²³그러나, 그의 주된 동기는 전화 메시지를 녹음하는 장치를 만드는 것이었다. 그는 사업상의 의사소통에서 녹음이 서면 메시지에 대한 대안을 제공할 수 있을 것이라고 생각하면서, 사업가들이 가장 먼저 그 장치를 사게 될 것이라고 믿었다. 이러한 점에서, 에디슨의 축음기는 현대 음성 메일의 전신이었다.

1877년 7월의 어느 날 밤, 에디슨과 그의 직원들은 실험실에서 녹음 기술을 고안해냈다. 그는 음파가 '진동판'이라고 불리는 얇은 막에 진동을 만들어낼 수 있다는 것을 알고 있었다. 그는 진동판에 바늘처럼 끝이 딱딱한 무언가를 붙이는 것을 통해 이 진동이 자국을 내는 데 사용될 수 있을지 궁금했다. 그래서 그는 한 직원에게 진동판에 그것을 붙여달라고 요청했고, 그 진동판 자체는 전화기 스피커에 부착되었다. 에디슨이 스피커에 대고 소리치자, 진동판은 진동했고, 이는 바늘이 움

---

직여서 아래에 있는 밀랍이 덮인 종이에 그 소리의 자국을 새기게 했다. 그 종이 위의 패턴이 바늘 아래에서 다시 움직여지자, 모두가 놀랍게도, 에디슨의 목소리가 다시 재생되었다.

에디슨은 곧 그의 축음기 디자인에 관한 기술 도안을 만들었고, 1877년 12월까지 그의 기술팀은 첫 번째 실용 모형을 만들었다. 그것은 '사이언티픽 아메리칸' 잡지의 출판 사무실에서 공개적으로 시연되었다. 당시에 이 출판물은 국내 신기술에 대한 가장 인기 있는 정보 출처였다. ²⁷엄청난 수의 군중이 이 말하는 기계를 듣기 위해 모였다. 하지만 이 최초의 디자인은 그저 진기한 물건일 뿐이었는데, 이는 그것의 상업적 가치가 제한적이었고 전시에만 적합했기 때문이었다. 그것이 단 1에서 2분 정도의 소리만 녹음할 수 있었기 때문에, 장시간 사용에는 실용적이지 않았다. 게다가, 소리의 품질이 나빠서, 일부 청자들은 스피커에서 나오는 말을 이해할 수 없었다. 따라서, 에디슨은 수정을 해야만 했다. ²⁸1887년과 1888년에, 그는 개선된 축음기와 완성된 축음기를 제작했고, 그것들을 에디슨 축음기 회사 이름으로 시장에 내놓았다. 비록 에디슨의 축음기가 상업적으로 성공하기는 했지만, 그것들의 가격은 결코 실제로 모든 이들에게 적당한 수준이 되지는 않았다.

phonograph 명 축음기    envision 동 상상하다    ultimately 부 결국
era 명 시대    motivation 명 동기    alternative 명 대안
precursor 명 전신, 선구자    contemporary 형 현대의
membrane 명 막    diaphragm 명 진동판    attach 동 붙이다
publicly 부 공개적으로    demonstrate 동 시연하다
assemble 동 모이다    curiosity 명 진기한 물건    suitable 형 적합한
practical 형 실용적인    extensive 형 장시간의, 넓은
modification 명 (개선을 위한) 수정    manufacture 동 제작하다

**21** 지문의 단어 "envisioned"와 의미가 가장 비슷한 것은?

(A) 깨달았다

(B) 예상했다

(C) 특징지었다

(D) 증명했다

**22** 지문에서 글쓴이는 왜 "contemporary voicemail"을 언급하는가?

(A) 에디슨의 시대 이후로 기술이 많이 변하지 않았다고 주장하기 위해

(B) 에디슨의 발명품과 유사한 최근의 예시를 제시하기 위해

(C) 에디슨의 디자인에 기반한 현대의 기술을 밝히기 위해

(D) 에디슨의 발명품이 매우 정교하지는 않았다는 것을 시사하기 위해

**23** 1단락에 따르면, 에디슨이 축음기를 만드는 데 주된 자극이 된 것은?

(A) 그는 그것을 부자들에게 홍보하려고 했다.

(B) 그는 음악 제작이 덜 비싸지기를 원했다.

(C) 그는 서면 의사소통을 없애려고 했다.

(D) 그는 전화 녹음 방법을 만들기를 원했다.

**24** 지문의 단어 "one"이 가리키는 것은?

(A) 바늘

(B) 끝

(C) 진동판

(D) 직원

**25** 아래 문장 중 지문 속의 음영된 문장의 핵심 정보를 가장 잘 표현한 것은? 오답은 문장의 의미를 크게 바꾸거나 핵심 정보를 생략한다.

(A) 종이 위의 패턴이 성공적으로 복제되었기 때문에 모두가 놀랐다.

(B) 바늘 아래에서 그 패턴이 두 번째로 그려짐으로써 에디슨의 음성 녹음이 재생되었다.

(C) 모두가 에디슨의 목소리가 반복되는 것을 들은 순간에, 그들은 놀라움과 함께 반응했다.

(D) 바늘이 에디슨의 음성을 녹음한 패턴을 종이에 만들어냈다.

26 지문의 단어 "modifications"와 의미가 가장 비슷한 것은?

(A) 제한
(B) 수정
(C) 제안
(D) 투자

27 3단락에 따르면, 에디슨의 첫 번째 축음기에 대한 반응은 무엇이었는가?

(A) 과학 출판물에서 홍보되었다.
(B) 언론에 의해 대체로 무시되었다.
(C) 많은 수의 사람들이 그것을 듣기 위해 모였다.
(D) 비평가들이 그것의 비싼 가격에 대해 불평했다.

28 다음 중 1887년과 1888년의 축음기에 관해 추론할 수 있는 것은?

(A) 2분 이하의 소리를 녹음할 수 있었다.
(B) 원형보다 더 높은 소리 품질을 가지고 있었다.
(C) 상업적 생산에 적합하지 않았다.
(D) 서로 다른 두 곳에서 제조되었다.

29 네 개의 네모[■]는 다음 문장이 삽입될 수 있는 곳을 나타내고 있다.

**당시에 이 출판물은 국내 신기술에 대한 가장 인기 있는 정보 출처였다.**

이 문장은 어디에 들어가는 것이 가장 적절한가?

30 지시: 지문 요약을 위한 도입 문장이 아래에 주어져 있다. 지문의 가장 중요한 내용을 나타내는 보기 3개를 골라 요약을 완성하라. 어떤 문장은 지문에 언급되지 않은 내용이나 사소한 정보를 나타내므로 요약에 포함되지 않는다. 이 문제는 2점이다.

> 에디슨의 축음기 발명이 녹음의 역사를 개시했다.
> · (A) 에디슨과 그의 직원들은 실험실에서 일하던 중에 녹음 방법을 알아냈다.
> · (B) 에디슨은 그의 축음기가 가정과 사업체 양쪽 모두에게 유용할 것이라고 생각했다.
> · (D) 모형을 설계하고 생산한 후에, 에디슨은 상업적 사용을 위한 추가적인 축음기들을 만들었다.

(C) 에디슨이 만든 축음기는 모든 이가 살 수 있을 정도로 충분히 저렴했다.

(E) 에디슨의 첫 번째 축음기는 전시에는 유용했지만 상업적 유통에는 유용하지 않았다.

(F) 에디슨이 그의 발명품을 언론에 발표했을 때, 거의 아무도 그것에 관심이 없어 보였다.

영어 실력을 높여주는 다양한 학습 자료 제공 HackersBook.com

**48**

# Actual Test 2

## Passage 1
본문 p. 184

1 (D)  2 (A)  3 (C)  4 (C)
5 (C)  6 (B)  7 (C)  8 (B)
9 (B)  10 (A), (D), (E)

### 나뭇잎의 변화

나뭇잎의 색깔 변화는 부분적으로 계절의 변화 때문이다. 계절이 변함에 따라, 식물은 각기 다른 색소를 생성한다. 잎에서 생성되는 세 가지 주요 색소 종류가 있는데, 바로 엽록소, 카로티노이드, 플라보노이드이다. ³ᴮ봄과 여름 동안에, 잎은 나무가 필요로 하는 대부분의 양분이 만들어지는 공장의 역할을 한다. ³ᴬ이 과정은 엽록소를 필요로 하며, 그것은 잎을 녹색으로 만든다. 그러나, 계절이 더 추워지면, 나무에서 일어나는 화학적 과정의 결과로 빨간색, 보라색, 주황색, 노란색이 혼합된 잎이 된다. 기온과 일광 길이의 변화는 잎으로 하여금 그것들의 양분 생산 과정을 멈추게 한다. ³ᴰ이 중단과 함께, 엽록소가 분해되고, 녹색이 사라지면서, 가을의 색으로 대체된다.

식물 내부의 화학적 상호작용뿐만 아니라 존재하는 색소의 양과 종류 또한 잎의 색을 결정할 수 있다. 봄과 여름 동안에는 엽록소가 풍부하기 때문에, 잎에 있는 다른 색소는 가려진다. 가을 동안에, 엽록소의 분해 속도는 그것의 생성이 느려지는 시기에도 일정하게 유지된다. 따라서, 잎의 녹색은 갑자기가 아니라 점진적으로 바래진다. ⁷잎 속의 더 많은 카로티노이드 색소의 양이 노란색을 내는 반면, 더 큰 플라보노이드의 비율은 빨간색, 파란색, 보라색, 자홍색을 낸다. 만약 잎에 동일한 비율의 카로티노이드와 플라보노이드가 있다면, 대개 주황색이 된다. 색소가 결핍되면, 다른 식물 화학 물질이 잎의 색에 영향을 줄 수 있다. 예를 들어, 타닌은 종종 떡갈나무 잎의 갈색을 낸다.

기온이 내려감에 따라, 탈리(분리)의 과정이 시작된다. ⁸초가을에는, 잎이 줄기에 붙은 지점에 탈리대라고 불리는 특수한 층이 발달한다. **이 층은 물과 양분이 나무의 주요 부분에서 잎으로 이동하는 것을 막는다.** 결국, 줄기는 더 이상 잎을 지탱할 수 없게 되며, 그것은 산들바람에 떨어진다. 그런 다음 나무가 그 절단 부위를 봉합하면, 한때 잎이 붙어 있던 자리에 상처가 생긴다. 나무는 긴 겨울잠을 위한 준비가 된 것이다.

pigment 명 색소  manufacture 동 생산하다
chlorophyll 명 엽록소  compound 명 합성물
take place 일어나다  daylight 명 일광  stoppage 명 중단
interaction 명 상호작용  determine 동 결정하다
abundant 형 풍부한  mask 동 가리다  decomposition 명 분해
fade 동 (색이) 바래다  gradually 부 점진적으로  abruptly 부 갑자기
magenta 명 자홍색  absence 명 결핍  abscission 명 탈리, 이탈
detachment 명 분리  seal 동 봉합하다, 밀봉하다

1 아래 문장 중 지문 속 음영 표시된 문장의 핵심 정보를 가장 잘 표현한 것은? 오답은 문장의 의미를 크게 바꾸거나 핵심 정보를 생략한다.

(A) 잎을 포함한 나무의 다양한 부분들은 그것이 필요로 하는 양분을 생산한다.

(B) 잎은 나무 한 그루가 일 년 동안 소비하는 양분의 주요 공급원이다.

(C) 봄과 같이 여름에도, 성장하는 잎이 많은 나무의 양분을 소비한다.

(D) 잎은 봄과 여름에 나무를 위한 대부분의 양분을 생산한다.

**2** 지문의 어구 "take place"와 의미가 가장 비슷한 것은?

(A) 발생하다
(B) 생산하다
(C) 바꾸다
(D) 계속하다

**3** 1단락에 따르면, 다음 중 엽록소에 관해 사실이 아닌 것은?

(A) 나무의 잎을 녹색으로 만든다.
(B) 식물을 위한 양분을 만드는 데 필요하다.
(C) 잎에 있는 유일한 색소이다.
(D) 가을에 분해된다.

**4** 지문의 단어 "its"가 가리키는 것은?

(A) 가을
(B) 분해 속도
(C) 엽록소
(D) 시기

**5** 지문의 단어 "abruptly"와 의미가 가장 비슷한 것은?

(A) 정확하게
(B) 즉각적으로
(C) 갑자기
(D) 반복적으로

**6** 글쓴이는 왜 "tannin"을 언급하는가?

(A) 나뭇잎의 색에 어떤 물질이 가장 큰 영향을 미치는지 언급하기 위해
(B) 잎의 색에 영향을 줄 수 있는 색소가 아닌 것의 예시를 제공하기 위해
(C) 색소와 나무에 의해 생성되는 다른 화학 물질들을 비교하기 위해
(D) 떡갈나무 잎의 색이 어떻게 변하는지 묘사하기 위해

**7** 2단락에 따르면, 붉은색 잎은

(A) 카로티노이드 생성의 증가가 원인이다
(B) 가을에 새로 만들어진 색소가 원인이다
(C) 더 많은 양의 플라보노이드가 원인이다
(D) 색소가 아닌 식물 화학 물질이 원인이다

**8** 다음 중 3단락에서 탈리에 관해 답변된 질문은?

(A) 나무에서 잎을 떨어뜨리는 바람은 얼마나 센가?
(B) 탈리대가 발달하는 곳은 어디인가?
(C) 탈리에 의해 생긴 상처는 어떤 기능을 하는가?
(D) 나무에서 잎이 떨어지는 데 얼마나 오래 걸리는가?

**9** 네 개의 네모[■]는 다음 문장이 삽입될 수 있는 곳을 나타내고 있다.

**이 층은 물과 양분이 나무의 주요 부분에서 잎으로 이동하는 것을 막는다.**

이 문장은 어디에 들어가는 것이 가장 적절한가?

**10** **지시:** 지문 요약을 위한 도입 문장이 아래에 주어져 있다. 지문의 가장 중요한 내용을 나타내는 보기 3개를 골라 요약을 완성하라. 어떤 문장은 지문에 언급되지 않은 내용이나 사소한 정보를 나타내므로 요약에 포함되지 않는다. **이 문제는 2점이다.**

---

**나뭇잎은 계절적인 변화를 겪는다.**

· (A) 엽록소는 따뜻한 계절에 나뭇잎에 녹색을 낸다.
· (D) 존재하는 색소의 종류와 양은 잎이 어떤 색깔이 될 것인지를 결정한다.
· (E) 잎과 줄기 사이에 형성된 층 때문에 잎이 떨어진다.

(B) 주황색 잎은 두 가지의 서로 다른 색소의 결합에서 생긴다.

(C) 이용 가능한 햇빛이 더 적어지면 잎은 양분 생산을 멈춘다.

(F) 잎이 떨어지면, 잎이 다시 형성되는 것을 막는 상처가 나무에 생겨난다.

---

**Passage 2** 본문 p.188

| | | | |
|---|---|---|---|
| **11** (D) | **12** (C) | **13** (C) | **14** (A) |
| **15** (B) | **16** (A) | **17** (D) | **18** (C) |
| **19** (B) | **20** (B), (D), (F) | | |

### 화성에서 온 운석

많은 운석들이 극지방에서 발견되는데, 그것들은 빙하 아래 깊숙이 묻혀 있다. 이는 그것들이 지구의 극지방에 떨어지는 빈도가 더 높기 때문은 아니다. 그렇다기보다는, 춥고 건조한 환경이 오랜 세월 운석들을 보존하고, 얼음으로 덮인 순백의 환경과 대비되어 그것들을 분간하는 것이 쉽기 때문이다. 1984년 12월 27일, 로베르타 스톤은 남극의 앨런 힐스에서 ALH84001이라고 불리는 화성 운석을 발견했다.

처음에, 그 운석은 디오제나이트로 분류되었고, 소행성대에서 왔다고 여겨졌다. 그것은 디오제나이트를 연구하는 한 미국 과학자가 연구를 위해 견본을 요청하기 전까지 10년 동안 보관되어 있었다. 그는 그것이 그가 연구해왔던 다른 디오제나이트들과 다르다는 것을 알아챘고, 동위원소 분석을 요청했다. 산소 동위원소 조성은 암석에 존재하는 $^{16}O$, $^{17}O$, $^{18}O$의 세 가지 산소 안정 동위원소의 상대적인 양을 가리킨다. 유사한 동위원소 조성을 가진 견본들은 같은 집단에 속하며, 아마 같은 모체에서 올 것이다. 그 운석의 산소 동위원소 조성이 지구 암석의 것과 달랐기 때문에, 그것은 우리의 고향 행성에서 왔을 리가 없었다. 달 또한 가능성에서 배제되었다. 인도에서 발견된 또 다른 운석은 화성에서 왔다고 여겨지는데, 이는 그것 역시 지구에서 발견되지 않는 산소와 질소의 동위원소 비율을 포함했기 때문이다. $^{13}$이 두 운석들의 탄산염 분석은 그것들이 화성의 대기와 접촉한 액체로부터 형성되었다는 것을 보여주었다.

추가적인 분석이 화성에 생명체가 존재했을 수도 있다고 시사했을 때, ALH84001은 전 세계의 헤드라인을 장식했다. 그 운석에 관한 많은 이론들이 제안되어 왔다. 과학자들은 그 자료에는 동의하지만, 그 실험 결과의 해석에 대해서는 의견이 다르다. $^{18}$어떤 이들은 45억 년 된 그 운석이 습한 환경에서 형성되었다고 믿는데, 이것은 지구에 물과 생명체가 존재하기 이전에 화성에 그것들이 존재했다는 것을 암시한다. 다른 이들은 심지어 그 운석이 화성 생명체를 이곳으로 옮겨왔을 수도 있다고 생각한다. 그들은 더 나아가 우리 모두가 화성 생명체의 후손일 수도 있다고 말한다. 이후의 실험들은 남극의 소금을 함유한 얼음이 그 운석들을 오염시켰을 수도 있다는 것을 밝혀냈다. 오늘날 과학자들은 ALH84001에서 나온 화성 생명체의 증거가 비록 설득력이 있기는 하지만, 결정적이지는 않다는 데 동의한다. $^{17}$그럼에도 불구하고, ALH84001은 지금까지 발견된 가장 오래된 운석들 중 하나이며, 운석들과 화성에 대한 새로운 정보를 계속 주고 있다.

meteorite 몡운석 　polar regions 극지방
incidence 몡빈도, 발생률 　preserve 동보존하다
distinguish 동구분하다 　asteroid belt 소행성대
request 동요청하다 　isotope 몡동위원소
composition 몡조성, 구성 　presumably 분아마
nitrogen 몡질소 　carbonate 몡탄산염 　indicate 동보여주다
put forward 제안하다 　interpretation 몡해석
experimental 혱실험의 　contaminate 동오염시키다
compelling 혱설득력이 있는 　inconclusive 혱결정적이 아닌
yield 동주다, 생산하다, 내다

**11** 지문의 단어 "incidence"와 의미가 가장 비슷한 것은?

(A) 풍부함
(B) 오류
(C) 가능성
(D) 발생

**12** 지문의 단어 "it"이 가리키는 것은?

(A) 디오제나이트
(B) 소행성대
(C) 견본
(D) 연구

**13** 2단락에 따르면, ALH84001과 인도에서 발견된 운석의 공통된 특징은?

(A) 둘 다 처음에는 디오제나이트로 분류되었다.
(B) 둘 다 지구의 것과 유사한 동위원소 조성을 가지고 있었다.
(C) 화성에서 왔다는 것을 암시하는 탄산염을 포함했다.
(D) 식별하기 어려운 동위원소를 포함했다.

**14** 지문의 어구 "put forward"와 의미가 가장 비슷한 것은?

(A) 제안했다
(B) 확인했다
(C) 요구했다
(D) 실험했다

**15** 지문에서 글쓴이는 왜 "salty ice"를 언급하는가?

(A) 그 운석이 화성에서 왔다는 것을 입증하기 위해
(B) ALH84001에 관한 일부 이론들이 틀릴 수도 있다는 것을 암시하기 위해
(C) 화성 생명체에 관한 주장의 예시를 들기 위해
(D) 운석들의 독특한 특징들을 밝히기 위해

**16** 지문의 단어 "compelling"과 의미가 가장 비슷한 것은?

(A) 설득력이 있는
(B) 확신하는
(C) 의도적인
(D) 광범위한

**17** 3단락에서 추론할 수 있는 것으로, 대다수의 운석들은

(A) 디오제나이트로 분류된다
(B) 주로 질소로 구성된다
(C) 화성에서 온 것으로 여겨진다
(D) 45억 년이 되지 않았다

**18** 3단락에서 글쓴이가 암시하는 것으로, ALH84001은

(A) 행성들 사이에서 물을 옮겼다

(B) 오늘날 화성에 생명체가 존재한다는 것을 입증한다
(C) 지구에서 생명체가 발달하기 전에 형성되었다
(D) 운석들의 나이에 관한 의문들을 제기한다

**19** 네 개의 네모[■]는 다음 문장이 삽입될 수 있는 곳을 나타내고 있다.

**달 또한 가능성에서 배제되었다.**

이 문장은 어디에 들어가는 것이 가장 적절한가?

**20** 지시: 지문 요약을 위한 도입 문장이 아래에 주어져 있다. 지문의 가장 중요한 내용을 나타내는 보기 3개를 골라 요약을 완성하라. 어떤 문장은 지문에 언급되지 않은 내용이나 사소한 정보를 나타내므로 요약에 포함되지 않는다. 이 문제는 2점이다.

> **극지방에서 발견된 많은 운석들 중 하나는 화성에서 기원했다.**
> ・ (B) ALH84001은 그것의 화학적 조성이 분석된 이후 화성 운석으로 확인되었다.
> ・ (D) 과학자들은 ALH84001이 화성 생명체를 지구로 옮겼을 지도 모른다고 추측했다.
> ・ (F) ALH84001에서 나온 화성 생명체에 관한 초기의 결론은 개연성이 낮은 것으로 밝혀졌다.

(A) 운석들은 한 표본이 지구에 얼마나 오래 있었는지를 계산하는 데 사용될 수 있는 동위원소를 포함한다.
(C) 로베르타 스톤에 의해 발견된 그 운석은 전 세계 언론에서 보도되었다.
(E) 인도의 운석은 화성과 큰 소행성 사이의 충돌에서 형성되었다.

## Passage 3 본문 p. 192

**21** (C) 　**22** (B) 　**23** (A), (D) 　**24** (C)
**25** (B) 　**26** (B) 　**27** (D) 　**28** (B)
**29** (D) 　**30** (A), (B), (F)

### 인쇄기의 발달

현대적인 인쇄기는 15세기에 독일에서 등장했다. [22]서양의 이전 인쇄 기술들과는 대조적으로, 이 인쇄기는 가동 활자를 포함했고, 그래서 많은 서로 다른 글자와 단어의 조합을 쉽게 만들어 낼 수 있었다. 비록 많은 사람들이 이 현대적인 인쇄기를 개발하기 위해 애썼지만, 일반적으로 요하네스 구텐베르크가 그것의 제작자로 인정받는다.

처음에, 구텐베르크는 더 효율적으로 인쇄물을 복제하는 방법을 연구했다. [23]그는 많은 실패를 경험했는데, 이는 특히 그가 필요로 했던 재료들이 비싸서 항상 투자자들을 필요로 했기 때문이었다. 일부 투자자들은 그의 인쇄 기술의 경제적 가치를 알고 있었고, 소송을 통해 그것을 차지하려고 했다. 따라서, 구텐베르크는 많은 시간과 돈을 변호사와 법정 비용에 썼고, 그의 프로젝트의 진전은 느렸다.

하지만, 1450년대에 그는 효율적인 인쇄기들을 만들어내는 데 성공했다. 이 인쇄기들은 2개의 열에 42개의 행의 활자를 넣어, 총 84개의 행을 만들어 내도록 고안된 틀을 가지고 있었다. [25]각각의 틀은 금속 활자를 담는 쟁반으로 맞춰질 수 있었다. 각 쟁반 안에는, 알파벳 글자를 나타내는 금속 활자가 단어와 행으로 조립되었다. 틀 전체가 채워지면, 종이 한 장이 잉크가 묻은 활자의 줄에 대고 세게 눌러졌다. 그런 다음, 그것이 인쇄기에서 다시 떼어지고 나면, 그것은 행과 열로 깔끔하게 배열된 완성된 글을 드러내 보였다. 금속 활자가 어떤 글이든 표현해 내도록 바뀔 수 있었기 때문에, 작업자들은 시간이나 노력의 큰 낭비

구텐베르크의 출판 방식은 사회와 지식에 극적이고 광범위한 영향을 가져왔다. 처음에, 그것은 구텐베르크 성서를 인쇄하기 위해 사용되었다. 28A이 성서는 1,200페이지 이상의 길이였고, 구텐베르크의 인쇄기는 필경사들이 전통적인 방식으로 한 부의 복사본을 만드는 데 걸렸을 시간과 동일한 시간 동안 수천 부의 복사본을 만들 수 있었다. 이후, 그 인쇄기는 마틴 루터에 의해 그의 95개조 의견서의 30만 부를 인쇄하는 데 사용되었는데, 이것은 가톨릭교회를 분열시켰고 종교 개혁을 일으켰다. 28C게다가, 그 인쇄기는 르네상스에 영감을 준 로마, 그리스, 아라비아 고전 문학의 광범위한 배포를 가능하게 했다. 28D그것은 또한 자연 과학자들이 그들의 과학적, 수학적 생각들을 더 자유롭게 공유하는 것을 돕기도 했다. 실제로, 인쇄기가 없었다면, 16세기와 17세기의 과학 혁명은 가능하지 않았을 것이다.

printing press 인쇄기    emerge 동등장하다
movable type 가동 활자    combination 명조합
acknowledge 동인정하다    reproduce 동복제하다
legal action 소송    advancement 명진전    metal type 금속 활자
assemble 동조립하다    alter 동바꾸다    represent 동표현하다
conveniently 부편리하게    reposition 동재배치하다
manuscript 명원고    dramatic 형극적인
far-reaching 형광범위한    conventional 형전통적인
distribution 명배포    inspire 동영감을 주다

21 지문의 단어 "acknowledged"와 의미가 가장 비슷한 것은?

(A) 요구되는
(B) 비판받은
(C) 인정받은
(D) 존경받는

22 다음 중 15세기 이전 유럽의 인쇄에 관해 추론할 수 있는 것은?

(A) 하나의 인쇄기에 의존했다.
(B) 가동 활자를 사용하지 않았다.
(C) 표준 절차가 없었다.
(D) 독일에 존재하지 않았다.

23 2단락에서 구텐베르크의 실패의 원인으로 제시된 두 가지 이유는? 두 개의 정답을 고르시오.

(A) 재료들의 높은 가격
(B) 이용 가능한 기술의 부족
(C) 변호사들을 고용할 능력의 부재
(D) 투자자에 대한 끊임없는 필요

24 아래 문장 중 지문 속의 음영된 문장의 핵심 정보를 가장 잘 표현한 것은? 오답은 문장의 의미를 크게 바꾸거나 핵심 정보를 생략한다.

(A) 금속 활자는 재배치하기에 편리했으나, 작업자들은 여전히 동시에 여러 페이지를 인쇄할 수 없었다.
(B) 책이나 원고의 각 페이지를 인쇄하는 것은 금속 활자를 바꿔야 하는 필요 때문에 많은 시간과 노력이 들었다.
(C) 금속 활자를 바꾸는 것이 편리했기 때문에 작업자들은 빠르고 쉽게 인쇄물의 각 페이지를 위해 그것의 위치를 바꿀 수 있었다.
(D) 작업자들은 현재 페이지를 인쇄하는 동안 다음 페이지를 위해 금속 활자를 재배치할 수 있었기 때문에 시간과 노력을 절약했다.

25 3단락에 따르면, 다음 중 1450년대에 구텐베르크가 개발한 인쇄기들에 관해 사실인 것은?

(A) 그것들은 최대 42개의 열을 만들어냈다.
(B) 그것들의 틀은 금속 활자를 위한 쟁반을 사용했다.
(C) 그것들의 행은 각각 정확히 한 개의 단어를 포함했다.
(D) 그것들은 잉크의 필요 없이 종이에 인쇄했다.

26 지문의 단어 "conventional"과 의미가 가장 비슷한 것은?

(A) 인정되는
(B) 전통적인
(C) 예측할 수 있는
(D) 특출난

27 지문에서 글쓴이는 왜 "the Scientific Revolution"을 언급하는가?

(A) 가톨릭교회가 분열된 이유를 강조하기 위해
(B) 구텐베르크의 인쇄기가 효율적이게 된 방법을 설명하기 위해
(C) 인쇄기의 성공에 대한 이유를 제시하기 위해
(D) 인쇄기의 장기적인 영향을 강조하기 위해

28 다음 중 4단락에서 구텐베르크 인쇄기의 영향으로 언급되지 않은 것은?

(A) 성서의 더 빠른 제작을 가능하게 했다.
(B) 가톨릭과 개신교의 사상을 통합했다.
(C) 고전 문학의 확산을 가능하게 했다.
(D) 과학 지식의 공유를 가능하게 했다.

29 네 개의 네모[■]는 다음 문장이 삽입될 수 있는 곳을 나타내고 있다.

그런 다음, 그것이 인쇄기에서 다시 떼어지고 나면, 그것은 행과 열로 깔끔하게 배열된 완성된 글을 드러내 보였다.

이 문장은 어디에 들어가는 것이 가장 적절한가?

30 지시: 지문 요약을 위한 도입 문장이 아래에 주어져 있다. 지문의 가장 중요한 내용을 나타내는 보기 3개를 골라 요약을 완성하라. 어떤 문장은 지문에 언급되지 않은 내용이나 사소한 정보를 나타내므로 요약에 포함되지 않는다. 이 문제는 2점이다.

> 구텐베르크의 현대적인 인쇄기는 인쇄 과정을 혁신했다.
> · (A) 구텐베르크의 인쇄기와 인쇄 방식은 중대하고 지속적인 방식으로 사회에 영향을 끼쳤다.
> · (B) 처음에, 구텐베르크는 더 나은 인쇄기를 개발하는 데 어려움을 겪었다.
> · (F) 15세기 중반에 구텐베르크는 생산적인 인쇄기를 만드는 데 성공했다.

(C) 현대적인 인쇄기는 종이 위에 인쇄가 가능한 최초의 기계였다.
(D) 구텐베르크가 그의 인쇄기에 대한 특허를 신청하려고 했을 때 그는 법적인 문제에 직면했다.
(E) 인쇄업자들은 르네상스 중에 고전 문학을 소개하기 위해 구텐베르크의 인쇄기를 이용했다.

# MEMO

# APEX
# READING
## for the
# TOEFL iBT® Basic

## Answer Book